THE FOOD52 COOKBOOK

Photography by Sarah Shatz

THE
FOOD52
COOKBOOK

140 WINNING RECIPES FROM EXCEPTIONAL HOME COOKS

AMANDA HESSER AND MERRILL STUBBS

and the Food52 Community

WM

WILLIAM MORROW

An Imprint of HarperCollins*Publishers*

HarperCollins books may be purchased for educational, business, or sales promotional use. For information please write: Special Markets Department, HarperCollins Publishers, 10 East 53rd Street, New York, NY 10022.

FIRST EDITION

Designed by Leah Carlson-Stanisic

Photography by Sarah Shatz except for the following: pages 57, 59, 62–63, 223, 225–256, 228–230, 307–309, 359–361, and 362–363 by Melanie Einzig. Contributor photographs are courtesy of the contributors except for Giulia Melucci by Sarah Shatz.

Library of Congress Cataloging-in-Publication Data

Hesser, Amanda.
   The Food52 cookbook / Amanda Hesser and Merrill Stubbs.—1st ed.
      p. cm.
      ISBN 978-0-06-188720-8
   1. Cooking.   2. Cookbooks.   I. Stubbs, Merrill.   II. Food52.   III. Title.
   TX714.H477 2011
   641.5—dc22

2010051727

11   12   13   14   15   OV/RRD   10   9   8   7   6   5   4   3   2   1

For home cooks, who inspire us every day.

{ Contents }

WINTER

191

SUMMER

11

FALL

103

SPRING

311

{ Introduction }

We met six years ago, when Amanda was looking for someone to help her with a dauntingly large cookbook she was writing for the *New York Times*. After testing more than 1,400 recipes together, eating countless dinners at 11 P.M., and doing all the necessary research and proofreading and dishwashing, we finished the book, which was published by W.W. Norton last year. We also became great friends and discovered how much we love cooking together.

Food52 grew out of an insight we had while working on *The Essential New York Times Cookbook*: many of the best recipes come from home cooks. It occurred to us that home cooks are both practical and inventive, and these qualities tend to lead to great recipes. At Food52.com, we recognize talented home cooks by giving them a place to show off their work, a place where cooks of all levels come to be inspired and to be part of a constructive and supportive community.

We love spending time in the kitchen, and we believe, like many cooks out there—both professional and amateur—that memorable cooking doesn't have to be complicated or precious. It's about discovering that frying an egg in olive oil over high heat gives the white a great crackly texture, that slashing the legs of a chicken before roasting allows the dark and white meat to cook evenly, that maple syrup adds not only sweetness but depth to an otherwise ho-hum vinaigrette.

We think cooking is really important—especially now. Over the past decade, many studies have shown that children from families who eat together do better in school, that eating "whole" foods is healthier, that eating sustainably will save the environment. But no one has pointed out that the only way to achieve all this in a comprehensive, lasting way is for people to cook.

Because:

- If you cook, your family will eat dinner together.
- If you cook, you will naturally have a more sustainable household.
- If you cook, you'll set a lifelong example for your children.
- If you cook, you'll understand what goes into food and eat more healthily.
- If you cook, you'll make your home an important place in your life.
- If you cook, you'll make others happy.
- If you cook, people will remember you.

This cookbook is the love child of the Food52 community, and the result of a year's worth of recipe contests—every recipe comes from one of our members and was chosen as a winner by his or her peers. It's not just the delicious concoctions, but the creativity and voice behind each recipe that make this cookbook truly special; no one chef could come up with this many great recipes in one year, and no one cookbook author could dream up this many entertaining backstories. We hope you'll get in the kitchen and have as much fun as we did making all of these terrific recipes and learning from talented home cooks from all over.

{ Test Run }

Before we even started building the website, we did an e-mail test among our friends and family. Merrill's mother, Veronica, dominated the field at a time when nepotism was still acceptable (two of the three winning recipes are hers). It turns out these early winners have stood the test of time—even after 52 weeks of official contests, we thought all three winners deserved to be included in the book.

- ◆ Your Best Salad Using Beets and Citrus
- ◆ Your Best Ragù/Bolognese
- ◆ Your Best Holiday Cookies

Red Leaf Salad with Roasted Beets, Oranges, and Walnuts

BY TERESA PARKER | SERVES 4 TO 6

A&M: Teresa wrote: "Seems to me beets and oranges are a classic winter salad combination that you see everywhere." But this is no run-of-the-mill beet and orange salad. Teresa explained, "My friend Sophie's dad, Jim Broderick, gave me the idea that really makes this salad great: fennel and orange rind in the dressing." She's right: this trick gives her winter salad lift and fragrance and makes you want to keep eating it.

2 medium beets, trimmed and scrubbed

Olive oil

½ teaspoon kosher salt, plus more for seasoning

⅓ cup coarsely chopped walnuts

1 head red leaf lettuce, rinsed, dried, and torn into pieces

2 navel oranges

1 tablespoon minced shallot

½ teaspoon fennel seeds, crushed in a mortar and pestle

2 tablespoons fresh lemon juice

¼ cup walnut oil

1. Heat the oven to 350°F. Lay the beets on one half of a large piece of aluminum foil. Sprinkle with olive oil and season with salt. Fold the foil in half to make a packet and roll the edges to seal. Lay on a baking sheet and roast until tender, 45 to 60 minutes. Let cool. Peel the beets and slice into ½-inch-thick wedges.

2. Keep the oven at 350°F; toast the walnuts on a baking sheet for a few minutes, 5 to 7, until they smell good. Remove the nuts and let them cool while you wash and dry the lettuce and tear it into a salad bowl.

3. Zest one orange—you need 1 teaspoon grated zest. Using a very sharp knife, cut the ends from the oranges, slicing just deep enough to expose the flesh. Cut off the remaining peel and pith. Then, working over a bowl, remove the segments, cutting between the membrane. Place the segments in a strainer to drain off excess juice.

4. Whisk together the dressing ingredients—the shallot, fennel seeds, and lemon juice—in a small bowl, adding the oil last, whisking as you pour it in so the dressing emulsifies a bit. Taste and adjust the seasoning.

5. Toss the nuts, beets, oranges, and the dressing with the salad, adjust the seasoning, and serve immediately.

TIPS AND TECHNIQUES

Teresa: "The oranges and beets are best tossed in at the last minute, when you dress the salad to serve it, lest the o-juice and beety color run amok."

ABOUT THE COOK

Teresa Parker is an expert on Catalonia and its cuisine, and runs culinary tours in Spain. She's a good friend of Merrill's and splits her time between New York City and Wellfleet, Massachusetts.

Pink Bolognese

BY VERONICA | SERVES 4 TO 6

A&M: Imagine if vodka sauce merged with Bolognese—this beautiful, aromatic pink sauce would be the conglomerate. We like how Veronica's use of ground turkey instead of beef keeps this simple to make but refined enough for a dinner party.

Veronica wrote: "The following list of ingredients looks daunting—it's not. Chances are, other than the ground meat, the fresh sage, and the cream, you might have all these lurking in your pantry/fridge."

½ pound ground pork

½ pound ground veal

½ pound ground turkey, preferably dark meat

2 tablespoons olive oil

1 medium carrot, finely chopped

1 medium yellow onion, finely chopped

2 garlic cloves, minced

2 small tomatoes, cored and finely chopped

1 cup red wine

1 quart homemade or organic store-bought chicken broth

1 tablespoon chopped sage, plus 2 sage leaves

½ teaspoon dried thyme

½ teaspoon dried oregano

½ teaspoon dried basil

½ teaspoon dried rosemary

Salt

2 tablespoons double-concentrate tomato paste, plus more to taste

1 cup heavy cream

2 tablespoons vodka

Freshly ground black pepper

1 pound short pasta, like penne rigate

---

1. In a large, heavy saucepan, brown the pork, veal, and turkey over medium-high heat. Keep stirring and separating the meat while cooking. Transfer the browned meat to a bowl and reserve. Return the pan to the stove.

2. Add the olive oil to the pan. Add the carrot, onion, and garlic and stir to combine. Reduce the heat to medium and cook until tender, 5 to 10 minutes. Return the meat to the pan. Stir in the tomatoes. Pour in the red wine and bring to a boil. Add the chicken broth, all the herbs, and a large pinch of salt, and simmer for 30 minutes, stirring occasionally.

3. Stir in the tomato paste and continue simmering for another hour, stirring every 10 minutes or so—you don't want any sticking or burning. The sauce should reduce and thicken.

4. Pour in the cream and vodka and cook until the sauce is the desired consistency. Season with salt and pepper. Taste, taste, taste—it's up to you.

5. Meanwhile, bring a large pot of generously salted water to a boil. Add the pasta and cook until al dente. Drain, then toss with the bolognese.

  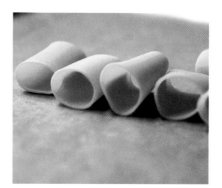

TIPS AND TECHNIQUES

Veronica: "The list of herbs is for dried—if using fresh (always better, but no big deal in this recipe) double the amount—more chopping for you!"

ABOUT THE COOK

Veronica Stubbs is a self-professed dilettante living in New York City. She is also Merrill's mother, and an excellent cook.

Her favorite recipe from a cookbook: "Trances de Jambon à la Crème from Julia Child's *Mastering the Art of French Cooking*. Use red wine and add some pre-soaked dried morels when you add the ham."

WHAT THE COMMUNITY SAID

Jestei: "This is good stuff, people. I used fresh sage and lots of it, and fresh rosemary, too. Funny how vodka seems so meaningless in the broader scheme of life, but it really does finish the dish nicely. A winner."

Secret Cookies

BY VERONICA | MAKES ABOUT 80 COOKIES

A&M: Merrill grew up eating these cookies every year at Christmas, but she swears she had nothing to do with the voting! As Veronica explained, "This recipe has truly been kept a secret for thirty years, but now is the time to release it. It was given to me by an elderly lady who had been given it by an even more elderly Swedish lady. The proviso: 'After I'm gone, you may give out the recipe.' The same proviso was given to me . . . so, here it is."

¾ **pound salted butter, softened**	**2 teaspoons vanilla extract**
1¾ **cups sugar**	3½ **cups all-purpose flour**
2 egg yolks	**Red, green, or multicolored sugar**

---

1. Heat the oven to 350°F. In a mixer fitted with a paddle attachment, cream the butter and sugar until light in color and fluffy. Add the yolks and vanilla, mixing well. Add the flour and combine thoroughly.

2. Use mounded teaspoonfuls and make balls of dough with your hands. Place on ungreased cookie sheets, then flatten the dough with the bottom of a patterned glass or jar dipped in colored sugar (don't mix the red and green!).

3. Bake for about 10 minutes (watch carefully, as they burn easily) until the cookies are lightly golden just around the edges. Let the cookies rest on the baking sheets for a minute or two and then gently transfer to baking racks to cool—they're fragile.

TIPS AND TECHNIQUES

It helps to lightly butter the bottom of the glass before dipping it in the sugar for the first time–this will help the sugar adhere.

Agamom: "Ran out of time to bake, so I rolled half the dough into a log in parchment and kept it overnight in the fridge. The next day: brushed the roll in beaten egg yolk mixed with a teaspoon of water, then sprinkled the colored sugar around the roll, then sliced (like sables) instead of rolling into balls. Not as pretty, but still delicious and very quickly made–and consumed!"

ABOUT THE COOK

For details on Veronica, as well as a peek at her winning Pink Bolognese recipe, turn to page 6.

WHAT THE COMMUNITY SAID

Agamom: "The real 'secret' to this recipe is how incredibly delicious the cookie tastes after the flavor has developed over a few days! Perfect for Christmas gift giving, if you can restrain yourself from consuming immediately. The vanilla scent is wonderful and the colors add to the beauty. Thank you for sharing!"

Savory Plum Tart

Summer

Summer Corn Chowder

BY NANCY JO | SERVES 6

A&M: This is an earthy, moody corn chowder that alternates between sweet and hot. We were intrigued by Nancy Jo's technique of cooking the vegetables in their own juices—without any extra liquid—before adding milk and cream, which seems to intensify all the flavors. Nancy Jo's inspiration for this recipe came from an issue of *Food & Wine*. "Not being a fan of bell peppers," she said, "I modified it by adding poblano peppers instead, and I think it tastes much better."

---

6 medium ears of corn

6 strips bacon, cut into ½-inch pieces

1 small onion, finely chopped

1 medium poblano pepper, finely chopped

1 jalapeño pepper, seeded and finely chopped

1 small celery rib, finely chopped

3 medium tomatoes, peeled, seeded, and finely chopped

2 medium boiling potatoes (about 1 pound), peeled and cubed

1 teaspoon salt, plus more to taste

⅛ teaspoon ground allspice

Pinch sugar

1 small bay leaf

2 cups light cream, at room temperature (or 1 cup milk and 1 cup heavy cream)

1 cup milk

Freshly ground black pepper

Chopped parsley, for garnish

---

1. Working over a bowl, cut the corn kernels from the cobs at about half their depth. Then, using the back of the knife, scrape the cobs over the bowl to release all the "milk"; set aside.

2. In a large saucepan, fry the bacon over medium-high heat, stirring occasionally, until crisp, about 10 minutes. Transfer the bacon to paper towels to drain. Crumble and reserve.

3. Discard all but 3 tablespoons of the bacon drippings from the pan. Add the onion and cook over medium heat until golden, 4 to 5 minutes. Add the poblano, jalapeño, and celery and cook until slightly softened,

about 2 minutes. Add the tomatoes, potatoes, salt, allspice, sugar, bay leaf, and the reserved corn kernels and their "milk" and stir well. Cook over medium heat until the mixture begins to sizzle.

4. Reduce the heat to low. Cover and cook, stirring occasionally, until the potatoes are tender, 35 to 45 minutes. Stir in the cream and milk and bring just to a boil. Remove from the heat and season with black pepper and more salt to taste. Ladle the chowder into bowls and garnish with the crumbled bacon and parsley.

TIPS AND TECHNIQUES

Nancy Jo occasionally roasts the poblano for a richer flavor. Broil the pepper on a baking sheet until blackened, turning it occasionally so that it blisters evenly. When cool enough to handle, peel off the skin and remove the seeds.

We admire Nancy Jo's purity, but we never–never!–peel or seed tomatoes. Some might call us lazy; we like to think of it as a firm conviction.

ABOUT THE COOK

Nancy Jo is a creative director living in New York City.

Her favorite recipe from a cookbook: "Marcella Hazan's Bolognese Sauce. Absolute perfection!"

WHAT THE COMMUNITY SAID

Elizacbrown: "Yummy. Easy to make and delicious. I did not have a poblano, but did have some of my own fresh roasted tomatoes. I added those, which gave it a nice smoky flavor."

BEHIND THE SCENES

In the early days, before Food52 was open to the public, all of the recipe entries came from family and friends–whom we sometimes had to cajole into participating. Nancy Jo is a friend of Merrill's, and she introduced us to Sarah Shatz, who took almost all of the beautiful photographs you see in the book and on Food52.com. The other winner this week was Merrill's sister, Abs; her cake is on page 16.

Not Red Velvet Cake with Fudge Glaze

BY ABS | SERVES 10

A&M: This cake has the wonderful, fluffy texture you get from boxed cake mixes, but with a made-from-scratch flavor they never manage to achieve. Abs leaves out the red food coloring usually found in red velvet cake, and she uses a chocolate ganache glaze instead of a traditional cream cheese icing. The glaze, which you spread and pour over the cake, is great for people intimidated by decorating with icing. The cake recipe was adapted from JoyofBaking.com.

CAKE

8 tablespoons unsalted butter at room temperature, plus more for buttering the pans

2½ cups sifted cake flour

1 teaspoon salt

2 tablespoons Dutch-processed cocoa powder

1½ cups sugar

2 large eggs

2 teaspoons vanilla extract

1 cup buttermilk

1 teaspoon white distilled vinegar

1 teaspoon baking soda

GLAZE

¾ cup heavy cream

8 ounces semisweet chocolate, chopped

Pinch of salt

---

1. Position a rack in the center of the oven and heat the oven to 350°F. Butter two 9-inch round cake pans and line the bottoms with parchment paper.

2. In a large mixing bowl, sift together the flour, salt, and cocoa powder. Set aside.

3. Using an electric mixer or hand beater, cream the butter on medium speed for about a minute. Add the sugar and continue to beat

until light and fluffy. Add the eggs one at a time, and then the vanilla, beating well after each addition and scraping down the sides of the bowl. Keeping the mixer running on low speed, beat in the dry ingredients and the buttermilk in several additions, alternating between the two and beginning and ending with the dry ingredients.

4. In a small bowl, stir together the vinegar and baking soda. When it starts to fizz, quickly fold it into the cake batter. Divide the batter evenly between the cake pans, smoothing with a spatula. Bake for 25 to 30 minutes, or until a toothpick inserted in the center of the cakes comes out clean. Cool the cakes in their pans on a wire rack for 10 minutes and then invert onto the rack to cool completely. Wrap each cake in plastic and put in the freezer for at least an hour. (This will make icing the cake easier.)

5. Using a double boiler, bring the cream just to a simmer over medium heat. Remove from the heat and whisk in the chocolate and salt. When the mixture has cooled and thickened slightly, use it to ice between the two cake layers and on top of the cake, letting the icing drip down the sides.

The red in most red velvet cakes comes from food coloring. Because this recipe doesn't call for any, it has a beautiful cocoa-marbled crumb.

You can substitute cream cheese frosting for the chocolate ganache: Beat together 8 ounces room-temperature cream cheese with 6 ounces (1½ sticks or ¾ cup) softened unsalted butter until light; add 1 teaspoon vanilla extract and then gradually beat in 2 to 2½ cups sifted confectioners' sugar, to taste.

ABOUT THE COOK

Abbie Burke is Merrill's sister and a nurse practitioner living in Washington, D.C. When she and Merrill were growing up, their mother tried to get them interested in cooking by offering to teach them how to boil artichokes—which surprisingly failed to entice them as tweens.

Her favorite entertaining tip: "Make good use of your oven so you can enjoy cocktail hour."

Lamb Burgers with Cilantro Yogurt

BY NAOMI | SERVES 8

A&M: Naomi, who wrote, "I love burgers but hate all the washing and chopping the fixings require," calls for ground lamb, which makes for a sumptuous burger requiring nothing more than a bit of salt and pepper. The tang of the cilantro yogurt sauce (which Naomi called her "single condiment solution") cuts the richness and keeps the lamb from tasting gamy.

---

2 pounds ground lamb

Salt and freshly ground black pepper

1 cup whole-milk yogurt (you need whole milk for the texture)

1 handful fresh cilantro leaves, washed, dried, and roughly chopped

2 small garlic cloves, very finely chopped

8 hamburger buns or Kaiser rolls

---

1. Heat your grill to medium-high. In a bowl, heavily season the lamb with salt and pepper and mix gently. Form into 8 patties.

2. In a small bowl, blend the yogurt with the cilantro, garlic, and salt to taste.

3. Cook the burgers on the grill (or in the broiler) to medium-rare or however you like them. After removing the burgers from the grill, toast the buns!

4. Place the burgers on the buns, top with some of the yogurt sauce, and serve the rest on the side.

TIPS AND TECHNIQUES

We shaved the garlic using a Microplane grater, which provided a more intense garlic flavor—if you decide to do the same, keep in mind you may only need one clove of garlic!

If you're feeling adventurous, try adding some minced garlic and fresh herbs to the lamb, and layer some roasted red peppers or arugula on top of the burgers before serving.

When shaping burgers, always flatten them more than you think—they puff up once they're on the grill.

ABOUT THE COOK

Naomi lives in New York City and is a wine expert.

Her favorite entertaining trick: "Casually slipping back into the kitchen during an effervescent dinner party, after the meal seems long done, and whipping up a batch of brownies while chatting back to everyone over one's shoulder. Big wow factor."

WHAT THE COMMUNITY SAID

BigGirlPhoebz: "I'm so glad you submitted this recipe—lamb burgers are my absolute favorite! The meat is always so much more flavorful than regular ground beef, and it gives you a lot more room to be creative with classic flavor combinations . . ."

Strawberries with Lavender Biscuits

BY SARA | SERVES 8

A&M: This dessert is a clever riff on strawberry shortcake. The biscuits contain whole wheat flour, but you won't believe how feathery and tender they are. Sara said: "The strawberries are from the farmers' market and stay pretty much unadulterated. You can adjust the sweetness factor to your specific batch of berries and taste!"

---

1 cup all-purpose flour

1 cup whole wheat pastry flour

4 to 6 tablespoons light brown sugar

2 teaspoons baking powder

1 teaspoon salt

1 tablespoon fresh lavender flowers
   (or ½ tablespoon dried)

8 tablespoons cold unsalted butter

1 cup heavy cream, plus more for brushing

Turbinado or raw sugar

2 quarts small fresh strawberries

6 to 8 tablespoons crème fraîche

Fresh mint sprigs and lavender flowers,
   for garnish

---

1. Heat the oven to 350°F. Combine the flours, 2 tablespoons of the light brown sugar, the baking powder, salt, and lavender flowers in the bowl of a food processor and pulse a couple of times to mix. Drop in the butter, one tablespoon at a time, while pulsing. Mix until the dough resembles coarse meal. Slowly add the cream, pulsing, until just incorporated. (The dough will be tacky.) Drop 8 large scoops of dough on an ungreased cookie sheet. Brush the tops with a bit of heavy cream, sprinkle with a little turbinado sugar, and bake for 18 to 20 minutes until lightly golden brown. Remove from the pan and let cool on a wire rack.

2. While the biscuits are baking, prepare the strawberries. Rinse the berries and stem and hull them. (I usually cut them in half because they are small to begin with.) Toss the berries with a few tablespoons of brown sugar—this part is a matter of taste. Try not to handle the berries too much—you don't want to mush them, but you do want their natural juices to come out. That's it.

3. Now it's time to assemble. Cut your biscuits in half. Lay the bottom of the biscuit in a bowl and spoon some berries and their juices over the biscuit. Add a dollop of crème fraîche (this too can be sweetened a

little, depending on personal taste—I like the sourness) and top with the other half of the biscuit. I like to garnish with some fresh mint and a lavender flower.

TIPS AND TECHNIQUES

Sara added that the biscuits "can morph into many forms–used for sweet or savory dishes. I've also shaped them like scones and passed them off that way."

If you can't find lavender, substitute an equal amount of fresh thyme.

ABOUT THE COOK

Sara is a food and health counselor and chef. A graduate of the Natural Gourmet cooking school in New York City, she lives in Brooklyn.

Her favorite cookbook: "*The Naked Chef* by Jamie Oliver."

Fasoolya Khadra (Beef and Green Bean Stew)

BY SUSAN | SERVES 6 TO 8

A&M: This is one of those recipes, like *pot-au-feu*, that seem to defy the laws of cooking by coaxing an intensely flavorful sauce from water rather than broth or wine. Here, beef and beans soften into lushness, enveloped by a silky gravy of tomatoes, garlic, coriander, and cumin. Susan wrote, "Many people (including me) put plain whole-milk yogurt on the side," and we encourage you to as well.

---

1 pound stewing beef, cut into 1-inch chunks

Salt and freshly ground black pepper

1 pound green beans

1 pound tomatoes (canned is okay)

2 garlic cloves, crushed

2 teaspoons ground coriander

2 teaspoons ground cumin

White rice, for serving

Yogurt, for serving

---

1. Season the beef generously with salt and pepper, place in a skillet large enough to hold the beef in one layer, and add enough water to just cover the beef. Cover and simmer gently over medium-low heat for about 10 minutes until the meat is no longer pink.

2. Remove the ends from the green beans. Cut them into 1½-inch pieces.

3. Remove 1 cup of the simmering liquid and reserve. Add the green beans to the skillet and simmer for 5 minutes.

4. Chop the tomatoes (if using fresh) and add them to the bowl of a food processor with the reserved beef broth and garlic. Pulse until smooth. Add this mixture to the green beans and beef. Season generously with salt and pepper, then stir in the coriander and cumin. Cover and simmer gently until the meat is fork-tender, 1½ to 2 hours. (Add more water if the pan gets dry—there should be half an inch of sauce at all times.) For the most delicious flavor, let the stew sit on the stove for a while after cooking and reheat later. Serve with rice and yogurt.

TIPS AND TECHNIQUES

Susan was studying abroad in Amman, Jordan, in 2005 when she learned this recipe from her host family. She says, "We usually ate it at lunch and then again from the fridge when we got home late on Saturday night."

Susan: "You can make it with fava beans as well, to make white fasoolya—this fasoolya is green fasoolya (khadra means green). People put cayenne or other chili pepper on white fasoolya sometimes, and I think it could be good on the green also, depending on your taste."

ABOUT THE COOK

Susan is a graduate student living in Tucson, Arizona.

Her favorite recipe from a cookbook: "Before I turned fourteen and developed an attitude, but after I could use the stove by myself, I used to make poached chicken from Pierre Franey's *60-Minute Gourmet* for family dinner. I was so proud of myself for helping my mom, and now of course I love that recipe."

WHAT THE COMMUNITY SAID

ThinkingChair: "We made this right after Christmas when we wanted something completely different from all that blandness. Both myself and my eleven-year-old son loved it!"

Tony S: "So simple but so good! Very similar to a Lebanese recipe called Lubee Ah Laham. Just replace the beef with lamb, and the coriander and cumin with cinnamon and perhaps a pinch of allspice."

Grilled Blade Chops over Greek Salad

BY HELEN | SERVES 2

A&M: This dish is fresh and intensely flavored: summer grilling at its finest. Helen advises "aggressive" seasoning throughout, and we heartily agree. She also pointed out: "Any feta will do here (although a mildly creamy Bulgarian feta is especially nice), but please do buy block feta and crumble it rather than buying the precrumbled stuff."

SALAD
1 large, ripe tomato
1 hothouse cucumber, peeled
1 green bell pepper (or red or yellow)
½ cup sliced red onion
1 tablespoon capers (rinsed if salt packed)
½ cup Kalamata olives
Pinch of dried oregano
Salt and freshly ground black pepper

3 tablespoons good-quality extra virgin olive oil, plus more for serving
2 tablespoons red wine vinegar
4 firm, fresh stuffed grape leaves
½ cup crumbled feta

LAMB
2 lamb blade chops
Kosher salt and freshly ground black pepper
Dried oregano
Ground coriander

---

1. At least an hour before you plan to eat, cut the tomato, cucumber, and bell pepper into bite-size pieces. Toss in a large bowl with the red onion, capers, olives, and oregano (don't overdo the oregano; it gets overwhelming quickly), aggressively season with salt and pepper, and dress with the olive oil and red wine vinegar. Allow to sit at room temperature while you cook the lamb.

2. Twenty minutes before you want to grill, pull the chops out of the fridge and heat the grill to medium-high. Season on both sides with salt, pepper, oregano, and coriander. Really press it in. Grill the chops until nicely charred on the outside and delightfully pink (medium-rare) on the inside, 4 to 6 minutes per side.

3. Divide the salad between two plates, and add 2 stuffed grape leaves to each. Crumble half the feta over each plate. Place the hot-from-the-grill lamb over each salad, and drizzle with olive oil to finish. Enjoy!

TIPS AND TECHNIQUES

Serve this with fresh pita and plenty of Greek yogurt.

Helen: "I like my salad to be a touch aggressive with the vinegar, as the fat of the lamb eventually mixes with it, rounding out, rather than dampening, the flavor."

ABOUT THE COOK

Helen lives in New York City. Fresh off the line at Prune restaurant in Manhattan, she was our first intern, establishing the all-hands-on-deck skill set for future Food52 interns—which includes speed shopping, recipe testing, dazzling e-mail correspondence, and even on-the-fly video editing.

Her favorite recipe from a cookbook: "Gordon Hamersley's roast chicken in *Bistro Cooking at Home*."

WHAT THE COMMUNITY SAID

lastnightsdinner: "We made this for dinner last Friday and it absolutely ROCKS. We love blade chops anyway (an underappreciated cut for sure), but the rub is fantastic, and in combination with the salad they are a pure win. We'll be making this often in the summer when our local tomatoes, cukes, and peppers are in season. Thanks for a great dish!"

Salted Almonds

BY LAUREN | SERVES 6 TO 8

A&M: This is more a concept than a prototypical recipe—which is one of the reasons we like it so much. By adding a mere suspicion of sugar to her recipe for roasted salted almonds, Lauren has come up with a clever twist on a traditional technique. She wrote that these are "perfect at cocktail hour, along with a stiff drink." We wholeheartedly agree—cheers!

---

1 pound shelled whole almonds

¼ cup olive oil

1 tablespoon kosher salt

1 teaspoon sugar

Heat the oven to 350°F. Toss the almonds in the olive oil, salt, and sugar until well coated. Spread on a baking sheet and bake for 10 minutes. Serve warm or at room temperature.

TIPS AND TECHNIQUES

The amount of sugar is just enough to ease the saltiness without actually making the nuts taste sweet.

Try the same technique with peanuts, pecans, walnuts, hazelnuts—whatever you have on hand. And if you want a little heat, add a pinch of cayenne.

ABOUT THE COOK

Lauren Shockey is a food writer who lives in New York City. Amanda has known Lauren since she was in college, when she worked as Amanda's intern at the *New York Times*. Lauren recently returned from a year living and cooking abroad, which inspired her first memoir, *Four Kitchens.* Here's her website: www.laurenshockey.com.

Her favorite entertaining tip: "Always have more wine/bubbly than you think you need. If for some reason dinner's a flop, just keep pouring and no one will know the difference later!"

By Week 3, we could see that the site was filling up with more great recipes than we could recognize through the contests. Thus, the Wildcard Winner was born. Whenever we came across a fantastic-sounding recipe, we'd try it out, and if it was truly excellent, we'd award it a trophy. We saw this as our opportunity to hand-pick some hidden gems throughout the course of the year.

Mom's Blueberry-Coconut Muffins

BY RHONDA35 | MAKES 1 DOZEN LARGE MUFFINS

A&M: This recipe comes from Amanda's mother, but was entered in this muffin contest by Amanda's sister, Rhonda. Although Amanda had never made them herself before we tested them, she grew up eating these light, cakey muffins every summer. Rhonda35 recalled, "My mother would take us blueberry picking every summer. We weren't always that enthusiastic about the picking, but with these muffins offered as our reward, we always seemed to muster the energy to get the job done!" The addition of toasted coconut is what sets these apart from other blueberry muffins, and the base isn't too sweet, allowing the tartness of the berries and the coconut to take center stage.

---

2 cups plus 1 tablespoon all-purpose flour

1 tablespoon baking powder

½ cup sugar

¾ teaspoon kosher salt

½ cup flaked coconut, toasted

1 egg, beaten

4 tablespoons unsalted butter, melted and slightly cooled

1 cup whole milk

1½ cups fresh blueberries (preferably small, wild ones if you can find them)

---

1. Heat the oven to 400°F. Line a 12-cup muffin tin with paper muffin cups. Set aside.

2. Sift together 2 cups of the flour, the baking powder, sugar, and salt. Stir in the toasted coconut.

3. Combine the egg, melted butter, and milk. Add to the dry ingredients and mix lightly until combined.

4. Toss the blueberries with the remaining 1 tablespoon flour. This prevents the blueberries from sinking to the bottom of the muffins. Fold into the batter.

5. Spoon the batter into the muffin cups. Bake for 17 to 20 minutes, or until a toothpick inserted in the center of a muffin comes out clean.

6. Remove from the oven and allow to cool in the pan for 10 minutes, then remove from the pan and finish cooling on a rack.

TIPS AND TECHNIQUES

If you can get coconut in larger flakes, do use it in this recipe—it'll add more texture.

ABOUT THE COOK

Although she enjoys entertaining, Rhonda Hesser Thomson, a mother and culinary consultant living in Easton, Maryland, has some simple favorites when cooking at home: "Spaghetti with fried eggs and garlic, or sometimes I just eat ice cream."

Her favorite entertaining tip: "When in doubt, serve generous pours and something made with cheese!"

WHAT THE COMMUNITY SAID

Catarina_castruccio_prince: "The coconut is such a perfect complement. My roommate ate two as soon as I could get them out of the muffin tin."

Ginger Sangria

BY REBECCAP | SERVES 12

A&M: If traditional sangria were a small, feisty brunette, this variation would be a tall, leggy blonde. RebeccaP wrote: "I recently adapted this recipe from *Country Living* (probably the closest I have ever come to country living)." This sangria deserves a pretty wineglass to showcase its pale elegance.

GINGER-INFUSED SIMPLE SYRUP
2 pieces ginger, about 3 inches long

1 cup sugar

GINGER SANGRIA
6 ripe peaches (white or yellow)

1½ cups brandy

½ cup Triple Sec

3 (750 ml) bottles chilled dry white wine

---

1. Make the ginger-infused simple syrup: Peel and cut the ginger into thin, long slices. Combine the ginger, sugar, and 1 cup water in a saucepan and bring to a boil. Let the mixture simmer for about 3 minutes and then cool to room temperature. Strain the syrup and store in the refrigerator. The syrup can be made up to 2 weeks in advance. I recommend doubling the recipe and saving some for other cocktails.

2. Make the sangria: Peel, pit, and slice the peaches. Add to a medium bowl, and then pour the brandy and Triple Sec over the fruit. Cover and store in the refrigerator for several hours. If you enjoy a strong brandy flavor, chill it overnight before using.

3. Several hours before drinking, combine the white wine, 1 cup ginger simple syrup, and the soaked peaches in a large punch bowl. Add ice cubes or a block of ice right before serving.

TIPS AND TECHNIQUES

RebeccaP: "In addition to boiling the ginger in the simple syrup, I added slices of ginger to the syrup to sit overnight to intensify the flavor. This is optional. To keep the sangria cool, fill an old orange juice quart container with water and freeze overnight. Cut the paper away from the ice and add the block of ice to the sangria before serving."

ABOUT THE COOK

Rebecca Palkovics is a recent graduate of NYU's Food Studies graduate program and was Food52's first publicist. She currently lives in New York City.

Her favorite cookbook: "*The Greens Cookbook* (and I'm not a vegetarian!)."

WHAT THE COMMUNITY SAID

Bladt: "Tasted this at a dinner party—quite good. The ginger is rather subtle and the brandy played nicely with the fruit."

Daddy's Carbonara

BY ERIC LIFTIN | SERVES ABOUT 6

A&M: A good carbonara is not easy to find—nor, for that matter, to make. We found Eric's silky, rich sauce (resulting from generous doses of bacon, egg, and cheese) totally addictive, and peas are a great addition. We also appreciate Eric's reasons for making this dish: "I refuse on principle to make pasta with butter (or powdered cheese) for my children. I prepared this version for my daughter's slumber party, and everyone loved it (even the vegetarian)."

---

1 pound dried spaghetti	4 eggs
1 pound bacon	1 cup freshly grated Parmesan
6 to 10 ounces frozen peas (according to your taste)	Freshly ground black pepper

---

1. Start cooking the pasta (I have long subscribed to the less-water method Harold McGee advocates—he experimented with cooking pasta in only a small amount of water to save energy and found the results to be satisfactory).

2. Take the bacon out of the package and cut across the slices into ½-inch-wide blocks. Cook in a skillet over medium heat, stirring and breaking up the blocks with a wooden spoon.

3. Dump the peas into a microwave-safe bowl with a little water and microwave for 3 to 4 minutes until they are warm, stirring halfway through.

4. While all the cooking is going on, whisk together the eggs, Parmesan, and pepper (to taste—it's best to use a lot, but for kids, maybe less) in a large bowl. It should have the consistency of a thick batter.

5. When the pasta is al dente, drain it quickly, reserving ½ cup of the pasta water. Whisk the reserved pasta water into the eggs to temper them, then dump the steaming spaghetti into the egg mixture and agitate well to cook the eggs. Add the bacon with a slotted spoon, leaving the fat behind. Some purists will just empty the skillet into the bowl, but that is too much. Mix in the peas, and you're done. The biggest challenge is to get the bacon and peas mixed in evenly—I recommend steel tongs.

Eric Liftin: "Modify quantities and proportions as you will. I totally prefer American bacon to pancetta for its crispness in this dish."

Ody, a Food52 member, recommended adding some chopped onion to the bacon when you sauté it.

ABOUT THE COOK

Eric Liftin is a New York–based architect and web developer with an affinity for seasonal ingredients—many of his Food52 recipes incorporate fresh picks from his garden. When he isn't building things (like the Food52 website!), he's cooking breakfast (pancakes), lunch (tomato tarts), and making dessert (lemon birthday cake) for his very lucky kids. Here's his website: Mesh Architectures (www .mesh-arc.com)

His favorite entertaining tip: "When cooking for others, one dish should be something you know will succeed, and one should be an experiment. Even if it doesn't succeed, it's a story that involves everyone."

WHAT THE COMMUNITY SAID

Elise: "Made this for dinner, and we loved it. Used whole wheat spaghetti to counter the delicious but unhealthier ingredients. Great for a quick meal because it took no time."

Salad Dressing

BY LESLIE | MAKES 1 CUP

A&M: We love that this dressing can be made in just a few minutes but contains a couple of surprises: the additions of both golden (or white) balsamic vinegar and Worcestershire sauce. (Why didn't we think of that last one?) But what thrills us the most is Leslie's suggestion to just throw everything in a jar and shake. It's an easy way to emulsify the ingredients, and storing leftovers is a snap. This is the perfect dressing for a salad of young, tender lettuces.

---

1 teaspoon Dijon mustard

1 garlic clove, peeled and lightly crushed with the side of a knife

¾ cup extra virgin olive oil

4 teaspoons balsamic vinegar

2 tablespoons golden (or white) balsamic vinegar

¼ teaspoon Worcestershire sauce

Salt and freshly ground black pepper

---

1. Place the mustard and the garlic clove in a bowl or glass jar.

2. Add the olive oil, vinegars, Worcestershire sauce, and salt and pepper (to taste), and mix well (or shake, if in a jar).

3. Taste for seasoning and add more of any of the ingredients to get the right balance.

TIPS AND TECHNIQUES

Leslie said not to refrigerate the dressing once you've made it, but it does benefit from some sitting time, which simultaneously intensifies and rounds out the flavors. Use the dressing within a day or two.

Tatiana131 suggested adding "a hint of apple cider vinegar."

Leslie Shatz is a retired development/marketing director for nonprofit arts organizations and lives in Stockbridge, Massachusetts. She's also our photographer's, Sarah Shatz's, mom!

Her favorite recipe from a cookbook: "Many, many years ago (1972) I bought a paperback edition of *The Elegant but Easy Cookbook*, by Marian Fox Burros and Lois Levine, and found I loved their recipe for fruit torte. My husband and children dubbed it 'the 24-hour cake,' since it's so tasty there are only a few stray crumbs left on the serving plate one day after I make it."

WHAT THE COMMUNITY SAID

sexyLAMBCHOPx: "I love using mason jars to make and store homemade salad dressings—less mess and fuss and inspires me to make my own more often. Can't wait to try this one!"

Roasted Duck Breast with Sour Cherries

BY SWEET ENOUGH | SERVES 4

A&M: Like sweet enough, we had never cooked with sour cherries before. The raw cherries were pristine, nearly translucent, and, well, sour! Simmering the cherries with the shallots, apricots, thyme, stock, and wine mellows their tartness and gives rise to a bright, fragrant sauce that complements the duck, an often gamy bird.

---

4 duck breasts, with skin on

Salt and freshly ground black pepper

4 fresh thyme sprigs

2 medium shallots, finely chopped

1 cup fresh or jarred sour cherries, pitted, stems removed

4 fresh apricots, pitted and quartered

½ cup chicken stock

⅓ cup apricot nectar

⅓ cup red wine (I used a Pinot Noir)

---

1. Heat the oven to 450°F. Rinse and pat dry the duck breasts and score the fat in a crosshatch pattern with a sharp knife. Sprinkle both sides with salt and pepper. Place them, fat side down, in a heavy pan over medium-high heat for about 7 minutes, or until the fat is golden brown.

2. Turn the breasts over and place a sprig of thyme under each. Place the pan in the oven and roast for 7 to 10 minutes, depending on how you like your duck cooked. Remove the breasts from the pan, place on a serving dish, and tent with aluminum foil.

3. Pour off all but about 2 tablespoons of the duck fat. Add the shallots to the pan and cook over medium heat for 3 to 4 minutes. Add the cherries and apricots and cook for about 1 minute; then add the stock, apricot nectar, and wine. Cook over medium heat until the sauce is reduced by about half. Discard the thyme sprigs and correct the seasoning.

4. Slice each breast and fan the meat on each plate. Spoon the sauce over the meat and serve.

TIPS AND TECHNIQUES

If you want a crisper layer of skin, keep the heat under the pan at a slow, steady burn, and (carefully) pour off the fat every once in a while so that the breasts don't start to deep-fry!

ABOUT THE COOK

Sweet enough is a literary agent living in New York City.

Her favorite recipe from a cookbook: "Linguine with pancetta, olive oil, chile, clams, and white wine from Jamie Oliver's *The Naked Chef Takes Off*. It's simple, perfect for one person or a crowd, and it's totally delicious."

WHAT THE COMMUNITY SAID

Naked Beet: "Love love the combination! (I'm a sour cherry fanatic.)"

El Chupacabra

BY JANEYMAX | MAKES 1 DRINK

A&M: This recipe was a finalist in the Best Summer Cocktail Contest. Although it didn't win, the race was very close, and we thought this excellent drink deserved a spot in the cookbook. A Pimm's Cup gone south of the border, the cocktail gets its name from a mythical creature whose name means "goat sucker." (Don't drink too many—we don't know what will happen!)

Janeymax calls for a couple of ingredients that may require a run to the local package store (Cynar, which is made from artichokes; blanco tequila; and Peychaud bitters), but it's well worth the field trip.

---

2 slices cucumber

1 ounce blanco tequila (Herradura, Dos Manos, and Gran Centenario all work)

1 ounce Pimm's No. 1

¾ ounce fresh lemon juice

¾ ounce simple syrup (see Tips and Techniques)

1 dash Peychaud bitters

1 splash soda water

⅛ to ¼ ounce Cynar

---

1. Muddle 1 cucumber slice at the bottom of a shaker.

2. Add the tequila, Pimm's, lemon juice, simple syrup, and bitters.

3. Add ice and shake.

4. Strain into a Collins glass with ice.

5. Top with soda water to taste.

6. Float the Cynar to taste.

7. Garnish the cocktail with the remaining cucumber slice and serve!

To make the simple syrup, combine ¼ cup sugar and ¼ cup water in a small saucepan. Bring to a boil, stirring to dissolve the sugar as it heats. Boil for 1 minute, then remove from the heat and let cool completely. Simple syrup may be stored in a container in the refrigerator for 2 to 3 weeks.

To "float" the Cynar in step 6, invert a spoon over the drink so the tip of the spoon is just touching the liquid, near the edge of the glass. Then slowly pour the Cynar over the inverted spoon so it floats atop the drink.

ABOUT THE COOK

Jane Lopes is a wine store manager and bartender living in Chicago, Illinois. Here's her blog: Lush Wine (www.lushwine.wordpress.com).

Her favorite entertaining tip: "Have places for people to sit, plenty of booze, and snacks out when friends arrive. People will be happy no matter what happens after that."

WHAT THE COMMUNITY SAID

Miss Ginsu: "Ha! The name makes me giggle. And I've never heard of Cynar, so that's worth the price of admission right there. Thanks for the education!"

Spicy Shrimp

BY HELEN | MAKES A BUNCH OF SHRIMP

A&M: We love Sriracha's heat, which is warm, lasting, and assertive without being overbearing. Helen combines the hot sauce with a few everyday ingredients—olive oil, Worcestershire sauce, sugar, and cilantro—to create a sublime marinade for shrimp. She was right when she said, "This is dead simple, and totally delicious." The oil and sugar give the marinade some viscosity, so it doesn't just season the shrimp but clings to it. But it's the sugar that makes this dish—on the grill it caramelizes, giving the shrimp a lacquered feel, and its sweetness balances the kick of the Sriracha. Buy some beer or tequila to drink with it.

⅓ **cup Sriracha**

⅓ **cup olive oil**

1 teaspoon Worcestershire sauce

3 garlic cloves, crushed

1 handful cilantro, roughly chopped, plus some minced for garnish

1 teaspoon sugar

Salt and freshly ground black pepper

2 pounds large shrimp (16 to 20 count), peeled and deveined

---

1. Combine the Sriracha, olive oil, Worcestershire sauce, garlic, chopped cilantro, and sugar in a 1-gallon plastic bag. Season aggressively with salt and pepper. Add the shrimp and mix together in the bag. Marinate in the fridge for 2 to 4 hours. Or longer.

2. Heat a grill to medium-high. Skewer the shrimp (4 to 6 shrimp per skewer) and grill until pink and delicious, 2 to 3 minutes per side.

3. Remove the shrimp from the grill, slide the shrimp from the skewer using a fork, and pile on a serving platter. Sprinkle with minced cilantro. Watch them disappear.

TIPS AND TECHNIQUES

Helen: "I tend to grill up millions of them, take them off the skewers, pile them on a platter, and stick toothpicks in a few. People get the idea pretty quickly, and they disappear . . . I like them good and spicy, but you can adjust the amount of Sriracha as you'd like."

ABOUT THE COOK

You can read about Helen, and find her recipe for Grilled Blade Chops over Greek Salad, on page 27.

WHAT THE COMMUNITY SAID

Lisa Schermerhorn: "I made this when I had company over Memorial Day weekend. We decided to put the shrimp over mixed greens and make a dinner salad. It was wonderful!!!"

Amagansett Corn Salad

BY PETER STEINBERG | SERVES 8

A&M: Peter Steinberg wrote, "Rather than do anything to mar the flavor of the sweet, sweet corn I make this absurdly easy, very delicious raw corn salad." This dish epitomizes the freshness of summer. Sweet raw corn kernels and their milk mix with the bright acid of tomatoes and the kick of red onion; a hint of balsamic vinegar adds a caramel tang. The flavors mellow and meld as the salad sits for a bit.

---

8 ears very fresh white or yellow corn

2 quarts cherry tomatoes

1 medium red onion

1 quart sugar snap peas (optional)

1 handful rough-chopped basil or flat-leaf parsley

3 to 4 tablespoons high-quality balsamic vinegar

Salt, preferably a large, flaky sea salt like Maldon

Freshly ground black pepper

---

1. Strip the raw corn from the ears. Yep, raw. You can use a fancy corn stripper, or just run your chef's knife down the side of each ear about 8 times.

2. Slice the cherry tomatoes in half or quarters, depending on your preference.

3. Chop the red onion into a large dice.

4. If using the sugar snap peas (they can be hard to find when the corn and tomatoes are available—their seasons barely overlap, and even then you're likely getting corn and tomatoes from the south and sugar snaps from the north), cut them in halves or thirds to make them more bite-size.

5. Toss all the vegetables and herbs in a large bowl, along with the vinegar (to taste), salt, and pepper. That's it. Enjoy!

TIPS AND TECHNIQUES

If you use the sugar snaps (which we recommend), blanch them briefly in salted boiling water and remove the strings before cutting them into halves or thirds. Also, if you prefer cooked corn, boil it for 2 minutes before stripping it from the cobs.

ABOUT THE COOK

Peter Steinberg is an entrepreneur living in Brooklyn, New York, who later joined Food52 as our Product Guy. Here's his book recommendation website: Flashlight worthy (www.flashlightworthybooks .com).

His best entertaining tip: "When throwing a big dinner party, always invite at least one good friend who you know will dive in and help in a table setting/salad making/dish cleaning crisis."

WHAT THE COMMUNITY SAID

ENunn: "I know this recipe has been up for a while, but I just made it this weekend for a rooftop cookout. It was absolutely delicious and we have enjoyed the leftovers for lunch. Bravo!"

Rosemary Thyme Pita Chips

BY MACHEF | SERVES 8 (DEPENDING ON THE SIZE OF YOUR PITA)

A&M: We know what you're thinking: a pita chip is a pita chip, right? Wrong. These chips are spread with both butter and honey before they're baked, making them extra rich and ever-so-slightly sweet. Also, the chips are dusted generously with dried herbs, which takes them from merely aromatic to downright fragrant (even more so after a day or two). Machef suggested eating these with cheese: "The honey and herbs pair well with the lemony, citrusy tang you often find in a young goat's milk cheese like Selles-sur-Cher or Valençay." The chips are pretty incredible on their own, too.

---

2 pitas	Sea salt
Unsalted butter, at room temperature	Dried thyme
Honey (preferably one that spreads easily and is not too runny)	Dried rosemary

---

1. Heat the oven to 350°F. Line a baking sheet with parchment paper or aluminum foil.

2. Cut the pita rounds into eighths or quarters. Pull those pieces in half so that each piece consists of only one layer of pita. Place the pita triangles on the baking sheet, rough side up.

3. Spread each piece of pita with a thin layer of butter, then honey.

4. Sprinkle each piece with a pinch each of sea salt, thyme, and rosemary (adjust according to taste).

5. Bake for 6 minutes. Rotate the baking sheet and bake another 6 minutes, or until the chips are browned and crisp. Keep a close eye on the chips toward the end of their baking time as they can quickly go from brown to burned. Let the chips cool and then enjoy!

TIPS AND TECHNIQUES

Machef said: "I like to go for very thin pita, which means a crispier chip!"

Tmmurphy suggested finishing them off with a few drops of lemon juice.

ABOUT THE COOK

Mary Murphy is a pastry chef living in Cambridge, Massachusetts. She and Merrill went to high school together and then later discovered they'd both gone to cooking school!

Her favorite cookbook recipe: "The Genoise cake recipe in my mother's *The Joy of Cooking*–it's the family birthday cake."

WHAT THE COMMUNITY SAID

Janneke Verheij: "I tried these last night and they were a big hit. I melted the butter with the honey so I only had to brush them once, and I cut the rosemary small so it doesn't stick between your teeth. Either way, they are delicious!"

Zucchini-Lemon Cookies

BY KELSEYTHENAPTIMECHEF | MAKES ABOUT 24 COOKIES

A&M: When we first saw this recipe, we knew we had to try it. KelseyTheNaptimeChef had come up with a concept we'd never considered before, and we were both intrigued and hopeful. These cookies are delicate and ultra-lemony, the crisp buttery base anchoring a tender, cakey dome. The zucchini is subtle, but every few bites it makes its presence known with a pleasant, vegetal undertone. We agreed that these brought to mind a modern-day English tea cake—we felt a hankering for a cuppa.

---

2 cups all-purpose flour

1 teaspoon baking powder

Pinch of coarse salt

¾ cup unsalted butter, at room temperature

¾ cup sugar

1 large egg

2 tablespoons freshly grated lemon zest

1 cup shredded zucchini

---

1. Heat the oven to 350°F.

2. In a bowl, combine the flour, baking powder, and salt. Set aside.

3. Combine the butter and sugar in the bowl of a standing mixer and beat until light and fluffy.

4. Add the egg and mix until incorporated. Add the lemon zest and zucchini, mixing until fully combined.

5. With the mixer on low, slowly add the flour mixture to the wet ingredients until all of the flour has been added and is completely mixed in. Do not overbeat.

6. Drop the dough by rounded teaspoons onto cookie sheets lined with parchment and bake for 14 to 16 minutes, or until the edges of the

cookies are golden. Cool for a minute or two on the cookie sheet, and then transfer to a wire rack to cool completely.

TIPS AND TECHNIQUES

The cookies are perfectly baked when they have a scattering of light brown "freckles" on top.

ABOUT THE COOK

Kelsey Banfield lives in Connecticut and writes the blog The Naptime Chef (www.thenaptimechef .com), and will be publishing a book of the same name in 2012. See her Double Chocolate Espresso Cookies on page 138 and her Chocolate Bundt Cake on page 249.

Her top entertaining tips: "Wine chills fastest in a bucket with half water/half ice. Always make sure your steak knives are sharpened *before* you serve meat to guests."

WHAT THE COMMUNITY SAID

Kabocha: "Just delicious! Airy and cake-like . . . perfect with tea or a latte in the morning, too."

Chilled Cantaloupe Soup

BY CHEF GWEN | SERVES 6

A&M: Cantaloupe soup is often overly sweet and one-dimensional. Not so with Chef Gwen's Chilled Cantaloupe Soup, which is from her *The Cool Mountain Cookbook*, and is adapted from the Topnotch Resort in Stowe, Vermont. She adds orange, lemon, and lime juice to the fruit, giving it a healthy blast of acidity, and then spices the soup with cinnamon and salt. When you taste it, you first get the sweet fruit, which seems impossibly bright and refreshing, and this is followed by gentle waves of cinnamon.

---

6 cups chopped cantaloupe, from about one 4-pound melon

1½ cups orange juice

¼ cup fresh lemon juice

¼ cup fresh lime juice

2 tablespoons honey

¼ teaspoon ground cinnamon

¼ teaspoon salt

½ cup whole-milk yogurt, thinned with a tablespoon or two of milk

1 fresh mint sprig

---

1. Place all of the ingredients except the yogurt and mint in a large bowl and stir.

2. Place half the mixture in a blender and puree until smooth. Pour the soup into a large pitcher, and repeat with the remaining mixture.

3. Taste and whisk in more cinnamon, honey, or lemon juice if desired. The soup should taste sweet and tart, with only a hint of cinnamon. Chill until ready to serve.

4. Remove the mint leaves from the stem and stack the leaves on top of each other. Roll lengthwise into a tight "cigar." Slice crosswise into thin strips.

5. Divide the chilled soup among 6 soup bowls. Garnish each with a swirl of the thinned yogurt and a sprinkle of mint and serve.

TIPS AND TECHNIQUES

The soup separates as it sits, so give it a stir before serving and make sure it's ice, ice cold. And don't forget the mint and yogurt, which aren't merely decorative—the yogurt enriches the soup and the mint adds a note of freshness.

Chef Gwen says: "Although it calls for cantaloupe, a really ripe honeydew melon would make a lovely substitution."

ABOUT THE COOK

Gwen Ashley Walters is a Phoenix-based food writer. Here's her website: Pen & Fork (www.penandfork .com).

Her favorite cooking tip: "Pureeing leftover vegetables with a little stock is a quick sauce-making tip. Just add an acid, like a splash of lemon juice or vinegar, and a pat of butter."

WHAT THE COMMUNITY SAID

ENunn: "I cannot wait to make this; I usually find cold soups and creative approaches to cantaloupe ridiculous: why not just eat the fruit? But this is right up my alley. Thanks for sharing it."

Foolproof Ice Cream

BY TAMMY | MAKES ABOUT 1¼ QUARTS

A&M: In her headnote, Tammy explained: "After making a number of ice cream recipes that did not turn out well, I dug into the 'science' of making ice cream at home." When we first read the recipe, we were slightly put off by the use of temperatures to determine doneness, as we tend to rely on sight and feel when it comes to making ice cream. When the method, which she adapted from an old *Cook's Illustrated* book, worked perfectly, we conceded that these details are really helpful for people who don't have much experience with custards—so get out your candy thermometer! Tammy's recipe makes a flawless, fragrant, and not-too-sweet vanilla ice cream, and she gives you the option to add your own flavors in the last step.

1½ cups whole milk

1½ cups heavy cream

¾ cup sugar

4 egg yolks

1 vanilla bean, split

---

1. Gently heat the milk and cream with half the sugar in a small saucepan to 175°F. (Use a candy thermometer!)

2. Meanwhile, beat the yolks with the remaining sugar for at least 2 minutes with an electric mixer (or 4 minutes with a whisk) until pale yellow.

3. Slowly pour a small amount of the heated milk-cream-sugar mixture into the egg yolks, whisking constantly as you pour.

4. Whisk the thinned egg yolks back into the saucepan containing the remaining milk, cream, and sugar.

5. Scrape the insides of the vanilla bean into the saucepan.

6. Heat the custard to 180°F, stirring constantly and making sure the egg doesn't start to scramble. The custard should thicken considerably.

7. Pour the cooked custard through a fine-mesh strainer into a container.

8. Chill the custard to 40°F or lower. (I usually make the custard right before I go to sleep so it can chill in my refrigerator overnight.)

9. Churn the custard in your ice cream maker for 30 minutes, or until frozen. If you have any add-ins, stir them into the ice cream in the last 30 seconds.

10. Put the ice cream in the freezer in an airtight container for 2 to 4 hours to harden completely.

11. Thirty minutes before serving, transfer the ice cream from the freezer to the fridge to soften a little.

TIPS AND TECHNIQUES

Tammy wrote: "The recipe is for vanilla, but you can adapt it to make lots of different flavors." After tasting the vanilla, we decided to play around, folding in ⅓ teaspoon strong peppermint extract (we used Boyajian), 10 finely chopped spearmint leaves, and 6 ounces finely chopped dark chocolate. Not to sound immodest, but it was some of the best mint chocolate chip ice cream we've ever had.

ABOUT THE COOK

Tammy is a technologist from New York. She has a crafting and cooking blog called TAH Handmade (www.tahhandmade.com).

Her kitchen pet peeve: "Dirty dishes sitting in the sink."

Simple Summer Peach Cake

BY SAVOUR | SERVES 8

A&M: We had high hopes for this peach cake, and it didn't let us down. Savour's inspiration came from childhood. "On summer mornings my mother would fix me a bowl of cut-up peaches with milk, sprinkled with sugar and a dusting of nutmeg," she wrote. "Although that's a pretty sublime combination, the flavors translate well to cake form." Indeed, they do. The cake is chock-full of juicy summer peaches, and the addition of ground almonds sets it apart from other simple butter cakes. It's luscious and a bit custardy in the areas surrounding the peaches—a texture that works when the cake is either warm or at room temperature. Don't be alarmed if the batter seems to curdle when you add the buttermilk, as it will come together again once you mix in the dry ingredients.

6 tablespoons softened unsalted butter, plus more for greasing the pan

1 cup all-purpose flour, plus more for dusting the pan

3 ripe peaches

¾ teaspoon freshly ground nutmeg

1 cup sugar

1 large egg

½ cup buttermilk

½ teaspoon vanilla extract

¼ teaspoon almond extract

½ cup almond flour (or finely ground almonds)

1 teaspoon baking powder

¼ teaspoon baking soda

Pinch of salt

Turbinado sugar

1. Heat the oven to 350°F. Butter and flour a 9-inch cake pan.

2. Cut the peaches into bite-size pieces. Toss the peaches with the nutmeg and 2 tablespoons of the sugar. Set aside.

3. In a large bowl, cream together the butter and remaining sugar with a wooden spoon or spatula. Add the egg, buttermilk, and extracts, and stir to combine.

4. In a medium bowl, combine the flours, baking powder, baking soda, and salt. Add this flour mixture to the butter mixture and mix until smooth (some lumps may remain). Pour into the prepared pan.

5. Press the peaches into the top of the cake. They can be nicely arranged, but I like to cram as many peaches as possible into the cake. Sprinkle turbinado sugar over the top.

6. Bake for 10 minutes, then reduce the oven heat to 325°F and bake for an additional 45 to 55 minutes, or until a toothpick in the center comes out clean. Cool in the pan for 10 minutes, than turn out onto a rack to cool completely.

TIPS AND TECHNIQUES

PerrySt: "I would recommend using a springform pan if you have one."

ABOUT THE COOK

Kate Wheeler lives in Los Angeles and writes a food blog called Savour Fare (www.savour-fare.com) and a home decor and design blog called Savour Home (www.savour-fare.com/savour-home).

Her favorite recipe from a cookbook: "I can always fall back on the chocolate chip cookie recipe from the 1963 edition of *McCall's Cookbook*. This was my childhood cookie recipe, and I have it memorized."

WHAT THE COMMUNITY SAID

Rhonda35: "Made this last night and threw in a good handful of blueberries along with the peaches. Delicious!"

The (Not Barefoot) Contessa's Fish Pasta

BY FISHERI | SERVES 4

A&M: Fisheri's recipe title—The (Not Barefoot) Contessa's Fish Pasta—caught our eye. Turns out the recipe comes from an actual contessa, a friend of fisheri's. "The mother of one of our boys' friends in Rome turned out to be a contessa, a title that only matters if other people care (and they seem to)," he wrote. "This is not a very fussy contessa; she doesn't mind sleeping on our couch. She can also cook for an army." The sauce reminded us of so much of the cooking we've seen in Italy, with vegetables and fish simmered for much longer than you'd expect. Here, the fish is sautéed in oil, and then it stays in the pan as wine is reduced and fresh tomatoes are added and simmered. We feared the fish would end up in shreds. Instead, we learned something: by adding the fish early on, its flavor infuses the whole sauce. And the capers and olives reinforce the flavor of the fish with brine. It ends up being a more vibrant version of puttanesca.

---

3 tablespoons olive oil

2 garlic cloves, crushed and chopped

1 pound white fish, such as striped bass or snapper, skinned and cut into bite-size chunks

Salt and freshly ground black pepper

Half a glass (⅓ cup) white wine

4 big, fresh tomatoes, roughly chopped

1 tablespoon salted capers

12 or so oil-cured olives, pitted and chopped

2 tablespoons roughly chopped flat-leaf parsley

1 pound linguine or spaghetti

---

1. Heat the olive oil in a large sauté pan over medium heat. Add the garlic and cook until soft, about 2 minutes. Add the fish, stirring carefully until browned. Try not to break it up.

2. Season the fish with salt and pepper, then pour in the white wine and turn up the heat to bring to a boil. Stir carefully until the wine is nearly evaporated.

3. Meanwhile, bring a large pot of generously salted water to a boil.

4. When the wine is nearly evaporated, reduce the heat, add the tomatoes, and cook until the sauce tightens slightly and becomes less liquid, about 10 minutes.

5. Stir in the capers (I prefer just to shake the salt off rather than wash them), olives, and parsley. Again, stir carefully; you don't want to turn this into fish puree. When the tomato juice is released and the sauce is just thickening, turn off the heat.

6. Cook the pasta al dente and drain it. Return the pasta to the pot.

7. Carefully add the sauce to the pasta over a little heat. Stir gently for a minute or two and serve.

TIPS AND TECHNIQUES

Fisheri said the sauce can be made with any flaky white fish, but "be careful when stirring the sauce: the fish should remain intact."

He also noted: "The tomatoes should be fresh and cooked al crudo, till the juices are released but they are still a little raw."

ABOUT THE COOK

Fisheri is an editor living in Brooklyn, New York.

WHAT THE COMMUNITY SAID

Likestocooklovestoeat: "This is more than the sum of its parts—so delicious, and now one of our favorite pasta dishes. Thank you for sharing the recipe!"

Steak for a Brooklyn Backyard Barbecue

BY GIULIA MELUCCI | SERVES 2

A&M: Giulia Melucci said this was an easy recipe, and it really is. We were drawn to it because we both like smoked paprika, which adds a toasted warmth to dishes. Everyone should have a steak rub that takes no time to make, something that you can throw together after work. If you don't already have such a recipe, make this one yours. You'll probably have leftover mint—sprinkle some over the sliced steak just before serving.

1 pound sirloin steak	1 ½ teaspoons smoked Spanish paprika
1 tablespoon olive oil	1 tablespoon chopped mint
1 teaspoon chopped garlic	1 teaspoon salt

1. Heat the grill to medium-high. Rub the steak with the olive oil, garlic, smoked paprika, mint, and salt. Allow the meat to come to room temperature, which should take 15 minutes or so, but if you don't have the luxury of time, it doesn't matter that much.

2. Grill over a very hot flame. (We did about 7 minutes per side for a perfect medium rare on a particularly thick piece of meat.)

TIPS AND TECHNIQUES

Giulia calls for a sirloin steak, but you can use any cut you like–porterhouse, skirt, you name it.
  We used sweet smoked paprika, but if you want a little heat, look for the "picante."

ABOUT THE COOK

Giulia Melucci is the author of *I Loved, I Lost, I Made Spaghetti: A Memoir of Good Food and Bad Boyfriends*. She lives in Brooklyn, New York.
  Here's her website of the same name: www.ilovedilostimadespaghetti.com.

WHAT THE COMMUNITY SAID

RayRay: "I find letting a steak get to room temperature is a great advantage to getting a perfect steak."

Smoky Pork Burgers with Fennel and Red Cabbage Slaw

BY LASTNIGHTSDINNER | MAKES 4 BURGERS, PLUS 2 CUPS OF SLAW

A&M: "Pork and fennel is one of my favorite flavor combinations, but the inspiration for putting them together in burger form came from, of all places, a food truck," wrote lastnightsdinner. "Chef Matt Gennuso of Chez Pascal restaurant here in Providence recently launched his Hewtin's Dogs Mobile food truck, which serves all manner of creative sausages and sandwiches, and one recent special was a revelation—a juicy slab of bacon-wrapped pork meat loaf served on a soft roll with a crunchy kohlrabi slaw."

Pork burgers always sound good in theory, but they don't necessarily turn out that way in practice. Ground pork can be dry and must be cooked just so. Lastnightsdinner came up with the perfect solution (and really the solution to so many of life's problems): just add bacon. She has you fold finely (and, as we learned, it needs to be really fine) chopped bacon into the ground pork, along with some great aromatics—fennel seed, onion, and smoked paprika. The bacon fat helps keep the burgers moist and adds its own layer of flavor. To go with the burger you make a tart little cabbage and fennel salad, just the right counterpoint to the rich burger. Lastnightsdinner added, "If a cheeseburger is your thing, a slice of melted Manchego wouldn't be out of place."

SMOKY PORK BURGERS
2 tablespoons fennel seeds
½ cup finely chopped onion
2 to 3 garlic cloves, minced
½ teaspoon kosher or sea salt
2 teaspoons smoked Spanish paprika
1 pound ground pork sirloin
1 cup finely chopped bacon, from 2 to 3 rashers
4 soft burger rolls or sandwich buns

FENNEL AND RED CABBAGE SLAW
2 tablespoons sherry vinegar
1 teaspoon apple cider vinegar
1 teaspoon Dijon mustard
½ teaspoon kosher or sea salt
1 tablespoon extra virgin olive oil
1 cup shredded fennel bulb
1 cup shredded red cabbage
1 tablespoon chopped fennel fronds

1. Gently toast the fennel seeds in a small, dry skillet until aromatic. Remove them from the pan and set aside.

2. In a large mixing bowl, combine the onion, garlic, fennel seeds, salt, and smoked paprika, stirring to combine.

3. Add the pork and bacon, tossing gently until the seasonings are well incorporated, but taking care not to overwork the meat.

4. Divide the seasoned pork into four portions and shape into patties. Place the patties on a plate or platter and chill for at least one hour.

5. Meanwhile, make the slaw: Combine the vinegars, mustard, and salt in a mixing bowl and whisk until the salt is dissolved.

6. Add the oil and whisk until the dressing is emulsified.

7. Place the shredded fennel and cabbage in the bowl on top of the dressing and toss to combine.

8. Add the fennel fronds, and toss again just before serving.

9. Heat a grill to medium high and cook the burgers: 6 minutes over the hot side of the grill, rotating them after the first 3 minutes, then flipping them and cooking them for another 3 minutes on the hot side before moving them to the cool side of the grill for the final 3 minutes. If you cut one open and it's light pink in the center, that's fine—if it's closer to rare, continue cooking the burger for a few more minutes.

10. Remove the burgers from the grill and allow them to rest briefly before serving.

11. Place the burgers on toasted or lightly grilled buns and top each one with a little of the fennel and cabbage slaw.

Many Food52ers suggested freezing the bacon so it's easier to slice.

Lastnightsdinner didn't specify whether you should use sweet or hot smoked paprika. If you like spicy food, you know which one to use.

ABOUT THE COOK

Jennifer Hess hails from Providence, Rhode Island, where she's a self-proclaimed "desk jockey by day, home cook and food blogger by night." While she eschews recipes on her blog, Last Night's Dinner– (www.lastnightsdinner.net), we're grateful that she bends her rules to share her cooking with all of us at Food52. See her Beef Chopped Salad on page 94, her Mussels for One (or Two) on page 234, and her Seared Scallops with Spring Onion and Tarragon Cream on page 349.

Her invaluable kitchen tip: "For cooking, it's so important to taste and season as you go. Recipes are great, but a dish has to please your palate, and the best way to make that happen is to taste and add salt and spicy or acidic components gradually."

WHAT THE COMMUNITY SAID

Bonnie59: "I made these for supper this evening and they were delicious! I even scraped off the foot of snow on the bbq to grill them!" (That's the kind of dedication we like.)

Watermelon and Goat Cheese Salad with a Verbena-Infused Vinaigrette

BY LOLI | SERVES 4

A&M: Not everyone is lucky enough to have lemon verbena growing in the backyard the way loli does, but this recipe is worth seeking some out. The herbal, citrus-scented vinaigrette lightly coats the sweet chunks of watermelon, and goat cheese adds a savory tang. We especially love the toasty crunch of the pistachios. We find that grinding the verbena with just a few drops of oil breaks it down quickly, and then the rest of the oil is easy to incorporate. We used only 4 ounces of goat cheese, but our watermelon wasn't huge and had a particularly thick rind. Adjust your proportions as needed.

---

1 handful fresh lemon verbena leaves (see Tips and Techniques for substitutions)

½ cup extra virgin olive oil

1 teaspoon coarse salt

½ seedless watermelon

½ cup unsalted pistachios

4 to 6 ounces fresh goat cheese

2 tablespoons red wine vinegar

Maldon (or other flaky) sea salt

Freshly ground black pepper

---

1. Roughly chop the verbena and place it in a mortar. Add the olive oil and coarse salt. Grind for 2 to 3 minutes and let it sit for about an hour at room temperature.

2. Cut the watermelon into 1-inch cubes and place in a salad bowl (or on a platter) in the refrigerator.

3. Place the pistachios in a small pan and set over low heat. Cook just until toasted, about 5 minutes. Remove the pistachios from the pan and chop them roughly. Set aside.

4. Crumble the goat cheese.

5. In a small bowl, whisk together the olive oil–verbena mixture and vinegar.

6. Take the watermelon out of the fridge, sprinkle on the goat cheese, drizzle on the vinaigrette, add the pistachios, and season with Maldon sea salt and pepper to taste. Mix gently and serve!

TIPS AND TECHNIQUES

If you don't have access to verbena, try either 1½ tablespoons minced lemongrass or a mix of lemon zest (from 1 lemon) and 3 tablespoons chopped basil.

In order to preserve the pristine beauty of this salad, you can skip mixing the salad in the last step and allow people to do this as they're eating it.

ABOUT THE COOK

Lauren Sozmen is an event planner living in Larchmont, New York.

Her best entertaining tips: "Prepare as much as you can in advance so you can enjoy the party too. Always have champagne in the fridge!"

WHAT THE COMMUNITY SAID

Bevi: "I assembled this for our pre-parade picnic, and it was fabulous! I took Amanda's suggestions and used lemon zest combined with basil leaves. The vinaigrette was refreshing and very sublime. I used the zest of one lemon and a handful of basil. Not only was this a tasty variation on the usual watermelon on the 4th, it was a beautiful presentation."

Lemon Basil Sherbet

BY SANDY SMITH | MAKES ABOUT 1 QUART

A&M: This sherbet is everything we want in a refreshing frozen treat. It's light and airy yet indulgent, with just the right balance of tart and sweet, and a hint of cream to round out the flavors. As if this weren't enough, Sandy Smith includes an inspired detail: she infuses the sherbet base with fresh basil leaves and then adds chopped basil before freezing the mixture. The results are subtle and bewitching. As Sandy noted in her recipe, the sherbet is best after a couple of hours in the freezer, as it emerges from the ice cream maker a bit soft.

---

1 cup half-and-half or light cream

⅔ cup sugar

2 tablespoons honey, plus more as needed

1½ tablespoons lemon zest

8 fresh basil leaves, divided

2 cups whole milk

Juice of 3 lemons, chilled

Pinch of fine sea salt

---

1. In a medium heavy-bottomed saucepan, combine the half-and-half, sugar, honey, and lemon zest. Bring to a simmer, stirring occasionally to dissolve the sugar. Remove from the heat and add 4 whole basil leaves. Using the back of a large spoon or ladle, bruise the basil leaves against the bottom of the pot. Cover and let steep 15 minutes.

2. Remove the basil leaves and discard, then whisk in the milk. Place the pan in an ice water bath or refrigerate until completely chilled.

3. Slice the remaining 4 basil leaves in very thin strips. Whisk the lemon juice into the chilled sherbet base, add the salt, and stir in the sliced basil. Taste for sweetness; adjust by adding an additional 1 or 2 tablespoons honey, if needed.

4. Freeze the sherbet mixture in an ice cream maker, following the manufacturer's instructions. For optimal flavor and texture, freeze the sherbet for a couple of hours before serving.

TIPS AND TECHNIQUES

Sandy said: "This technique works great for all manner of herbs and spices, and teas too. If you're using a dried herb, though, you'll only need about one-third as much."

ABOUT THE COOK

Sandy Smith is a food writer, editor, and baker living in the Hudson Valley, New York. Here's her blog: Real Food for Real People (www.realfoodforrealpeople.blogspot.com).

Her favorite cookbook recipe: "If I can pick only one, I'll go with a fundamental: Dorie Greenspan's Sweet Tart Dough from her phenomenal *Baking: From My Home to Yours.*"

BLT Panzanella

BY MEREDITH SHANLEY | SERVES 4

A&M: What struck us immediately about Meredith Shanley's recipe was its clever origins—one night, her husband wanted a grilled steak for dinner and she wanted a BLT, so she grilled the steak and made the BLT into a salad. We're also biased toward any recipe that calls for bacon. In a smart maneuver, Meredith not only uses cubed bacon in the salad, but she saves some of the drippings for the dressing, a bright lemony affair made creamy with Dijon mustard and a touch of mayo. The juices from the tomatoes meld with the dressing, helping to make a little go a long way, and peppery arugula keeps the salad from being too rich. Resist the temptation to use too much bread, or the salad won't be balanced the way it should be.

SALAD

½ loaf ciabatta bread, cubed

3 ounces slab bacon, cut into ¼-inch cubes

3 small to medium tomatoes, diced large

3 large handfuls arugula, roughly chopped

CREAMY LEMON DRESSING

½ lemon, juiced

Zest of ¼ lemon

1 teaspoon Dijon mustard

Salt and freshly ground black pepper

3 tablespoons extra virgin olive oil

2 teaspoons mayonnaise, preferably Hellmann's

---

1. Heat the oven to 350°F.

2. Place the cubed bread in a single layer on a cookie sheet. Toast in the oven until golden and completely dry, 15 to 20 minutes.

3. In a medium sauté pan, cook the bacon until slightly crisp and nicely browned. Remove to paper towels; reserve 1 teaspoon drippings.

4. To make the dressing, combine the lemon juice, zest, Dijon mustard, and salt and pepper.

5. Whisk together the bacon drippings and olive oil, then add in a slow stream to the Dijon mixture, whisking as you pour.

6. Once the dressing is emulsified, whisk in the mayonnaise until it's fully incorporated and slightly creamy.

7. Toss the tomatoes, bacon, bread, and salt and pepper with the dressing.

8. Just before serving, toss in the arugula. Check for seasoning and serve.

TIPS AND TECHNIQUES
Keep the bread cubes smaller than 1 inch.

ABOUT THE COOK
Meredith Shanley is a private chef and caterer living in New York City. Here's her blog: What's for Lunch, Dot? (www.whatsforlunchdot.com).

Her favorite recipe from a cookbook: "The Coconut Cake with Lime Curd from *The Gourmet Cookbook* is pretty much the perfect birthday cake."

WHAT THE COMMUNITY SAID
Leslie: "A superb salad: fun to prepare, well balanced, colorful, and exceptionally tasty! Yum!"

Zucchini Pancakes

BY DAGNY | SERVES 2

A&M: These pancakes almost didn't get photographed because we began eating them, dabbed with Greek yogurt, as they emerged from the frying pan. A little grated potato binds the cakes and gives them the crispness of latkes, while the zucchini is fresh and lively, perfumed with lemon zest and parsley. Dagny said to squeeze out any extra moisture from the potatoes and zucchini with a towel, and you should definitely take this extra step. The pancakes will be crisper and lighter, and you, too, will devour them straight from the pan.

---

3 medium zucchini, trimmed

1 medium white potato, peeled

Salt

1 large egg

1 tablespoon chopped parsley

1 teaspoon grated lemon zest

Freshly ground black pepper

Pinch of bread crumbs

1 tablespoon unsalted butter, plus more as needed

2 tablespoons sour cream or Greek-style yogurt (optional)

---

1. Grate the zucchini and potato using the largest hole on your grater. You'll need 2 cups grated zucchini and ½ cup grated potato. Salt generously and let stand in a colander for at least 30 minutes to drain. The finished pancakes will hold together better if you drain out as much moisture as possible.

2. In a bowl, beat the egg, parsley, and lemon zest. Add a pinch of salt and pepper to taste.

3. Roll and squeeze the zucchini-potato mixture in a towel to soak up moisture. Add a pinch of bread crumbs to soak up any leftover wetness.

4. Combine the zucchini-potato mixture with the egg mixture. Stir well to coat.

5. Heat the oven to 200°F and place a cookie sheet lined with aluminum foil in the oven to keep your pancakes warm as you make them.

6. Heat a large skillet over medium-high heat. Melt the butter. You can use olive oil if you prefer, but butter is delicious. When the foam subsides, drop tablespoonfuls of your pancake mixture in the pan. You don't really need to form the pancakes in advance, but pat them with a spatula (or spread them with a fork) and try to flatten them out as much as possible—they'll be crispier that way.

7. Cook the pancakes until golden brown on each side, then place in the oven to keep warm while you make additional pancakes. Serve as soon as possible, and, if you like, with a dollop of sour cream or drained Greek-style yogurt on top for extra richness.

TIPS AND TECHNIQUES

If the batter seems too dry, you can add an extra egg to help it come together.

ABOUT THE COOK

Dagny Prieto is a Brooklyn, New York–based user-experience designer. Here's her website: www .dagnyprieto.com.

Her most treasured kitchen possession: "My Le Creuset braising pot."

WHAT THE COMMUNITY SAID

Camelotcook: "All I can say is *wow*! These bring back memories of what my mother used to make for me, and I will now make these for my grandson."

BEHIND THE SCENES

This was the first time we didn't cook together for our photo shoot. Amanda, out in Wainscott, Long Island, with her family, went it alone, and Sarah's photos came out distinctly different because of the new beach house setting–which, in our opinion, was very cool.

Sweet and Savory Tomato Jam

BY JENNIFER PERILLO | MAKES 1 ½ PINTS

A&M: We're huge fans of tomato preserves, but we'd never made one quite like this. Jennifer Perillo's recipe calls for vinegar, cumin, coriander, onion, and salt, which we expected to translate into a chutneylike preserve. But there's enough sugar in this jam to keep it balanced—deliciously—between sweet and savory. It made us realize that tomatoes really need an acid like vinegar to underline their sweetness; the vinegar also adds a crucial sense of richness to the jam. Jennifer noted that it has "just enough sweetness to toe the line between a condiment for roasted and grilled meats and a treat to slather on toasted baguette." The only issue with this recipe is that it makes just 3 half pints; we'd like to share it and yet we find it difficult to part with any of them.

3½ pounds tomatoes, coarsely chopped

1 small onion, chopped

½ cup lightly packed brown sugar

1½ cups sugar

1 teaspoon salt

½ teaspoon ground coriander

¼ teaspoon ground cumin

¼ cup cider vinegar

Juice of 1 lemon

Put all the ingredients in a 2-quart pot. Bring to a gentle boil, then reduce the heat to a simmer. Cook until thickened and jamlike in consistency, stirring occasionally, about 3 hours. Transfer to sterilized glass jars and store in the refrigerator for up to 2 weeks, or process in a hot-water canning bath for 15 minutes for long-term storage.

ABOUT THE COOK

Jennifer Perillo is a recipe developer and food editor from Brooklyn, New York. She writes a food blog called In Jennie's Kitchen (www.injennieskitchen.com).

Something she'd like a chance to eat: "There's a 100-year-old bottle of balsamic vinegar that costs $750 at a local Italian shop."

WHAT THE COMMUNITY SAID

Melissav: "I made this last week and it was delicious. Even my husband (a recovering tomato hater) admitted it was yummy. We plan on serving some at our next wine tasting on top of goat-cheese-slathered crostini."

Blackberry Caipirinha

BY MISSGINSU | MAKES 1 DRINK

A&M: A classic caipirinha is made with cachaça (distilled from sugarcane), sugar, and lime juice. MissGinsu's version doesn't stray far—she adds fresh blackberries, which dye the drink a deep purple. It's bright and a little austere. The recipe calls for 1 teaspoon of sugar, but you may want to add more to taste if your blackberries are tart. Add any extra sugar after the drink is shaken, and shake it again to dissolve the added sugar. If you can't find cachaça, you can use white rum.

---

6 to 8 plump blackberries

1 teaspoon sugar

½ lime, cut into 3 wedges

2 ounces cachaça (or white rum)

¾ cup ice cubes

---

1. In a shaker or pint glass, muddle/mash up the blackberries and the sugar with 2 of the lime wedges.

2. Add the cachaça or rum and the ice. Cover well and shake vigorously.

3. Remove and discard the crushed lime wedges. Pour the mixture into a rocks glass and use the remaining wedge of lime as a garnish.

TIPS AND TECHNIQUES

MissGinsu said: "If you want to, you can run a little water or lime around the rim of the rocks glass and dip it in sugar before you pour in the cocktail to give it a pretty edge."

And: "Keep in mind, this is a drink that requires a good, fierce muddling." So don't hold back.

ABOUT THE COOK

Leitha Matz is a Web-content manager and writer living in New York City. Here's her blog: Miss Ginsu (www.missginsu.com).

Her favorite entertaining tip: "Whether you're at a fancy party or a basic shindig, pigs in blankets are always one of the first things to go. Even if they're made with veggie dogs or beef franks. People just go crazy for tiny sausages wrapped in pastry."

Seriously Delicious Ribs

BY JENNIFER PERILLO | SERVES 4 TO 6

A&M: The recipe title doesn't lie: these ribs are seriously delicious. Jennifer Perillo's low and slow braising method ensures tender meat, and broiling the ribs at the end caramelizes the glaze beautifully. We love the addition of Prosecco, which gives the glaze a faintly boozy flavor that's hard to put your finger on. And the combination of instant espresso and chipotle in the rub lends smoky depth. We reduced the glaze until it was very thick and syrupy, and found that it really clung to the ribs. We made these ribs twice, using both a grill and a broiler for the last step, and both work equally well.

DRY RUB
½ cup light brown sugar

2 teaspoons sweet paprika

1 teaspoon garlic powder

½ teaspoon freshly ground black pepper

1 tablespoon kosher salt

1 teaspoon instant espresso powder

¼ teaspoon allspice

1 teaspoon chipotle powder (optional)

2 slabs pork baby back ribs (3 to 3 ½ pounds total)

BRAISING LIQUID/BBQ GLAZE
1 cup sparkling white wine, like Prosecco

2 tablespoons apple cider vinegar

2 tablespoons Worcestershire sauce

1 tablespoon honey

---

1. Heat the oven to 250°F.

2. Add all the dry rub ingredients (from brown sugar to chipotle powder) to the bowl of a food processor. Pulse until the ingredients are combined, about two or three 1-second pulses. Rub the mixture evenly all over each rack of ribs, making sure to coat the top and bottom. Place the ribs, in a single layer, on 2 rimmed baking sheets or in a roasting pan and let sit, covered, in the refrigerator for 1 hour.

3. Meanwhile, place the braising liquid ingredients in a small pot and cook over medium heat until just hot. Alternately, you can add them to a microwave-safe bowl and cook on high for 1 minute.

4. Remove the ribs from the refrigerator. Pour the braising liquid over the ribs, wrap tightly with heavy-duty aluminum foil, and place the pan(s) in the oven, side by side if possible. Cook for 2½ hours, or until

the meat is very tender and easily pulls away from the bone. Rotate the pans halfway through if cooking on separate racks in the oven.

5. Remove the pans from the oven, discard the foil, and pour or spoon the braising liquid into a medium saucepan. Bring to a boil, then reduce to a vigorous simmer and let cook until the liquid reduces by half and has a thick, syrupy consistency, 20 to 30 minutes.

6. Heat the broiler. Brush the glaze on top of each rack of ribs. Place the ribs under the broiler until the glaze begins to caramelize, 1 to 2 minutes (watch carefully, or all your waiting will be spoiled by burned ribs!). Slice and serve with the remaining glaze on the side.

TIPS AND TECHNIQUES
Jennifer's ideal drink pairing? "An old-fashioned made with Eagle Rare single-barrel bourbon is the perfect partner."

ABOUT THE COOK
To learn about Jennifer Perillo, and to see her winning recipe for Sweet and Savory Tomato Jam, turn to page 80.

WHAT THE COMMUNITY SAID
Blim8183: "Made these today and they were a huge hit with my friends. I will definitely be making these again . . . often . . ."

Classic Southern Buttermilk-Bathed Fried Chicken

BY CHEF JAMES | SERVES 6

A&M: Chef James wrote that this recipe took nearly twenty years to develop, and we think it shows. The result is intensely flavorful and expertly spiced chicken with a crisp, dark skin reminiscent of parchment. The meat gets coated in a lively spice rub before being doused with buttermilk and hot sauce, which adds another layer of heat. The brine tenderizes the dark meat, and then it's time for a quick dusting of flour and a date with the fryer.

SPICE RUB

1 teaspoon dried thyme

1 teaspoon dried marjoram

2 teaspoons onion powder

2 teaspoons garlic powder

½ teaspoon cayenne pepper

3 tablespoons salt

1 tablespoon freshly ground black pepper

6 chicken legs (legs and thighs
    separated)

BUTTERMILK BRINE

2 quarts buttermilk

¼ cup vinegar-based hot sauce, like Tabasco or
    Cholula

6 cups all-purpose flour

Salt and freshly ground black pepper

Peanut or canola oil for frying

---

1. For the spice rub: In a medium bowl, mix all the dry spices. Add the chicken pieces and toss until well coated. Refrigerate for 1 hour.

2. Pour enough buttermilk over the chicken to cover completely and stir in the hot sauce. Leave on the counter for 1 to 2 hours, or refrigerate up to 24 hours. Pour the chicken legs into a colander and allow the excess buttermilk to drain away.

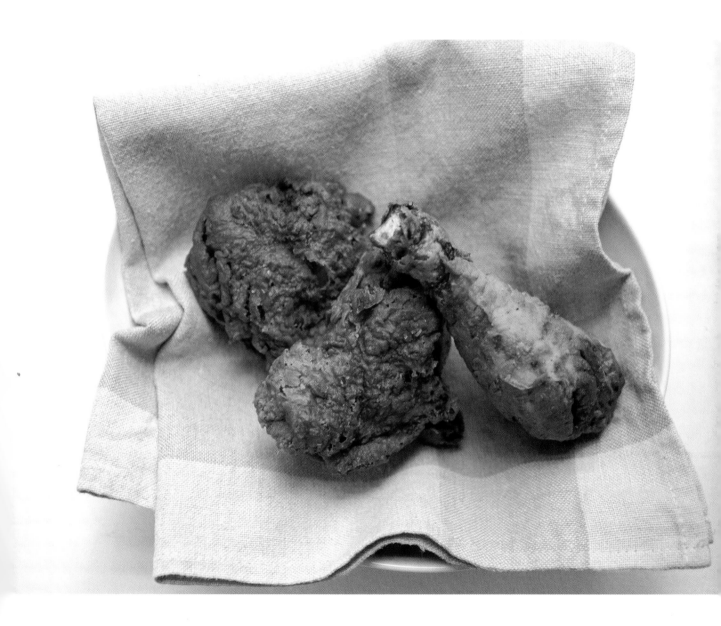

3. In a large bowl, mix the flour with salt and pepper to season well. One by one, add the chicken pieces, making sure they are thoroughly coated with flour on all sides. Leave them in the bowl with the excess flour while you wait for the oil to heat up.

4. Fill a very large saucepan 4 inches deep with oil and heat over medium heat to 325°F. Grab each piece of chicken and slap it back and forth between your hands a few times to knock off the excess flour before slipping it into the oil. As the legs go into the oil, the temperature will drop. Turn the flame to high to increase the temperature to 350°F as the chicken cooks. Cook until golden brown and at least 160°F at the bone, 12 to 18 minutes. Remove to a rack to drain and season immediately with salt. Cool for a few minutes and serve.

TIPS AND TECHNIQUES

Chef James said: "The trick to frying is starting with a lower temperature that increases through cooking to ensure perfect crispness and the right amount of browning." He calls for heating the oil to 325°F and letting it gradually climb to 350°F, but we found that our chicken ended up a bit dark. For our second batch, we started at 300°F and maxed out at about 340°F, which produced a perfect mahogany crust. All fryers are different, though, so just keep an eye on the browning and adjust your temperature accordingly.

ABOUT THE COOK

James Briscione is a chef-instructor and writer living in New York City. He and his wife, Brooke Parkhurst, have just completed their first cookbook, appropriately titled *Just Married and Cooking*. Here's their website of the same name: www.justmarriedandcooking.com.

His number one cooking tip: "Keep your knives sharp!"

Eggplant Parmesan

BY NANCY JO | SERVES 6

A&M: All of the cooking here is centered around getting the eggplant and tomatoes to the right texture so that when you fuse them, neither is the sauce watery nor the eggplant soggy. Nancy Jo accomplishes this by baking slabs of flour-dusted eggplant in the oven with just a trace of oil. They come out as stiff as cards. And the tomatoes are cooked down in the pan until pulpy. When the two meet in a baking dish, the eggplant soaks up some tomato juices but retains its own character, so you get distinct layers. And Nancy Jo adds the mozzarella as a center layer, so you get the warm melted cheese right in the belly of the dish. Use fresh mozzarella, which is creamy and even a little sweet.

EGGPLANT
3 pounds eggplant
Salt
Generous amount of olive oil
1 cup all-purpose flour
1 cup grated Parmesan
½ pound buffalo mozzarella

SAUCE
Enough olive oil to cover the base of the pan
3 garlic cloves, thinly sliced
Two 28-ounce cans whole, peeled tomatoes
  (San Marzano, or any brand you like)
Salt

1. Peel the eggplant and slice lengthwise into ¼-inch slices.

2. Sprinkle each layer with salt and place in a colander, overlapping and salting as you go. Each slice should be salted. After you fill the colander, lay a plate on top and weight it with a heavy pan or a teakettle filled with water. Let the eggplant sweat for 30 minutes or more.

3. While the eggplant sweats, make the sauce. Coat the bottom of a large saucepan with olive oil and heat over medium-high heat. Add the garlic and cook until it sizzles (do not let it brown). Add the tomatoes and their juice and a large pinch of salt. Stir and chop coarsely using a potato masher or two knives

cutting crosswise. Lower the heat and simmer until reduced by almost half. Taste and adjust the salt if necessary.

4. Remove the eggplant from the colander and thoroughly pat dry each slice.

5. Set a rack in the top third of the oven, then heat the oven to 450°F. Coat the bottom of a baking sheet (or two—you need enough space to hold all the eggplant in a single layer) with olive oil.

6. Dredge the eggplant slices in flour, shaking off any excess. Arrange on the baking sheets and drizzle each slice with olive oil. Bake until brown on one side (about 15 minutes or so), then turn over and brown the other side. Repeat until you have cooked all the eggplant. Lower the heat to 400°F.

7. Using a 7×11-inch baking dish (I like ceramic or earthenware, but you can use stainless steel as well), spread a thin layer of sauce on the bottom and layer the eggplant until it completely covers the bottom (it's like a puzzle!).

8. Sprinkle generously with the Parmesan. Add another layer of sauce and then the eggplant. Continue to build the layers until you are about two layers from the top, then add a single layer of sliced mozzarella. Finish with a couple of more layers of eggplant, sauce, and Parmesan. Finish the top with Parmesan.

9. Place the dish on the rack in the top third of the oven. Check it after it's been in for 20 minutes. You may find that it throws off more liquid as it bakes. If so, press down on the eggplant and draw off any excess liquid. Cook for another 15 minutes or so. Let stand for a good 15 to 20 minutes before serving.

TIPS AND TECHNIQUES

When selecting eggplants, choose ones that are large, smooth, and firm. If possible, Nancy Jo said, "go for male eggplants. They have fewer seeds and a rounder, smoother bottom."

If you want extra sauce for leftovers, Nancy Jo recommended adding another can of whole, peeled tomatoes to the recipe.

ABOUT THE COOK

For details on Nancy Jo, as well as a peek at her winning Summer Corn Chowder recipe, turn to page 13.

WHAT THE COMMUNITY SAID

Jennifer Perillo: "I made this last night using your technique and it was wonderful. The eggplant was indeed crispy and I loved the hidden surprise of fresh mozzarella in the center. A nice lesson in moderation compared to other eggplant parms."

Tuscan Grilled Zucchini and Summer Squash

BY STEFANO COPPOLA | SERVES 4 TO 6

A&M: This dish is a great example of the whole equaling more than the sum of its parts. At first glance, the recipe seems like one we've all seen before, but we've never tasted grilled zucchini quite like this. The porous squash soaks up the lemon, garlic, herbs, and chile in the marinade, and after a quick char on the grill, it's throbbing with flavor. Add the mellow sweetness of red onion grilled in its own skin and you've got a bowl of vegetables that's irresistible. You'll have leftover marinade, which is a good thing: reuse it to grill more veggies or drizzle over a salad.

Sturdy skewers	½ cup red wine vinegar
5 garlic cloves, minced	2 cups extra virgin olive oil
Leaves from 4 rosemary sprigs, chopped	2 zucchini, cut into 1-inch cubes
1 oregano sprig, chopped	3 summer squash, cut into 1-inch cubes
½ tablespoon crushed red pepper flakes	2 red onions, unpeeled and halved
3 lemons, zested and juiced	Salt and freshly ground black pepper

1. If using wood skewers, soak them in hot water. Make the marinade: Combine the garlic, herbs, red pepper flakes, lemon juice and zest, and vinegar in a mixing bowl. Whisk in the oil.

2. Place the zucchini and squash into a large resealable plastic bag, pour the marinade over, and seal. Allow to marinate for at least 30 minutes, preferably for a few hours.

3. Heat the grill to high.

4. Remove the zucchini and squash from the marinade and place on skewers (4 to 5 pieces to a skewer).

5. Grill the onions, turning occasionally, until they are charred on the outside, about 15 minutes. Place them in a bowl and cover it with plastic wrap to steam the onions.

6. Grill the zucchini and squash until tender, 5 to 6 minutes total, turning occasionally.

7. Peel and slice the onions. Pull the zucchini and squash off the skewers, toss with the onion, and season with salt and pepper. Serve.

TIPS AND TECHNIQUES

Stefano: "The marinade can be tweaked with any woodsy herb and by substituting a different vinegar or citrus juice. A super-hot grill and sturdy skewers are key."

We marinated the squash at room temperature. We also seasoned it generously with salt and pepper before throwing the skewers on the grill, adding a bit more seasoning later along with a tablespoon of oil from the marinade.

ABOUT THE COOK

Stefano P. Coppola is a culinary arts student on the East Coast.

His favorite cookbook recipe: "Thomas Keller's Confit Pork Belly from *Ad Hoc*."

WHAT THE COMMUNITY SAID

Lastnightsdinner: "This is really one of those perfect summertime dishes."

Beef Chopped Salad

BY LASTNIGHTSDINNER | SERVES 4

A&M: Beef and blue cheese are always an appealing match. And when you throw potatoes, tomatoes, peppery greens, homemade pickled onions, and garlic croutons into the mix, how can we say no? While it has many different components, we love the way this salad comes together; all of the vegetables and the meat end up coated in a creamy blanket of dressing and blue cheese.

Lastnightsdinner saves time by dividing the same mixture of red wine, sherry vinegar, and olive oil and using it to both marinate the steak and serve as the dressing for the salad. The onions (we used shallots), which pickle gently in salt, sherry vinegar, and juniper berries while you prepare the rest of the salad, contribute subtle acidity and sweetness. Lastnightsdinner calls for bottom round, which is relatively inexpensive but has excellent flavor with a tender bite.

BEEF AND SALAD

¼ cup dry red wine

¼ cup sherry vinegar

Kosher or sea salt and freshly ground black pepper

⅓ cup plus 1 teaspoon extra virgin olive oil

½ pound bottom round, about 1 ½ inches thick (we buy grass-fed)

2 tablespoons chopped garlic

1 cup waxy potato chunks (½ to 1 inch)

1 cup halved small cherry or grape tomatoes

¼ pound firm blue cheese, such as Maytag Blue, cut into ½-inch chunks

4 cups young arugula or spinach leaves

1 cup chunky garlic croutons, homemade or store-bought

QUICK PICKLED RED ONIONS

1 teaspoon kosher or pickling salt

1 teaspoon juniper berries

¼ cup sherry vinegar

½ cup thin rings of small, young red onion or shallot

---

1. In a large measuring cup, combine the wine, sherry vinegar, 1 teaspoon salt, and 2 teaspoons pepper, whisking to dissolve the salt. Whisk in ⅓ cup of olive oil until emulsified.

2. Set aside ¼ cup of this mixture, then pour the remainder over the beef in a glass container or zip-top plastic bag. Add the garlic and refrigerate, allowing the meat to marinate at least 1 hour. Pour the reserved red wine mixture into a large salad bowl.

3. Meanwhile, make the pickled red onions. Combine the salt, juniper berries, and sherry vinegar in a small bowl, whisking to dissolve the salt. Add ¼ cup water and the sliced onions and let sit at room temperature for 1 hour. (Use right away, or store in their brine in the refrigerator. These stay good for at least a few days, and are great on salads, sandwiches, and burgers or as an accompaniment to grilled meats.)

4. Boil the potato cubes in salted water until just tender. Drain the potatoes, and while they are still warm, add them to the salad bowl and toss with the dressing.

5. Remove the meat from the marinade and allow it to come to room temperature. Discard the marinade.

6. Heat the oven to 350°F. Add the remaining teaspoon of oil to an iron skillet. Use a small basting brush to distribute the oil evenly and heat over medium heat until the oil is almost smoking.

7. Pat the meat completely dry with paper towels, add to the hot pan, and sear until it is well browned on all sides, 1 to 2 minutes per side. Transfer the skillet to the oven. Cook the meat for 6 to 8 minutes, turning it halfway through, until the internal temperature reaches 130°F to 135°F for medium-rare. Remove the beef from the skillet, place on a plate, and tent loosely with aluminum foil so that the meat can rest for 10 minutes.

8. Chop the beef into ½- to 1-inch chunks and add to the salad bowl. Add the tomatoes, blue cheese, greens, and croutons and toss gently to combine. Serve in deep bowls, scattering pickled onions over the top and grinding on additional black pepper at the table.

TIPS AND TECHNIQUES

To make our garlic croutons, we rubbed two thick slices of stale country bread with a clove of garlic, cut the bread into 1-inch cubes, and toasted them in the oven at 350°F for about 10 minutes.

ABOUT THE COOK

For more on lastnightsdinner, as well as her recipe for Smoky Pork Burgers with Fennel and Red Cabbage Slaw, turn to page 66. See her Mussels for One (or Two) on page 234 and her Seared Scallops with Spring Onion and Tarragon Cream on page 349.

WHAT THE COMMUNITY SAID

Recipegal: "Sounds delicious, and I might use leftover oven-roasted potatoes along with rib-eye steak."

Savory Plum Tart

BY JACKIEK | MAKES ONE 9-INCH TART

A&M: One mark of a great recipe is when each component is terrific in its own right. The pastry for this tart is beautiful and lovely to work with (as long as it's chilled). The caramelized onions are delicious. And the way the plums are cooked—quickly sautéed with sugar added during the last moments—is a great technique for sautéing fruit. The edges brown, the fruit warms through without falling apart, and the tiny sprinkling of sugar forms a light glaze. JackieK's tart would make an impressive hors d'oeuvre—one whose components can be made in advance, then assembled just before guests arrive—or a last course for people who aren't big dessert eaters.

TART SHELL (BASIC PÂTE BRISÉE)

1 cup all-purpose flour

½ teaspoon salt

8 tablespoons unsalted butter, chilled and cubed

1 large egg

PLUM FILLING

1 tablespoon extra virgin olive oil

½ yellow onion, thinly sliced

Pinch of salt

1 tablespoon unsalted butter

2 firm plums, pitted and thinly sliced

1 teaspoon sugar

1 tablespoon mascarpone

1 teaspoon honey

1 teaspoon balsamic vinegar

1 tablespoon thinly sliced fresh basil

---

1. To make the tart shell: Combine the flour and salt in the bowl of a food processor. Add the butter and pulse for about 5 seconds until well combined. Pour in ¼ cup ice water and pulse just until the dough forms a ball. Note: This can also be done by hand. Use your fingertips to blend in the butter, but be sure to work quickly so it doesn't melt.

2. Form the dough into a ball and wrap in plastic. Freeze 1 hour or refrigerate overnight.

3. Heat the oven to 400°F. Roll out the dough onto a floured work surface to create a circle ⅛ inch thick. Invert a 9-inch plate over the dough to measure the size of the tart and cut out a circle. Set the dough onto

a silicone baking sheet or a baking sheet lined with parchment paper. Crimp the edges of the dough to make a decorative edge. Don't worry if the tart doesn't look perfect—it's supposed to be rustic.

4. Set a piece of aluminium foil over the dough and fill with dried beans. Leave the edges exposed. In a small bowl, whisk together the egg and 1 tablespoon water. Use a pastry brush to lightly coat the edges with egg wash.

5. Bake the tart dough for 8 minutes. Remove the foil and the dried beans, and use a fork to dock the bottom of the tart. Return the tart to the oven and bake for 10 minutes, or until cooked through and lightly browned. Cool to room temperature.

6. To make the plum filling: Heat the olive oil in a large sauté pan set over medium heat. Add the onions, season with salt, and cook, stirring often, until soft and caramelized, 15 to 18 minutes. Remove the onions from the pan.

7. Increase the heat to medium-high. Melt the butter in the pan, then add the plums. Cook, stirring often, until lightly roasted, about 5 minutes. Stir in the sugar and cook 2 minutes longer, then remove from the pan and cool to room temperature.

8. To assemble the tart: Begin by spreading the mascarpone over the cooled tart shell. Top with a layer of caramelized onions, then arrange the plum slices in a fan shape. Drizzle the honey and balsamic vinegar over the top and garnish with the thinly sliced basil. Serve at room temperature.

TIPS AND TECHNIQUES

JackieK said: "This tart is delightful as an appetizer or as dessert." If serving it for dessert, sprinkle on a little more honey and a little less balsamic vinegar.

Chicago-based Jaclyn Kolber wears many hats: "Chef, food writer, recipe tester, food stylist, and culinary instructor for kids." Here's her blog: Foodie Reflections (www.foodiereflections.com).

Her favorite cookbook: "The Flavor Bible."

WHAT THE COMMUNITY SAID

MrsWheelbarrow: "I've been dreaming of this tart since last summer when I think I made it ten times during plum season. Plums are not quite in the markets yet, so this week I made the tart with apricots. *Yum.* It's a brilliant recipe and I expect I'll make it at least ten more times this year."

Mediterranean Octopus Salad

BY SASA STUCIN + JAN VRANJEK | SERVES 4

A&M: Marinated octopus is a dish we're always delighted to see on an antipasti table—so why don't we make it at home? Sasa and Jan convinced us to give it a try. And it's so painless—no different from boiling a vegetable and dressing it with oil and herbs. With octopus, you just boil it for a little while longer. As Sasa and Jan noted, this salad is "refreshing and light" and brings out the fresh buttery flavor of octopus, marinating it with a pared-down dressing of lemon, onion, parsley, and olive oil—flavors that are intrinsic to the Mediterranean.

OCTOPUS

2 bay leaves

3 garlic cloves

Whole peppercorns

Salt

1 pound fresh, cleaned octopus

SALAD

Small bunch flat-leaf parsley, finely chopped

1 small onion, finely chopped

Juice of ½ lemon (or more to taste)

Extra virgin olive oil

Salt and freshly ground black pepper

1. Bring a large pot of water to a simmer. Add the bay leaves, garlic cloves, a few whole peppercorns, salt, and the octopus and cover. Let the octopus simmer for about an hour, until tender but not overcooked. Drain, discarding the bay leaves, peppercorns, and garlic.

2. Cut the octopus in half and try to remove the slimy outer layer of the octopus with your hands, until left with a pinkish white meat.

3. Cut the entire octopus into cubes. The size is not very important since the meat should be very tender by now; I recommend about ¼ inch. Place the prepared octopus in a bowl.

4. Assemble the salad: Add the parsley, onion, and the juice of half a lemon or more, depending on your preference. Add a good tablespoon of olive oil and season with salt and a little pepper.

5. Mix well, cover, and leave to rest for at least 1 hour in the fridge. Serve chilled, but not straight out of the refrigerator.

TIPS AND TECHNIQUES

Shop for octopus with thin tentacles, which will cook faster and be more tender. We cut our octopus into larger pieces (1 inch) and were happy with the results.

ABOUT THE COOK

Sasa Stucin and Jan Vranjek live in Slovenia. She's a designer, he's an economist. Here's Sasa's blog: sasastucin.blogspot.com.

　　Her entertaining tip: "Keep it simple. Have a good time."

BEHIND THE SCENES

While most Food52ers live in the United States, by this point in the contest year, we began attracting cooks from around the world, including this stylish couple from Slovenia. Just as it's a useful travel tip to dine where the locals eat, it's always a treat to receive recipes from locals in faraway places.

Southwestern Spiced Sweet Potato Fries with Chili-Cilantro Sour Cream

Fall

Savory Bread Pudding

BY KAMILEON | SERVES 4

A&M: Think of this as strata gone wild. Kamileon, who wrote that this recipe was "born from some leftover ham and boredom one Sunday morning," has concocted a rich, custardy bread pudding containing everything but the kitchen sink that somehow doesn't feel overwrought. A couple of details really make this dish stand out. First, you toast the bread cubes before combining them with the rest of the ingredients, which ensures a crunchy top layer. Second, you add raw, chopped shallot, which mellows slightly in the oven but still retains a nice, subtle kick. Prosciutto, goat cheese, and Gruyère or Parmesan make any additional salt gratuitous, while sliced mushrooms and copious amounts of fresh thyme give the bread pudding some depth. We found that mixing the dry ingredients in a large bowl before putting them in the baking dish helped prevent spillover, and our bread pudding spent a mere 25 minutes in the oven. If you poke it in the center and it bounces back, you know it's set!

3 cups cubed bread (1-inch cubes)

4 large eggs

1 egg yolk

½ cup whole milk

1 cup heavy cream

3 ounces prosciutto, diced

2 shallots, minced

4 crimini mushrooms, sliced

1 teaspoon chopped fresh thyme

Freshly ground black pepper

4 ounces chèvre, finely crumbled

¼ cup grated Gruyère or Parmesan (optional)

1. Heat the oven to 350°F. Toast the bread cubes in the oven for 10 minutes or so, stirring halfway through. Remove and set aside, leaving the oven on.

2. In a medium bowl, mix together the eggs, yolk, milk, and cream until thoroughly blended.

3. In a 9×9-inch square baking pan, toss together the bread cubes, prosciutto, shallots, mushrooms, thyme, and a few grinds of pepper to taste. Gently stir in the chèvre.

4. Pour the egg mixture over the bread cubes. If desired, garnish with Parmesan or Gruyère, for a golden crust. Bake for 25 to 40 minutes, or until a thermometer inserted into the center reads 145°F.

TIPS AND TECHNIQUES

The heavy cream gives the pudding a hint of crème brûlée texture, Kamileon pointed out, but of course you can make it with something lighter, like 2% milk.

Flavoristabarr: "I made this tonight with roasted butternut squash instead of the mushrooms and ricotta instead of the goat's cheese and it was *fantastic*! Toasting the bread makes a welcome difference, and the prosciutto is key."

Maryvelasquez added: "I found that the size of the pan was pretty important. The bread needs to be submerged in the custard. When I used a slightly larger rectangular baker, the bread cubes were a little dry. Flavors were still great, though."

ABOUT THE COOK

Kamileon is a grad student living in California.

Her favorite cooking tip: "From *Cook's Illustrated,* I learned to parcook vegetables in the microwave and pat them dry before browning. They brown faster and take up less oil."

WHAT THE COMMUNITY SAID

Helen: "This is a fantastic, no-fail dish. Definitely one I'll return to for those Sundays when I agree to entertain, but I'm a little, uh, worse for the wear. And as a side note, it's seriously delicious, even cold out of the fridge."

Paulkog: "Just made this today (with bacon instead of prosciutto) and the family loved it. Parmesan added a very nice melty touch! Thank you for this, now added to my repertoire."

Linguine with Bread Crumbs and Kale

BY HOTPLATE GOURMET | SERVES 2 TO 3

A&M: Hotplate Gourmet made her ambitions very clear—this linguine dish is to be a respectable weeknight dinner, something easy but good. She said, "This is a perfect leftover meal. You can use whatever greens you have lying around, and one- or two-day-old bread makes the best bread crumbs." Well, it's more than just that—we think it's terrific. Like an old Italian *nonna*, Hotplate Gourmet has you use the pasta water to help cook the kale and has you add bread crumbs to the kale to fortify the pasta. You sauté the bread crumbs in oil, then add garlic and kale, and not too much of either. The garlic gently scents the kale and the greens add substance and sweetness, without making you feel like you're eating kale for the sake of eating kale. You pull the dish together with some fresh olive oil and grated Parmesan and you have a wonderful fall dinner.

Salt and freshly ground black pepper

2 slices day-old bread, cubed

½ cup olive oil

2 garlic cloves, minced

½ large bunch kale, ribs and stems removed, leaves chopped

½ pound linguine

¼ cup grated Parmesan

---

1. Bring a large pot of salted water to a boil. Process the bread in a food processor until it's about the consistency of coarse cornmeal.

2. Heat ¼ cup of the oil in a frying pan over medium heat and add the bread crumbs. Once the bread crumbs are slightly toasted and golden brown, add the garlic and continue to stir until well toasted. Remove the bread crumbs from the pan; keep the pan on the stove.

3. Add the chopped kale to the frying pan with a little bit of the pasta water and sauté until wilted, about 3 minutes. Meanwhile, when the pasta water boils, add the pasta to the pot and cook until al dente. Drain.

4. Toss the kale mixture with the drained pasta and add salt and pepper to taste. Add the rest of the oil as needed. Mix in the Parmesan and bread crumbs and serve.

JenMach: "I added anchovies to the garlic and oil, a little lemon zest at the end, and topped each dish with a poached egg. Totally fast (and cheap) way to dress it up for guests."

ABOUT THE COOK

Erin Culbreth works in publishing in New York City and, on her blog Hotplate Confidential (www .hotplateconfidential.com), she writes about cooking meals for two with nothing but a hotplate, a toaster oven, and a mini-fridge.

Her favorite recipe from a cookbook: "Ina Garten's Peanut Butter Chocolate Chunk Cookies from *Barefoot Contessa Parties.* They are so delicious, and the recipe is absolutely foolproof!"

WHAT THE COMMUNITY SAID

SarahS: "I've made this two nights in a row . . . it's really delicious."

pierino: "The bread crumb thing is very southern Italy; they call it "mollica" and add it to pastas, especially ones that have bitter ingredients such as rapini or other dark greens."

Michelle_SF: "Pasta with kale is a standby of mine—but I never thought of adding bread crumbs! Now we're talkin'! (I usually add walnuts.)"

BEHIND THE SCENES

This was our first week open to the public. We knew we were onto something when we got written up in GOOP, DailyCandy, the *New York Times*, and TechCrunch!

Rum Apple Cake

BY COLOMBEDUJOUR | SERVES 8

A&M: When we tasted colombedujour's apple cake, our first thought was: this is an apple cake for grown-ups. Rich and buttery, delightfully boozy and chockfull of tender apple pieces, this cake makes a sophisticated ending to a fall meal. The recipe calls for ground almonds instead of flour (we tried regular and blanched almonds, and both were good). Maple sugar, which has the same molasses tones as brown sugar, is drier and prevents the cake from being soggy. Folding whipped egg whites into the batter (a technique that reminded us of making French macaroons) keeps it from being too dense. We used both an 8-inch and a 9-inch springform and found we liked the results with the 9-inch better. If you do use an 8-inch pan, you may want to cook the cake for a bit longer than suggested so that the fruit is tender throughout.

---

12 tablespoons unsalted butter, plus more for greasing the pan

2 Granny Smith apples

Juice of 1 lemon

¾ cup maple sugar (you may substitute raw sugar, or muscovado is great)

3 large organic eggs, separated

1⅓ cups ground almonds

1 teaspoon baking powder

2 tablespoons rum, brandy, or Calvados

Confectioners' sugar, for dusting

Whipped cream or ice cream, for serving

---

1. Heat the oven to 300°F. Butter an 8-inch springform cake pan with a removable base.

2. Peel, quarter, and core the apples. Cut two of the quarters into thin slices, toss in a bowl with a splash of lemon juice, and set aside.

3. Slice the remaining apple quarters more thickly into ¼-inch cubes. Toss in a separate bowl with a splash

of lemon juice. Sprinkle with 1 tablespoon of the maple sugar and set aside for 10 minutes.

4. Cream the butter and remaining maple sugar together until light and fluffy. Beat in the egg yolks and then incorporate the ground almonds and baking powder, working the mixture as little as possible to keep it light. Transfer the mixture to a large bowl.

5. In another bowl, beat the egg whites until stiff. Fold half into the cake mixture and then fold in the remainder. Add the rum and any juice given out by the thicker chunks of apple. Gently fold the chunks into the mixture. Transfer to the prepared cake pan and smooth the surface.

6. Drain the reserved apple slices and arrange on top of the cake, fanning out the slices in a circle. Bake for 1 hour and 15 minutes, or until the cake is golden and a skewer comes out clean.

7. Run a knife around the edge of the cake and leave it to cool for several hours before serving. If you'd like to serve it warm, you may reheat it. It keeps well in a covered container. Dust the cake with confectioners' sugar and serve with whipped cream or ice cream.

TIPS AND TECHNIQUES

Colombedujour said her cake is also excellent with brandy or Calvados instead of rum, and that serving it with ice cream or whipped cream is essential. We couldn't agree more!

She also pointed out that the cake comes out wonderfully crumbly and tender, but you need to allow it to cool completely or it may be too crumbly to slice.

ABOUT THE COOK

Colombe Jacobsen is a personal chef and food consultant living in New York City (you may also recognize her from season 3 of *The Next Food Network Star*). Here's her blog: Colombe du Jour (www .colombedujour.com).

Her favorite entertaining tip: "I like to freeze premade cookie dough so that I can bake warm cookies to order. I make the batter and portion them out with a 1-ounce ice cream scooper and freeze them in a container. This way I have something on hand for last-minute guests—they can also be served with ice cream, warm right out of the oven as an impromptu dessert."

WHAT THE COMMUNITY SAID

Minami_nyc: "I made this cake today with hazelnuts instead of almonds, because I am slightly allergic to almonds. It was fantastic! Also, instead of Granny Smiths I used Braeburn apples, and added an extra tablespoon (and splash or so) of rum. It's lovely to eat a flourless cake that is not chocolate-based! It was very special."

Individual Sweet Potato Gratins with Crème Fraîche, Onions, and Bacon

BY APARTMENTCOOKER | SERVES 2 AS A SIDE DISH

A&M: Sweet potatoes are often made even more sweet using ingredients like maple syrup, brown sugar, molasses, and even marshmallows. We like that apartmentcooker goes definitively in the other direction by adding bacon, Parmesan, onion, garlic, and a crème fraîche béchamel, while still paying homage to more traditional recipes (she adds a tablespoon of brown sugar to the béchamel, with great results). Thinly sliced sweet potatoes are layered in the baking dish (we used one dish big enough for two rather than individual ones) with béchamel, crisped bacon, and raw onions and garlic, which infuse the gratin with their fragrance.

---

4 slices bacon, diced

½ cup chopped onion

1 teaspoon minced garlic

2 tablespoons unsalted butter

2 tablespoons all-purpose flour

1 cup whole milk

3 tablespoons crème fraîche

½ teaspoon ground nutmeg

1 tablespoon light brown sugar

Salt and freshly ground black pepper

2 cups thinly sliced sweet potatoes
(⅛ inch thick)

¼ to ½ cup grated Parmesan

---

1. Lightly grease 2 individual baking dishes (I used ovenproof bowls that hold roughly 1½ cups). Heat the oven to 350°F.

2. In a small sauté pan, cook the bacon over medium heat until crisp. Remove from the heat and toss with the onion and garlic.

3. In a small saucepan, melt the butter over medium heat. Stir in the flour and cook until the mixture is

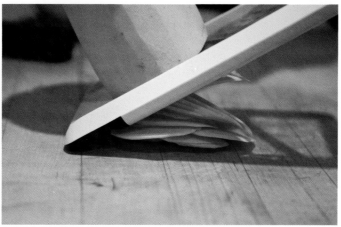

well combined but still pale. Stir in the milk and crème fraîche.

4. Reduce the heat to low and bring the béchamel to a simmer. Cook until thickened, about 5 minutes. Stir in the nutmeg, brown sugar, salt, and pepper.

5. Layer 4 to 6 slices of sweet potato on the bottom of each of the prepared baking dishes. Top with a few tablespoons of béchamel and a few spoonfuls of the bacon mixture. Repeat with another layer of each. Add one last layer of potatoes and spoon the remaining béchamel over the potatoes. Sprinkle with the grated Parmesan.

6. Bake the gratins until they are bubbly around the edges and cooked through, 15 to 25 minutes.

TIPS AND TECHNIQUES

A sprinkling of Parmesan on top helps with browning, but if you want a little more color, pop the gratins under the broiler for a few minutes at the end.

We found that 20 to 25 minutes' baking time was perfect for a two-person baking dish.

"Individual portions mean I can make a big batch," apartmentcooker wrote, "and reheat it later as a last-minute side dish."

If you're serving more than two people, you can easily double or triple this recipe.

ABOUT THE COOK

Erin Jeanne McDowell is a recent graduate of the Culinary Institute of America in Hyde Park, New York. On her blog, The Apartment Kitchen, she writes about leaving the well-equipped kitchens at school behind and cooking in her tiny first apartment.

Her favorite recipe from a cookbook: "My great-great-great grandma's sugar cookie recipe. It appeared in the town church cookbook that's now barely held together by a string."

WHAT THE COMMUNITY SAID

Losangel: "I've made this five times already, and now I have friends calling me for the recipe."

Pudding Chômeur

BY CAMILLE | SERVES 6

A&M: If you crossed sticky toffee pudding with pancakes and maple syrup, you would get *chômeur*, a buttery biscuit submerged in a bath of maple syrup and cream. Pudding Chômeur, a traditional cake from Québec, takes no time to prepare: you mix the dough in 10 minutes and refrigerate it, and then the next day, you drop it into ramekins, pour over the syrup and cream, and pop it into a very hot—450°F—oven. As the syrup mixture boils, it poaches and glazes the biscuit. This makes it both a great no-stress dinner party dessert and fun baking project to do with your kids. The recipe calls for 6 ramekins. The pudding is so rich you might want to make it in 10 to 12 small ramekins, baked for slightly less time, about 20 minutes. The batter should half-fill the ramekins, and the syrup should come no closer than ¼ inch from the rim, or it will boil over. We learned this the hard way!

10⅔ tablespoons unsalted butter, at room temperature

1 cup sugar

2 large eggs

2⅓ cups all-purpose flour

1 teaspoon baking powder

2 cups maple syrup

2 cups heavy cream

---

1. In a large bowl (or in a mixer), beat the butter and sugar until smooth.

2. Add the eggs one at a time.

3. Add the flour and baking powder and stir just until the flour is completely incorporated.

4. Cover the dough and chill for at least 24 hours.

5. Heat the oven to 450°F. In a medium saucepan over low heat, bring the syrup and cream to a boil.

6. Divide the dough among six 8-ounce ramekins and place the ramekins on a baking sheet. Pour the cream and syrup mixture over the dough, dividing it evenly among the ramekins.

7. Bake until bubbling and lightly browned, 20 to 25 minutes.

TIPS AND TECHNIQUES

Camille said you can make a less expensive version substituting brown sugar for the maple syrup.

"It is rich and decadent and a perfect winter dessert," she wrote. "With more heavy cream on top, it's even better!"

Next time, we plan to make it with salted butter to balance the sweetness.

ABOUT THE COOK

Camille Béland-Goyette is a student living in Montréal.

Her ideal meal: "Fresh pasta with a cream and mushroom sauce and a thin and caramelized tarte Tatin."

WHAT THE COMMUNITY SAID

Tspbasil: "The description of *chômeur* enticed me to make this dessert . . . now . . . way past dinner and dessert time!"

Creamy Mushroom Soup

BY MRSWHEELBARROW | SERVES 6

A&M: With this dish, MrsWheelbarrow takes a classic home cook recipe and elevates it to elegant dinner party fare. First, she has you make a reinforced stock by simmering the mushroom stems in chicken broth. Then, in a move that evokes the fastidiousness of culinary school, she instructs you to "beautifully and precisely chop" 1½ pounds of mushroom caps into a ½-inch dice. Halfway through, you will likely be cursing both her and us, but trust us: it's worth it. And the rest is easy. The resulting soup is a balance of delicately creamy and intensely mushroomy, with layered undertones of herbs and Cognac.

---

1 pound mixed mushrooms, cleaned, stems separated from caps

1 pound cremini mushrooms, cleaned, stems separated from caps

4 cups rich homemade chicken stock

3 tablespoons olive oil

½ cup minced shallots

6 thyme sprigs

1 rosemary sprig

Salt and freshly ground black pepper

¼ cup Cognac

¼ cup whipping cream

¼ cup chopped chives

---

1. Roughly chop the mushroom stems and simmer them, covered, in the chicken stock for about 1 hour.

2. In the meantime, heat the oil in a large skillet and sauté the shallots until transparent. Add the herbs, and salt and pepper liberally.

3. Beautifully and precisely chop the mushroom caps into a ½-inch dice. Add them to the shallots as they are chopped. Keep the heat very low and cook gently until the mushroom liquid is released and reabsorbed; 20 to 30 minutes. Shake the pan so they don't stick. Remove the thyme and rosemary.

4. Turn up the heat and add the Cognac. Flame it if you're feeling really chef-y.

5. Cook the mushroom cap–shallot mixture down until the liquid is well reduced and the mushrooms are starting to turn a little golden on the edges.

6. Strain the mushroom stems from the chicken broth. Add the beautiful mushroom cap and shallot mixture to the strained broth and heat gently.

7. Swirl in the cream and chives, and serve. Or serve in small sipping cups topped with chives and lightly whipped cream, if you want to get fancy.

TIPS AND TECHNIQUES

MrsWheelbarrow: "I often find amazing mushrooms, both wild and cultivated, at our local farmers' market. I've made this soup with cremini, shiitake, button, hen of the woods, oyster, chanterelle, and many other local wild types."

ABOUT THE COOK

Cathy Barrow is a landscape designer living in Washington, D.C. She also writes the food blog Mrs. Wheelbarrow's Kitchen (www.mrswheelbarrow.com), teaches classes on cooking and canning, hosted a Food52 potluck brunch in D.C., and later led the Food52 Canorama in central Pennsylvania. When we featured her in a Cook Spotlight, the response, not surprisingly, was overwhelming: thirty-plus enthusiastic comments named her "the heartbeat of Food52" and "Mrs. Wonderwoman," among other accolades. See her recipe for Salmon in Sorrel Sauce on page 377.

Her favorite recipe from a cookbook: "It's a toss-up between Marcella Hazan's *The Classic Italian Cookbook*–the spectacularly easy Tomato Sauce III with tomato, butter, sugar, and onion–and Thomas Keller's Gnocchi with Mushrooms and Butternut Squash from *Bouchon*."

WHAT THE COMMUNITY SAID

Hope.thurman: "Ever since I saw the movie *Julie and Julia*, I've been wanting to make something with mushrooms. She kept saying, 'Don't crowd the mushrooms,' and it just made my mouth water for a little taste! This soup looks great, light and hearty at the same time. Going to get ingredients tomorrow!"

Smoky Fried Chickpeas

BY ALIWAKS | SERVES 4

A&M: If you were to put out a bowl of these crunchy, smoky, spicy little nuggets at a cocktail party, it's likely they'd be gone in five minutes. Aliwaks, who was inspired to create this dish while "making a Spanish/Moroccan/Moorish sort of dinner for friends one night," has taken an already brilliant idea (fried chickpeas with smoked paprika) and run with it. You also fry strips of lemon zest, fresh thyme leaves, and, later, thinly sliced garlic to mix with the chickpeas, paprika, and salt. This leads to an array of crispy little bursts of flavor, each more fragrant than the last.

Two 1-pound, 13-ounce cans chickpeas

1 cup olive oil

1 tablespoon lemon zest, in thin strips

1 fresh thyme sprig

4 garlic cloves, sliced

1 tablespoon smoked paprika (sweet or hot, depending on your taste)

Coarse salt

---

1. Drain the chickpeas and set on paper towels in a colander to dry thoroughly. (This can be done 1 day in advance.)

2. Heat the oil in a large pan (preferably cast iron) to 350°F, or until the oil makes bubbles around a single chickpea when you drop it in.

3. Add the lemon zest, thyme sprig, and chickpeas in batches so the pan doesn't crowd. Fry each batch for about 5 minutes until the chickpeas darken and are crunchy.

4. Remove the chickpeas, zest, and thyme from the oil with a slotted spoon and drain well over a colander or sieve. After you've fried the last batch, add the garlic to the oil and fry briefly until golden. Remove and drain.

5. Toss the chickpeas and garlic with the smoked paprika and salt, adding more to taste. Serve right away while still warm and crisp.

TIPS AND TECHNIQUES

Make sure the chickpeas are as dry as you can get them and do be careful while frying (use a splatter screen if you have one). It's worth a little experimenting to find a brand of chickpeas that spit the least while frying but still stay tender in the middle.

ABOUT THE COOK

Ali Waks is a chef living in South Philadelphia. Her excellent porchetta recipe (page 329) went on to do battle with *Cook's Illustrated*'s best roasted pork shoulder (and nearly won!). You can also see her Cowboy Rubbed Rib-eye with Chocolate Stout Pan Sauce on page 182.

Her favorite recipe from a cookbook: "It's from *A Platter of Figs* and goes something like this: select beautiful ripe figs and arrange on a platter."

WHAT THE COMMUNITY SAID

Friskier: "A hit. Somehow turned out much lighter and better than what we had sampled at a pricey tapas place."

BEHIND THE SCENES

Little did we know that this contest theme would unleash a torrent of paprika recipes—sweet, smoked, spicy, you name it! Paprika was clearly *the* ingredient of 2009/2010.

Braised Moroccan Chicken and Olives

BY SONALI | SERVES 4

A&M: This is a pitch-perfect take on a classic dish. Sonali assembles a mouth-tingling spice mixture of ginger, garlic, coriander, cumin, paprika, turmeric, cayenne, and saffron, and then adds green olives and preserved lemons to the party. The chicken is browned in oil and then coated in the spice base before simmering gently in chicken stock until tender. Adding the lemons and olives toward the end helps retain their integrity and perfume.

4 tablespoons canola oil

2½ pounds chicken legs and thighs

Kosher salt and freshly ground black pepper

1½ cups finely diced onion

1 teaspoon minced ginger

1 teaspoon minced garlic

1 tablespoon ground coriander

1 tablespoon ground cumin

1½ teaspoons paprika

½ teaspoon turmeric

½ teaspoon cayenne pepper

2 to 3 cups chicken stock

¼ teaspoon saffron threads

½ cup green olives, rinsed

2 preserved lemons, pulp removed and discarded; rind cut into strips

2 tablespoons chopped cilantro, plus more for garnish

Couscous, for serving

1. Heat 2 tablespoons of the oil in a Dutch oven or a large, deep skillet over medium heat. Dry the chicken pieces and season them with salt and pepper. Working in batches, place them in the skillet and brown on all sides, 8 to 10 minutes per batch (take your time with this step, and don't be tempted to turn up the heat, as you do not want the chicken pieces to burn). Remove the chicken and place on a plate.

2. Add the onion to the skillet and cook until slightly softened. Add the ginger, garlic, coriander, cumin, paprika, turmeric, and cayenne, and stir together. Add the chicken pieces and stir to coat with the spice mixture. Pour the chicken stock into the skillet so that two-thirds of the chicken is submerged. Add the saffron and stir to combine. Bring the liquid to a simmer, cover the skillet, turn the heat to medium-low, and simmer for 20 minutes. Add the olives and preserved lemons. Cover and cook another 10 minutes, or until the chicken is cooked through. Remove the chicken and turn the heat to high. Cook for another 6 to 8 minutes until the sauce reduces slightly. Stir in the cilantro. Adjust the seasoning to taste.

3. Serve the chicken on a bed of couscous. Spoon the sauce over the top. Garnish with additional cilantro.

TIPS AND TECHNIQUES

You may want to discard some of the fat after browning the chicken (this will depend on the meat you buy)—we kept about 2 tablespoons. And couscous is a must. We used our favorite couscous (M'hemsa from Les Moulins, Mahjoub; available online), and it was such a perfect foil for the rich, spicy sauce that we couldn't resist forking up every last grain.

Cordelia said: "I would recommend that if you don't have preserved lemons, just use fresh unpeeled lemon slices and add them in earlier when cooking. If you want to make sure they won't be too bitter, you can poach the slices in boiling water for a few minutes before adding them to the chicken."

ABOUT THE COOK

Sonali Ruder is a physician at a trauma center in Manhattan and culinary student who has a knack for winning cooking competitions, at Food52 and elsewhere. See her Autumn Celeriac (Celery Root) Puree on page 133 and her Mashed Potatoes with Caramelized Onions and Goat Cheese on page 261. Here's her blog: The Foodie Physician (www.thefoodiephysician.com).

Her favorite cooking tip: "Toast your own spices and then grind them—they'll be so much more aromatic than buying preground spices."

WHAT THE COMMUNITY SAID

Maryvelasquez: "I made this last night and I loved it. It was worth the effort to get a hold of the preserved lemons. I've never cooked with them before, but I will always have them around the house from now on."

Toasted Coconut Gelato

BY NICOLECLANG | SERVES 4 TO 6

A&M: Coconut ice creams are often too rich and too sweet—not this one! NicoleCLang's toasted coconut gelato hits all the right notes, with layers of fresh and toasted coconut, the freckling of vanilla bean, and a milk custard that keeps it all nimble. We love her backstory, too: "When I was young I loved the texture of the coconut chocolates sold at the Fannie Mae kiosks in the local mall. The coconut was very finely cut and all throughout the chocolate. The texture was sublime. I wanted to re-create that sensation in an ice cream that was as rich as I remembered that confection to be."

2 cups unsweetened dessicated coconut

1 cup sugar

4 egg yolks

2 cups whole milk

1 vanilla bean, split down the middle

1. Heat the oven to 350°F. Spread 1 cup of the coconut on a baking sheet and toast it in the oven for 5 to 10 minutes, or until golden, stirring 2 or 3 times to get it evenly browned.

2. In a bowl, combine the sugar and egg yolks; stir until incorporated.

3. In a medium saucepan, heat the milk and vanilla bean over medium heat until scalded. Whisk a little of the hot milk into the sugar-egg mixture, then whisk the eggs back into the rest of the hot milk. Add the remaining 1 cup coconut (not toasted) and continue to cook, stirring constantly, over medium heat (if custards make you nervous, take the pan on and off the heat so you don't end up with scrambled eggs). When the mixture is thick and glossy and coats the back of a spoon, remove from the heat and cool. Cover and refrigerate for at least 4 hours, or overnight if you can.

4. When you are ready to freeze the mixture, strain out the vanilla bean and coconut and discard. Pour the mixture into an ice cream maker and follow the manufacturer's instructions. When it reaches the consistency of soft serve, add the toasted coconut. Put into a container and freeze until ready to eat.

TIPS AND TECHNIQUES

NicoleCLang: "In order for it to be the right texture, you have to use unsweetened dessicated coconut. Leaving the untoasted coconut in the base overnight really intensifies the coconut flavor."

ABOUT THE COOK

Nicole Lang lives in Richmond, Virginia, and writes three different blogs: Food Punk (www .foodpunk.wordpress.com); Tentacles (nicolelang.blogspot.com); and Dessert of the Month Club (dessertofthemonthclub.blogspot.com).

Her favorite recipe from a cookbook: "The stuffed mushroom recipe from *Joy of Cooking*. It's what got me into food as a child."

WHAT THE COMMUNITY SAID

nannydeb: "I made this for myself for my birthday and it was delish! Of course, everyone else (even those who said that they didn't like coconut) gobbled it up. I'll make this one again!"

Chicken with Creamy Dijon Mustard Sauce

BY MARIA TERESA JORGE | SERVES 6

A&M: You will sop up every last bit of this sauce with bread because it is so delicious. Maria Teresa Jorge, who was cooking for dinner guests in rural Tuscany, took this classic dish and amplified its flavor by adding not a few sage leaves and garlic cloves, but ten and twelve respectively. We liked the touch of Cognac in addition to the wine, and the flour and cream slurry that goes in at the end to smooth out the sauce.

2 tablespoons unsalted butter	½ cup white wine
3 tablespoons extra virgin olive oil	⅓ cup Cognac
10 sage leaves	2 tablespoons Dijon mustard
12 garlic cloves with skin on	Salt and freshly ground black and white pepper
8 chicken thighs	½ cup heavy cream
1 cup chicken stock (or water)	1 tablespoon all-purpose flour

1. In a large pan over medium heat, melt the butter with the olive oil and add the sage leaves and garlic. When the butter starts to sizzle, add the chicken thighs, skin side down, and let them get golden brown. Carefully turn them with a spatula, so as not to rip the skin, and brown the other side for a total of about 8 minutes. The chicken will be cooked through later; you just want to get a nice golden brown color now.

2. Heat the chicken stock in a small saucepan over low heat.

3. Remove the chicken from the pan and set aside on a plate. Add the white wine and Cognac to the pan to deglaze it, scraping any brown bits stuck on the bottom. Cook until the alcohol has evaporated completely, then whisk the mustard into the sauce.

4. Add the chicken thighs to the pan and pour in the hot chicken stock to two-thirds of the height of the chicken thighs. Season with salt and pepper and simmer over low heat, covered, for 20 minutes.

5. Remove the cooked chicken thighs and keep warm. Let the sauce simmer over low heat to reduce to about ¾ cup. Squeeze the garlic cloves into the pan, mash them and the sage with the back of a wooden spoon or spatula to release more flavor; then discard the sage leaves.

6. Place 3 tablespoons of the cream in a medium bowl and sift in the flour. Whisk the flour into the cream, then add the remaining cream and whisk. Whisk in a bit of the hot sauce, then slowly pour the cream mixture into the pan, whisking constantly over very low heat. Keep whisking so that the sauce doesn't stick to the bottom of the pan.

7. Let the sauce thicken and reduce again to the amount you need, always stirring. You will need about a cup of sauce to serve with the 8 chicken thighs.

8. Pour the hot sauce over the chicken thighs and serve immediately.

TIPS AND TECHNIQUES

We poured off the fat after browning the chicken, and our little chicken pieces cooked in half the time. Keep an eye on those buggers. And if you want to skip the flour you can—the sauce may not emulsify as perfectly, but it'll still taste great.

Maria Teresa Jorge recommended serving this with mashed potatoes, which would do just as good a job as bread at sopping up the delicious sauce.

ABOUT THE COOK

Maria Teresa Jorge formerly ran a cooking school in Tuscany, but recently moved back to her native Portugal to open a restaurant with her husband.

Her favorite recipe from a cookbook: "Pear and Almond Tart (Torta di Pere e Mandorle) from *The River Café Cookbook* by Rose Gray and Ruth Rodgers."

WHAT THE COMMUNITY SAID

Mt97: "Just made this dish tonight. Coupled it with crisp roasted potatoes and a nice garden salad. Went over very well with my lady. She even asked for more of the sauce to dip the remaining potatoes. I will definitely add this to my repertoire."

Gale: "I have a recipe similar to this, but this one is so much better. It is so adaptable—make it for 8 or for 2—and it's also good with thyme rather than sage. I, too, have chickens that run around the farm and are less fatty and take a bit longer to cook. This one is a real keeper."

Autumn Celeriac (Celery Root) Puree

BY SONALI | SERVES 4

A&M: A lovely change of pace from simple mashed potatoes, this puree sings with bright, clean flavor. Although she handles it like a pro, Sonali wrote that she "recently discovered celeriac, also known as celery root." The celery root and apple both contribute tartness (there's even a mysterious lemony element, although no lemon is used), while the potato smooths out any rough edges. Cream and butter make the puree luscious, so that it feels like a treat rather than just a healthy dose of veggies.

---

1 medium celeriac (about 1 ¼ pounds), peeled and cut into ½-inch pieces

1 small Idaho potato (about 6 ounces), peeled and cut into 1-inch pieces

Kosher salt

1 Granny Smith apple, peeled, cored, and cut into 1-inch pieces

½ cup heavy cream

2 tablespoons unsalted butter

1 bay leaf

Freshly ground black pepper

---

1. Place the celeriac and potatoes in a large pot of salted cold water. Bring to a boil. Boil for 10 minutes, then add the apple. Continue to cook until all are tender, another 10 to 12 minutes.

2. While the vegetables are cooking, heat the cream, butter, and bay leaf in a small saucepan over medium heat. Do not boil.

3. Drain the cooked vegetables and apple and return them to the hot, dry pot. Stir them over low heat for

2 minutes until they are dry. Pass the ingredients through a food mill into a large bowl. Gently stir in the hot cream and butter mixture until smooth (remove the bay leaf). Alternatively, you can puree the

vegetables and apple together with the cream and butter mixture in a food processor. Season the puree with salt and black pepper to taste. Serve warm.

TIPS AND TECHNIQUES

Sonali said: "Because I like to start both the celery root and potatoes in cold water and the celery root takes slightly longer to cook, I cut it into smaller pieces so that everything will finish cooking at the same time."

Ody: "I don't have a food mill, but recently I've started using my stand mixer for mashed-tuber dishes–I make sure to get the roots good and mushy and also preheat the mixer bowl with hot water so that the mash stays hot during mixing. The paddle attachment gives it the perfect texture."

ABOUT THE COOK

Learn more about Sonali and see her recipe for Braised Moroccan Chicken and Olives on page 125; see her recipe for Mashed Potatoes with Caramelized Onions and Goat Cheese on page 261.

WHAT THE COMMUNITY SAID

Broyals: "Looks delicious. Comfort food with a gourmet twist."

Prosciutto and Fontina Panini with Arugula Pesto

BY BIGGIRLPHOEBZ | MAKES 4 SANDWICHES

A&M: This is a sophisticated sandwich with a couple of extra steps that are simple and totally worthwhile. BigGirlPhoebz admitted to a particular fondness for prosciutto and Fontina, adding, "I found that the ultimate complement was a smooth, creamy arugula pesto that leaks into all the notches of the bread, and a scattering of sweet pickled shallots to give the sandwich some acidity."

SANDWICH
¼ cup cider vinegar

2 tablespoons sugar

½ teaspoon salt

1 large shallot, thinly sliced

1 ciabatta loaf, sliced in half lengthwise

⅓ pound Fontina, thinly sliced

⅓ pound prosciutto (about 10 slices)

PESTO
¼ cup toasted pine nuts

2 garlic cloves, peeled

2 cups packed baby arugula

Juice of ½ lemon

½ teaspoon salt

¼ cup olive oil

1. To make the pickled shallots: Bring the cider vinegar, sugar, and salt to a boil in a small saucepan over medium heat. Simmer for a minute until the sugar has dissolved, then pour the hot liquid over the shallots in a small bowl or jar so they are fully submerged. Allow to sit for 20 minutes, then place in an airtight container until ready for use. This can be done up to a week ahead.

2. To make the pesto: In a small food processor, pulse the pine nuts and garlic until coarsely chopped. Add the arugula, lemon juice, and salt and pulse to combine. Stream in the olive oil and continue to blend until all the ingredients are finely chopped and the pesto is smooth and creamy. Taste for seasoning and add more salt if necessary.

3. Turn on the broiler. Place the two ciabatta halves, crust side down, on a baking sheet and toast for 3 to 5 minutes until the bread is beginning to crisp but not totally browned. Slather the bottom half of the bread

evenly with pesto and arrange the cheese slices in a single layer on top. Return just this slice of bread to the oven and continue to toast until the cheese has melted, 3 to 5 minutes.

4. Slather the other slice of bread with the remaining pesto and arrange the pickled shallots on top, followed by the prosciutto. Sandwich the halves together.

5. Heat a large skillet over medium-high heat. Depending on the size of your pan and the size of the ciabatta, you may have to cut the sandwich in half. Set the sandwich, top side down, in the pan and weight it with a smaller skillet and/or a heavy bowl so that the bread is flattened as it toasts. When the bread has browned, repeat on the other side. When finished, the panini should be browned, crisped, and flattened, and should have cheese oozing from it. Toast the remaining half (if necessary), and then cut it again to create 4 sandwiches.

TIPS AND TECHNIQUES

BigGirlPhoebz calls for baby arugula, but good, meaty leaves from the greenmarket worked well, too.

If you can't find Fontina, a mild melting cheese like mozzarella or Muenster would be a good substitute.

ABOUT THE COOK

Phoebe Lapine is one-half of the duo that writes the blog Big Girls, Small Kitchen (www.biggirlssmallkitchen .com). The other half is Cara Eisenpress, or SmallKitchCara as we know her at Food52—you can see her Secret Ingredient Beef Stew on page 257. The two published their first book, *In the Small Kitchen*, in 2011.

WHAT THE COMMUNITY SAID

Pete: "To be honest, I never cook; I leave that up to my amazing wife, Sonali (a fellow Food52 member and previous winner). However, the other night she was working late, so I figured I'd try to surprise her and give this recipe a whirl. It was a smashing success—the panini were delicious! Not only did I impress her, but I also gave myself a big confidence boost in the kitchen. Who knew I could make pickled shallots and arugula pesto! Thanks for the great recipe!"

Double Chocolate Espresso Cookies

BY KELSEYTHENAPTIMECHEF | MAKES 50 TO 55 COOKIES

A&M: Two warnings about these cookies: don't give them to young children before bedtime and don't leave them lying around, if you want any left for yourself. These cookies are crisp on the edges and have a chewy middle strewn with pockets of soft chocolate. The espresso powder, as KelseyTheNaptimeChef noted, amplifies the chocolate, but not the sweetness, making it a grown-up cookie. When making any cookies, make sure to cream the butter really well—this aerates the cookies and integrates the sugar—but be conservative with your mixing once the dry ingredients are added.

---

18 tablespoons (2¼ sticks) unsalted butter, at room temperature

1 cup sugar

1 cup light brown sugar

2 large eggs, at room temperature

2½ cups all-purpose flour

¾ cup unsweetened cocoa powder

1 teaspoon baking soda

1 teaspoon kosher salt

2 tablespoons instant espresso powder, like Medaglia D'Oro, or similar

12 ounces semisweet chocolate chips

---

1. Heat the oven to 350°F.

2. In a large bowl, cream the butter and sugars until light and fluffy. Add the eggs one at time, mixing after each addition to make sure they are well combined.

3. In a separate bowl, combine the dry ingredients: flour, cocoa powder, baking soda, salt, and espresso powder. I use a whisk to make sure they are well blended.

4. With the mixer on low, slowly add the dry ingredients to the wet ingredients, scraping down the sides of the bowl as needed. Mix everything until the ingredients are fully combined, but do not overbeat. Using a wooden spoon, stir in the chocolate chips.

5. Line a baking sheet with a Silpat mat or parchment paper. Using a 1 ½-inch ice cream scoop or a rounded teaspoon, drop the dough on the sheet 2 inches apart. Bake for 10 to 12 minutes, or until the tops look dry. Do not overbake, or the cookies will not be chewy. Cool on a wire rack and serve.

Kelsey said: "If you don't have instant espresso, you can use instant coffee. Add a little more coffee than the 2 tablespoons of espresso powder in the recipe, since it is not as strongly flavored."

Readers recommended various additions, including cacao nibs, coarse salt, peanuts, and white chocolate chips. Have fun, kids!

Maryvelasquez said: "I froze the remaining double chocolate espresso cookie dough—I formed it into a log shape, wrapped it in freezer paper, and then put the whole in a Ziploc freezer bag. I hack off a chunk of the log every now and then and bake a small batch."

ABOUT THE COOK

Learn more about KelseyTheNaptimeChef and see her recipe for Zucchini-Lemon Cookies on page 52; see her Chocolate Bundt Cake on page 249.

WHAT THE COMMUNITY SAID

HSP: "A true adult treat, so refined, but so good you'll swear you were a kid again."

Oui, Chef: "These are amazing! Made a triple batch (no easy feat, mind you) of these lovelies to add to our holiday goody bags this year. Keeping a nice little tin for myself, thank you very much."

Blueberry Almond Breakfast Polenta

BY ONE HUNGRY MAMA | SERVES 3 TO 4

A&M: One Hungry Mama gave us the history of this dish: "This recipe came to me right as I was about to overextend myself: I was eight months pregnant and, with a day of cooking ahead of me, almost decided to whip up impromptu blueberry corn muffins for breakfast. As I stared at the cornmeal trying to gear up to bake, it struck me: *breakfast polenta*!" Inspired by a Martha Stewart recipe, she blends almond meal with the polenta and cooks the two together, later adding vanilla, fresh blueberries, and cardamom. A bit of honey lends just the right amount of sweetness—a light touch keeps it from being cloying.

4 cups whole milk

¾ cup quick-cooking polenta

½ cup almond meal

4 tablespoons unsalted butter

⅓ cup honey

1 cup blueberries, plus more for serving

½ teaspoon vanilla extract

Pinch of cardamom (or up to ¼ teaspoon)

Crème fraîche or sour cream

1. Bring the milk to a simmer in a medium saucepan over high heat.

2. Reduce the heat to low and add the polenta, whisking constantly until smooth. Add the almond meal and continue whisking for several minutes until the polenta thickens to a creamy consistency. Add the butter and whisk until it melts completely.

3. Turn the heat off and whisk in the honey, blueberries, vanilla, and cardamom. Serve with a dollop of crème fraîche or sour cream and an extra sprinkle of blueberries.

TIPS AND TECHNIQUES

We tried this with hazelnut meal instead of almond meal, too, and loved it just as much. You can also be flexible with the fruit: use whatever berries are in season.

ABOUT THE COOK

Stacie Bills lives in Brooklyn, New York, and writes about food and parenting on her blog, One Hungry Mama (www.onehungrymama.com).

Her favorite recipe from a cookbook: "Mark Bittman's Orzo Risotto from *How to Cook Everything* because it's simple, endlessly adaptable, can be fed to anyone (even a six-month-old!) and, of course, is utterly delicious however you personalize it."

WHAT THE COMMUNITY SAID

CASJ: "I am eating a bowl of this right now—it is wonderful—I never would have thought to add the almond meal. Thanks for the great recipe!"

Bubbly Manhattan

BY COLLIN | SERVES YOU, YOU LUSH

A&M: Usually when you drink a Manhattan, all the warmth comes from the hit of booze, but here a nutty and bitter IPA gives the drink depth and a warming feeling throughout. Collin uses the beer to replace the classic bitters and in doing so gives the drink a little fizz, a little life, we think. He said, "I also think that an orange slice brings out the flavors of the whiskey better than the traditional maraschino cherry." Drink it cold as can be—if you're up to it, chill the rye and vermouth before assembling.

2 ounces good rye whiskey (which of course you have on hand, right?)

½ ounce sweet vermouth

1 ounce India pale ale (the bitterer the better)

1 thin slice of orange (or a kumquat)

1. Measure the rye and vermouth into a mixing glass with ice.

2. Shake and strain into a chilled martini glass, adding the ale at the same time.

3. Top with an orange slice or kumquat.

4. Look cool, because you are.

TIPS AND TECHNIQUES

Collin said: "I don't shake the beer together with the whiskey and vermouth, because I think it loses just a bit of that effervescence that you're adding the beer for."

ABOUT THE COOK

Collin is an attorney from Los Angeles, California, whose recipes on Food52, such as lamb chili and cochinita pibil, are unmistakably hearty, but lightened with sweet elements like cider and sweet potato.

His ideal meal: "Tuna and caper pizza at Chez Black in Positano, a bottle of wine, and my wife beside me."

WHAT THE COMMUNITY SAID

Tamio888: "I'm not, by nature, a cocktail guy. I made this one, though. I felt like I was transported to *Mad Men.* A man's man's cocktail."

Grilled Brussels Sprouts

BY KITCHENWITCHCOOKIE | SERVES 2 AS A SIDE DISH

A&M: We were drawn to this recipe because it approaches Brussels sprouts in a way we'd never tried before. "My husband turned me into a huge Brussels sprouts fan with this recipe," said kitchenwitchcookie. "He varies it a little each time, but the result is always delicious." First you blanch the sprouts in boiling salted water, and then you coat them in a mixture of olive oil, celery salt, onion powder, garlic powder, salt, and pepper before charring them lightly on the grill. Another toss in the seasoned oil, and they're ready to eat. Grilling the Brussels sprouts gives them some smokiness and really wakes up the flavors in the onion and garlic powders.

12 small to medium Brussels sprouts

2 tablespoons olive oil

Kosher salt

½ teaspoon cracked black pepper

½ teaspoon onion powder

½ teaspoon garlic powder

½ teaspoon celery salt

1 handful cooked, crumbled bacon (optional)

1 teaspoon lemon zest (optional)

1 tablespoon grated Parmesan (optional)

1. Heat the grill so that it's nice and hot.

2. To clean the sprouts, trim the cut ends back without interfering with the leaves and peel any withered leaves off the bulbs. Score the bottoms; one cut will suffice.

3. Blanch the sprouts in boiling, salted water for no more than 5 minutes. *No more!*

4. Drain the sprouts and place them in a medium bowl. Drizzle them with oil and add 1 teaspoon salt and the pepper, onion powder, garlic powder, and celery salt. Toss them well to coat.

5. Grill the sprouts for 12 minutes, turning every 4 minutes or so, until well browned on the tips. Return them to the seasoning bowl and toss to coat with any remaining seasoning.

6. If desired, add any or all of the optional ingredients (bacon, lemon zest, and Parmesan).

TIPS AND TECHNIQUES

Of the optional ingredients, we chose to add only the lemon zest and really liked the extra bit of perfume. The choice is yours!

Kitchenwitchcookie rightly insists that you blanch the sprouts for no more than 5 minutes—if you like your sprouts a bit firm, as we do, you can get away with a minute or two less.

If you don't have an outdoor grill (or if you're making these in the dead of winter), a grill pan will work just fine.

Menumaniac: "I like to put them on skewers to grill; it makes it easier to turn them."

ABOUT THE COOK

Casey Benedict-Pendergast is a blogger living in Malvern, Pennsylvania. She launched Kitchen Witch, a business selling ready-to-bake cookies and other sweets, after growing weary of the ingredients in processed foods. Here's the website: www.kitchenwitchcookie.com.

Her favorite entertaining tip: "Keep it simple and write out your menu to refer to while you're prepping and during your party."

WHAT THE COMMUNITY SAID

Meg226: "I made these for Thanksgiving dinner and managed to break my mom's thirty-plus-year refusal to eat Brussels sprouts. They were wonderful! Quite possibly one of my new favorite foods. Thanks!"

MrsWheelbarrow: "I just made what I thought would be enough Brussels sprouts for the two of us. It took great restraint to share. Fantastic recipe."

Moroccan Carrot Salad with Harissa

BY CORDELIA | SERVES 8 TO 10

A&M: As Cordelia noted, this "classic Moroccan salad" is all about tang and fragrance. It's one of those dishes that really wake up your senses: the garlic keeps on giving (in the best possible way), the harissa lends both sweetness and heat, and the perfume of the preserved lemon lingers after each bite. We love the plump little rounds of carrot, which grab on to just the right amount of dressing. And, yes, it is even better the next day.

---

10 medium carrots, peeled

Salt

2 tablespoons harissa

4 tablespoons chopped preserved lemon
(about 1 lemon)

5 garlic cloves, chopped

¼ cup extra virgin olive oil

2 tablespoons white vinegar

¼ bunch cilantro, chopped

Freshly ground black pepper

---

1. Cut the carrots into rounds about ¼ inch thick.

2. Bring 4 cups of water to a boil in a medium saucepan over medium heat and add some salt. Boil the carrots until they're soft but still have some bite, about 10 minutes. Drain, let dry, and cool.

3. In a large bowl, mix the carrots with the rest of the ingredients. Cover and refrigerate at least overnight.

4. Before serving, check and see if the salad needs more salt or vinegar. Serve at room temperature.

TIPS AND TECHNIQUES

If you don't have preserved lemon, Cordelia gave this suggestion: "You can cut a lemon (including the peel) into small pieces and cook it for 1 minute in a little water in the microwave." Discard the water, and you're good to go.

You can control the heat by choosing a milder or more spicy harissa.

ABOUT THE COOK

Cordelia lives in Seattle and, just after the official launch of the site, she began adding dozens of recipes that caught our attention, from Shakshuka to Orange Pancakes with Poppyseeds. See her Hot Spiced Drunken Apple Cider on page 194.

Her favorite cookbook: "The one I will write one day, and until then *Haim Cohen Cooks* (Hebrew)."

WHAT THE COMMUNITY SAID

Kgaines: "Tried this—had great luck with it. I was using a blend of beautiful orange and purple carrots, and in Shanghai, I haven't ever found the right ingredients for harissa, so I substituted chipotle in adobo. I also added some black mustard seeds that I fried up. A very nice recipe to play with! We ate it both as a salad and as a vegetarian pita stuffing with some feta cheese and lettuce. We'll definitely be making this again."

Ciabatta Stuffing with Chorizo, Sweet Potato, and Mushrooms

BY MELISSAV | SERVES 6 TO 8

A&M: Melissav has bucked tradition with this recipe, and we're all for it. She has you make homemade garlic herb croutons and recommends nibbling on them as you cook. Then you sauté chorizo until crisp, followed by sliced shiitakes, which take on a russet hue as they absorb the paprika-tinted fat from the sausage. Red onion and sweet potato are gently caramelized, and finally everything is tossed together with some stock and an egg and baked. At the last minute, you broil the stuffing so that the crust becomes crunchy and golden while everything beneath stays soft and tender.

9 cups ciabatta bread, cut into 1-inch cubes

14 sage leaves, divided into 4 whole and 10 chopped

2 tablespoons chopped fresh rosemary

2 garlic cloves, pressed or chopped

2 tablespoons olive oil, plus more for sautéing

Salt and freshly ground black pepper

1 cup diced dried chorizo

5 cups shiitake mushrooms (or your favorite mix), sliced

1 medium red onion, diced

3 cups diced sweet potato (about 1 large potato, peeled)

2 to 2½ cups chicken or turkey stock (or broth)

1 large egg

4 tablespoons melted fat (butter, schmaltz, or turkey drippings)

1. Heat the oven to 375°F.

2. Toss the bread cubes with the 4 whole sage leaves, the rosemary, garlic, olive oil, salt, and pepper. Spread on a baking sheet and bake, stirring once, until golden and toasty, 10 to 15 minutes. Place the croutons in a large bowl or container. (They are great for a little snack as you continue with the recipe.)

3. In a large pan, sauté the chorizo in 1 or 2 teaspoons olive oil until golden. (The chorizo is already cooked, but I like to render the fat and get it a little crispy.) Remove the chorizo with a slotted spoon to the bowl with the bread.

4. Next, sauté the mushrooms over medium-high heat in the chorizo fat, adding a little olive oil if necessary, and add salt and pepper to taste. Brown them lightly. Remove to the bowl with the bread.

5. Add some olive oil, as the mushrooms will most definitely have sucked up all the fat. Sauté the onion until soft and golden and add salt and pepper to taste. Add to the bowl with the bread.

6. Last, sauté the sweet potato, adding oil as necessary, and salt and pepper to taste. You don't need to cook the potato through, as it will cook in the oven, but I like to get a little color on it.

7. Whisk 2 cups of the stock or broth with the egg and some salt and pepper. Pour into the bowl of stuffing ingredients, add the remaining sage and 2 tablespoons of the fat, and toss thoroughly until evenly moistened. You may need to add up to an additional ½ cup stock, but don't overdo it. You have been seasoning all along, but you may want to taste for seasoning and adjust the salt and pepper.

8. Pour into a 9 × 13-inch baking dish or oval gratin pan. Cover and refrigerate for at least 1 hour. This allows the bread to really absorb the stock and makes for a moist interior and crunchy top (or at least that is what I once read in *Food & Wine*, and it seems to hold true).

9. Cover the pan with aluminum foil and bake for 30 minutes. Remove the foil, brush the top with

the remaining 2 tablespoons fat, and bake for 15 more minutes. I like to broil the top for the last few minutes so it gets nice and crispy, but be sure to watch it carefully.

TIPS AND TECHNIQUES

Melissav said: "My favorite lazy Sunday morning breakfast is a quick hash made from sautéed chorizo, sweet potato, red onion, shiitake mushrooms, and rosemary, topped with a fried egg or two. I decided to incorporate those flavors into a stuffing fit for the Thanksgiving table. Not only is it a great side for the turkey but the leftovers still rock for breakfast the next morning topped with an egg." We tried it and concur!

Feel free to use hot or sweet chorizo, depending on your preference.

ABOUT THE COOK

Melissa Villaveces is a lawyer living in Fort Lauderdale, Florida. She also owns a local wine shop with her husband. See her recipe for Grilled (or Broiled) Oysters with a Sriracha Lime Butter on page 252.

Her favorite recipe from a cookbook: "Pasta with Bolognese Sauce from *Cook's Illustrated*'s *The New Best Recipe*. This is the one recipe from a cookbook I make over and over. I always make a double batch and freeze it in small portions. It is perfect for a quick dinner after a busy day."

WHAT THE COMMUNITY SAID

JuliaBeck: "Thank you, Melissa. This was an outstanding addition to my Thanksgiving table. It was the 'fave newbie,' hands-down. Congrats on winning a spot here on my table for next year!"

jifferb: "I made this at a Thanksgiving themed dinner party yesterday . . . and promptly died. It was fantastic. Making this again for the real Thanksgiving, and ever after."

BEHIND THE SCENES

Right before Thanksgiving, we got to demonstrate this and the other stuffing finalist on the *Today* show with Al Roker!

Pear, Brandy, and Walnut Cranberry Sauce

BY NOTLAZY.RUSTIC. | MAKES 6 TO 8 SMALL SERVINGS

A&M: Notlazy.rustic. wrote: "Growing up, my mom always made a cranberry and orange relish for Thanksgiving. But it wasn't until I was working at a magazine, taste testing for a November issue, that I realized all the cranberry possibilities." In this cranberry sauce, you won't find any of the punishing tartness you get in many—this one's all silk and fragrance. The pears, which are shredded, melt into the sauce. The cranberries soften and soak up the brown sugar, cinnamon, and black pepper. Walnuts add crunch, and the brandy tightens up any wrinkles.

⅓ cup plus 2 to 3 tablespoons brandy

2 cinnamon sticks, each broken in half

8 black peppercorns

12 ounces fresh cranberries, picked over

¾ cup packed light brown sugar

2 medium Bartlett pears, peeled

½ cup chopped walnuts, toasted

---

1. Measure ⅓ cup brandy in a liquid measuring cup; add enough water to reach ½ cup liquid total. Set aside. Place the cinnamon sticks and peppercorns in the center of a small piece of cheesecloth or into a large tea bag and tie closed using kitchen twine.

2. In a medium saucepan, combine the cranberries, brown sugar, and cinnamon-pepper bundle. Using the large holes on a box grater, grate the pears into the saucepan. Stir in the brandy-water mixture.

3. Bring to a boil over high heat, reduce the heat to medium and cook, stirring occasionally, for 10 to 12 minutes, or until the cranberries have burst and the mixture has combined. Remove from the heat.

4. Stir in the remaining 2 to 3 tablespoons brandy. Let cool. Remove and discard the cinnamon-pepper bundle. Stir in all but 1 tablespoon of the toasted walnuts. Transfer the mixture to a small serving bowl and sprinkle with the remaining walnuts.

TIPS AND TECHNIQUES

We've made the sauce with grated apple and it's just as delicious. We've also served it over fresh ricotta—make sure you have some leftovers so you can try this! The sauce can be made a day or two ahead.

Notlazy.rustic: "When choosing the pears, I look for ones that are ripe, but still firm. And, feel free to play with the brandy to make the sauce as boozy (or not) as you want."

ABOUT THE COOK

After leaving her job as a food editor at a women's magazine, Brooke Herman went back to culinary school and started the food blog Not lazy. Rustic (www.notlazy-rustic.blogspot.com). She lives in Fort Lee, New Jersey.

Her favorite cooking tip: "My life changed when I learned to thinly coat a measuring cup with cooking spray or oil before measuring sticky ingredients, like honey."

WHAT THE COMMUNITY SAID

Dagny: "I made this exactly as in the recipe for Thanksgiving, and my whole family loved it, so I thought I'd do it again for Christmas. I tried it with pecans instead of walnuts this time, and I also added a lemon peel to the tea bag (actually I used a tied coffee filter) and a bit of orange and lemon zest. I actually liked the contrast of the walnuts better than the pecans, but the lemon peel and zest added a really nice zing to the mix."

Pink Greens

BY MARISSA GRACE | SERVES 2

A&M: This may be the most thoughtful sautéed greens recipe we've ever encountered. Beet greens (we agree with Marissa Grace that they deserve more attention in the kitchen) are usually wilted in hot olive oil with a little garlic, and they're delicious this way, but Marissa Grace plotted out ways to amplify the greens' sweetness while tempering it with chiles. She has you brown garlic with shallot and red pepper flakes, then layer in sugar, black pepper, and salt before adding the greens and wilting them. Just before serving, you splash the beet greens with sherry vinegar, which electrifies the whole dish. The key here is the sugar, which caramelizes with the garlic and tightens up the sauce, so by the time the greens are cooked (and beet greens really should be cooked), it wraps them in a cloak of sweet and fiery sauce.

---

1 large bunch beet greens

2 teaspoons chopped garlic

1 shallot, chopped

¼ teaspoon crushed red pepper flakes

1 teaspoon olive oil

½ teaspoon coarsely ground black pepper

2 teaspoons sugar

¼ teaspoon salt

2 teaspoons sherry vinegar

---

1. Wash and trim the beet greens. If the stems are very thick, it's worth trimming them back a bit.

2. In a large sauté pan over medium heat, sauté the garlic, shallot, and red pepper flakes in the olive oil until slightly browned. Add the black pepper, sugar, and salt.

3. Place the beet greens in the pan, pour ¼ cup water over them, and immediately cover. Once the greens have cooked down, 1 to 2 minutes, remove the lid and stir. Cook for another 1 to 2 minutes, allowing the water to evaporate.

4. Just before serving, pour the vinegar over the greens. Serve and enjoy!

TIPS AND TECHNIQUES

If you double the amounts as we did, so that it serves 4 people, add vinegar to taste. Twice the amount may be too much.

You could use the same technique with spinach, arugula, chard, or any other dark leafy green.

ABOUT THE COOK

Marissa Grace Desmond and her husband, Ian Kaminski-Coughlin, live in Cambridge, Massachusetts.

Their favorite entertaining tip: "For dinner parties, we share online spreadsheets with our guests, so everyone can see who has responded. It also makes it much easier to coordinate who is bringing what and whether or not we need more wine!"

WHAT THE COMMUNITY SAID

Alli51: "This recipe would work great for various types of Asian greens (which I typically just cook with a bit of oil, kosher salt, and some soy/fish sauce and maybe some chicken broth). This will be much more interesting!"

Southwestern Spiced Sweet Potato Fries with Chili-Cilantro Sour Cream

BY TASTEFOOD | SERVES 4

A&M: The brilliance of the sweet potato fry is that with all the sugar in the potatoes, you can really lay on the seasonings. Here, TasteFood has you use chili powder, cumin, cayenne, and paprika, which, as she pointed out, "complement the natural sweetness of the potatoes." You might want to double the recipe so you'll feel better about sharing. You'll want to eat the first batch plain and the second tempered with the tangy sour cream sauce.

POTATO FRIES

2 large sweet potatoes, cut in matchsticks/
    batons, approximately ¼×2 inches

2 tablespoons olive oil

2 teaspoons salt

1 teaspoon ground cumin

1 teaspoon chili powder

1 teaspoon paprika

1 teaspoon freshly ground black pepper

½ teaspoon cayenne pepper, or to taste

CHILI-CILANTRO SOUR CREAM

1 cup sour cream

1 tablespoon freshly squeezed lime juice

2 teaspoons sweet chili sauce

1 small garlic clove, minced

½ teaspoon salt

½ teaspoon freshly ground black pepper

1 heaping tablespoon chopped cilantro

1. Heat the oven to 425°F.

2. Toss the sweet potatoes and olive oil in a large bowl.

3. Combine the salt, cumin, chili powder, paprika, pepper, and cayenne in a small bowl.

4. Add the spices to the potatoes and toss to coat.

5. Arrange the potatoes in one layer on a large baking sheet.

6. Bake on the lowest rack of the oven until the undersides are browned, 12 to 15 minutes. Turn the potatoes with a spatula and bake for 10 more minutes.

7. Meanwhile, make the sour cream sauce. Combine all the ingredients except the cilantro in a medium bowl and whisk together. Stir in the cilantro.

8. Remove the potatoes from the oven, cool for a few minutes, and serve with the sour cream.

TIPS AND TECHNIQUES

TasteFood says: "When I make these I always double the batch, because they are gobbled up faster than you can say 'Southwestern Spiced Sweet Potato Fries.' I don't peel the sweet potatoes, because the skin adds extra texture and nutrients."

Maryvelasquez says: "This spice mixture and dipping sauce also taste delicious when used with regular potatoes, which I found out tonight."

As we discovered the hard way, cayenne's heat varies a lot—start with ¼ teaspoon and add more if you like.

ABOUT THE COOK

Lynda Balslev is a food blogger who generously hosted the first Food52 potluck at her home in the California Bay Area, inspiring spinoffs across the country. See her Smoked Ham with Pomegranate Molasses, Black Pepper, and Mustard Glaze on page 201; her Whole Baked Fish in Sea Salt with Parsley Gremolata on page 224; and her Broccoli Rabe, Potato, and Rosemary Pizza on page 371. Here's her blog: TasteFood (www.tastefoodblog.com).

Her favorite recipe from a cookbook: "Big Chocolate Cake recipe from Ruth Reichl's *Comfort Me with Apples*. It is hands-down no-fail; it pleases kids, adults, a crowd, and it tastes delicious."

WHAT THE COMMUNITY SAID

More please by Margie: "Made these for dinner last night . . . was kicking myself for not doubling the recipe. Irresistible."

Arugula, Pear, and Goat Cheese Salad with Pomegranate Vinaigrette

BY BRIGIDC | SERVES 6

A&M: Although this salad has lots of different ingredients, it's somehow not overly busy or complicated. Brigidc's inspiration was the pomegranate molasses (she first encountered it in a Persian cooking class), and its fragrance and sweetness mollify the tartness of the sherry vinegar in the dressing. We love how the shallots lightly pickle in the vinaigrette as you make the rest of the salad. Mellow pears, salty goat cheese, crunchy pomegranate seeds, and toasted pistachios ensure that every bite contains a party of flavors and textures.

VINAIGRETTE
1 large shallot, halved and thinly sliced
1 tablespoon pomegranate molasses
2 tablespoons sherry or apple cider vinegar
½ teaspoon kosher salt
¼ teaspoon freshly ground black pepper
⅓ cup extra virgin olive oil

SALAD
4 cups arugula, lightly packed
4 cups romaine, torn into bite-size pieces
2 ripe pears, cored and cut into ½-inch cubes
⅓ cup pomegranate seeds
3 ounces cold fresh goat cheese or feta, crumbled
¼ cup pistachios, toasted and coarsely chopped

1. To make the dressing: In a small bowl, combine the shallot, pomegranate molasses, vinegar, salt, and pepper, and whisk until the salt is dissolved. Whisk in the olive oil and let the vinaigrette stand at room temperature until the salad is assembled.

2. To make the salad: Combine the arugula, romaine, pears, and half of the pomegranate seeds in a large bowl. Crumble half of the goat cheese over the ingredients in the bowl (this works best if the cheese is very cold).

3. Whisk the vinaigrette until uniform and add all but 2 tablespoons of it to the bowl. Gently toss the salad with your hands or salad tongs, coating the ingredients well with the vinaigrette. If the salad seems dry, add the vinaigrette in small increments until it is dressed to your liking.

4. Crumble the remaining cheese over the salad and sprinkle the remaining pomegranate seeds and the pistachios over the top. Serve immediately.

TIPS AND TECHNIQUES

If you don't have pomegranate molasses, you can reduce sweetened pomegranate juice until it's syrupy.

Lenny recommended trying ricotta salata instead of goat cheese, and biceinparadise suggested goat's milk feta. We think any soft, mild, salty cheese would be great.

ABOUT THE COOK

Brigid Callinan lives in Petaluma, California, and works as a cooking instructor for the U.S. Coast Guard Training Center. She has co-authored two cookbooks, *Fondue* and *The Mustards Grill Napa Valley Cookbook*.

Her favorite entertaining tip: "Invite friends who are good cooks/Martha Stewart types and don't be afraid to task them."

WHAT THE COMMUNITY SAID

Melissav: "I finally made this and wish I hadn't waited until the end of pomegranate season to try it. This is a really beautiful salad! Thank you for the recipe."

Herb and White Wine Granita

BY ROBYNMICHELLELEE | SERVES 2

A&M: This recipe was submitted the week we held our Best Frozen Dessert contest, and while we loved it, we didn't feel it fit the category perfectly. Yes, you could serve this granita on its own as a not-too-sweet dessert, but we think its clean, herbal notes would be perfect for a palate-cleansing middle course, or as the wow factor in a multi-component dessert (think poached pears or a fruit galette with ice cream).

⅓ cup sugar

4 rosemary sprigs, plus 2 more for garnish

⅔ cup white wine (ours was an organic bottle from the south of France, part Rolle and part Ugni Blanc)

1 splash freshly squeezed lemon juice

1. Bring 1 cup water, the sugar, and 4 of the rosemary sprigs to a boil in a small saucepan. Turn off the heat, cover, and let stand.

2. When the syrup has cooled and is infused with the scent of rosemary, remove the rosemary and stir in the wine and lemon juice.

3. Freeze the liquid in an open container for at least 3 hours, scraping often with a fork as it solidifies.

4. Serve garnished with a sprig of rosemary.

TIPS AND TECHNIQUES

Robynmichellelee wrote: "It is possible to vary this recipe each time by using different wine and different herbs. One possibility is to use mint rather than rosemary, and lime juice rather than lemon juice."

ABOUT THE COOK

Robyn Michelle-Lee Thompson is a lifestyle photographer, English teacher, and student living in Vancouver. Here's her blog: This is Life (www.robynmichellelee.com).

Her favorite entertaining tip: "When entertaining, fresh-cut flowers and sparkling water on the table always add a touch of elegance!"

Cooking biut: "WOW."

Cider-Brined Pork with Calvados, Mustard, and Thyme

BY OUI, CHEF | SERVES 2

A&M: Oui, Chef has proven himself to be an accomplished cook, especially talented at taking a simple concept and elevating it to new heights. Here, inspired by a meal he had while traveling through Brittany, he brines thick chops in cider and herbs so that they stay juicy and develop a rich, caramel crust as they sauté. He then constructs a quick pan sauce by building on the ingredients of the brine. Starting with the drippings, he deglazes with Calvados, then adds shallots, thyme, more cider, and cream for suppleness. A spoonful of Dijon lends a subtle bite.

CIDER BRINE
2 cups apple cider

¼ cup kosher salt

¼ cup lightly packed light brown sugar

1 tablespoon black peppercorns

2 teaspoons yellow mustard seeds

3 fresh thyme sprigs

CHOPS AND PAN SAUCE
Two 1-inch-thick, bone-in, center-cut pork chops

Canola oil

Salt and freshly ground black pepper

¼ cup Calvados

2 tablespoons unsalted butter

1 shallot, minced

1 tablespoon minced fresh thyme

½ cup heavy cream

⅓ cup apple cider

2 teaspoons Dijon mustard

1. Place all of the brine ingredients and 1½ cups water in a medium saucepan and stir over low heat until the salt and sugar have dissolved. Remove from the heat and let cool.

2. Place the chops in a single layer in a shallow pan, cover fully with the brine, cover, and refrigerate overnight. When ready to cook, remove the chops from the brine, rinse well under cold water, and dry with paper towels before continuing.

3. Heat 1 to 2 tablespoons canola oil in a large, heavy skillet over medium-high heat. Season the pork with a little salt and freshly ground pepper. Add the pork to the skillet and sauté until just cooked through, about 4 minutes per side. Transfer to a plate; cover with aluminum foil and keep warm.

4. Pour off the excess oil and, over medium heat, deglaze the pan with the Calvados, scraping the bottom of the pan well and letting the brandy reduce to a glaze. Add the butter, shallot, and thyme and sauté for 2 minutes. Stir in the cream and cider; boil until the mixture thickens to sauce consistency, about 3 minutes. Stir in the mustard and season with salt and pepper to taste. Remove from the heat and serve with the pork.

TIPS AND TECHNIQUES

It may seem like this recipe makes a lot of sauce for two servings, but trust us: you'll be mopping up the last creamy ribbons with your final bite of pork. If you don't have Calvados, regular brandy will do.

Oui, Chef: "I like the dish with a nice thick chop, but it would also work well with a cutlet, or pork tenderloin."

ABOUT THE COOK

Steven Dunn is a writer living in Massachusetts. He chronicles teaching his five children how to cook on his food blog, Oui, Chef (www.ouichefnetwork.com), which he launched after taking a two-year professional hiatus to attend culinary school in France.

His favorite recipe from a cookbook: "Short Ribs Braised in Red Wine with Celery Duo from Daniel Boulud's *Café Boulud Cookbook.*"

WHAT THE COMMUNITY SAID

Mt97: "Chef, I made this recipe tonight and it absolutely rocked. Your magic helped me turn out the best chop of my life thus far. I could not get over how the apple cider spice permeated the meat. And the sauce . . . the sauce was both rich and light. My girlfriend would not stop gnawing at the completely stripped rib bones! Kudos to you, chef. Kudos to you . . ."

Scgoble: "I have made this recipe twice now, once with a tenderloin and this week with chops. Absolutely amazing both times. This week, I didn't have brandy and used Jim Beam and apple juice—I'm sure that's not what you had in mind but it was delicious anyway! Even my two-year-old had to make sure that each bite of pork chop had some sauce on it."

Lemony Cream Cheese Pancakes with Blueberries

BY ENUNN | SERVES 6

A&M: ENunn rightly noted, "A world without lemons would be a very sad one." And for those who crave the purity of a plain pancake but occasionally find themselves wanting more, ENunn's recipe might be the perfect compromise: lemon's perfume (from both the juice and zest) permeates these light, fluffy buttermilk pancakes. The real magic lies in the addition of chunks of cream cheese, blended into the batter until they are reduced to about pea-size, resulting in salty, creamy pockets scattered throughout the cooked pancakes.

1½ cups all-purpose flour

1 tablespoon sugar

1 tablespoon baking powder

½ teaspoon baking soda

Pinch of salt

2 large eggs, separated

1 cup buttermilk

6 ounces cold cream cheese, cut up

1 tablespoon melted butter, plus additional for the pan

1 teaspoon vanilla extract

2 tablespoons lemon juice

Zest of 1 large lemon

1½ cups fresh or thawed frozen blueberries

Honey, maple syrup, or jam, for serving

---

1. In a medium bowl, mix together the flour, sugar, baking powder, baking soda, and salt. In a separate bowl, whisk together the egg yolks and buttermilk. Add the cream cheese and mix until it has separated into uniformly small lumps, about the size of large cottage cheese curds. Stir in the melted butter, vanilla, lemon juice, and lemon zest.

2. Add the dry ingredients to the wet ingredients, then stir to combine. In a medium bowl, whisk the egg whites until stiff but not dry; fold them gently into the batter.

3. Heat a griddle or cast-iron pan over medium-high heat until a drop of water sizzles. Lower the heat to medium and butter or oil the pan. Drop the batter into the pan by ⅓ cupfuls, making sure not to crowd the pancakes. Once the batter has spread, drop in the berries. (You might want to drizzle some batter over to cover them.) These need to be cooked a bit longer than you might expect; they won't bubble as quickly or as much as plain pancakes. Turn down the heat if necessary to keep them from overbrowning, and let them puff up to their full extent after you turn them, which will take 2 to 3 minutes. Serve with honey or maple syrup or jam.

TIPS AND TECHNIQUES

ENunn admitted that she also likes these pancakes plain. We think a swipe of salted butter never hurts.

ChezSuzanne used homemade candied lemon zest, with great results. A few readers wondered whether these would be good with chocolate chips instead of blueberries—we say, why not?

ABOUT THE COOK

Emily Nunn is a former editor at *The New Yorker* and the *Chicago Tribune*. She currently lives in Chicago and works as a freelance writer and food blogger at Cook the Wolf (www.cookthewolf .blogspot.com). See her Faulknerian Family Spice Cake with Caramel Icing on page 358.

Her favorite recipe from a cookbook: "Red and Yellow Bell Pepper Sauce with Sausages, from Marcella Hazan's *Essentials of Classic Italian Cooking*. She insists that you peel the peppers; the resulting dish is transportive and characteristically simple. I love her."

WHAT THE COMMUNITY SAID

Melissav: "Made these a few weekends ago for breakfast and they were so good that I made another batch a few nights later for dinner!"

Turkey Pho

BY WINNIEAB | MAKES 2 BIG BOWLS OF SOUP

A&M: Anyone who knows pho knows that it's all about the broth. WinnieAb uses turkey leftovers (meat and stock, which should really be homemade for this) to coax the most out of this soup. She also adds some warm spices—coriander, cloves, star anise, and cinnamon—which she toasts beforehand to amp up the broth. Chopped kale is an unusual ingredient that adds some welcome heft—we preferred 1 cup rather than 2. As with any pho, don't forget to squeeze in some fresh lime juice just before eating—its hit of acidity really wakes up the dish.

SPICES
2 tablespoons coriander seeds

4 whole cloves

4 whole star anise

1 cinnamon stick

TURKEY PHO
1 quart homemade turkey stock (or homemade or store-bought chicken stock)

1 bunch scallions (green top parts only), chopped

One 3-inch chunk of ginger, sliced and smashed with the side of a knife

1 teaspoon light brown sugar, or more to taste

1 tablespoon fish sauce, or more to taste

1 to 2 cups kale, chopped into bite-size pieces

½ pound leftover turkey breast, shredded

1 bunch (about 2 ounces) cellophane or bean thread noodles (or enough flat dried rice noodles to serve 2)

1½ tablespoons chopped cilantro, for garnish (optional)

1½ tablespoons minced scallions (white parts only), for garnish (optional)

Sriracha hot sauce

½ lime, cut into wedges

---

1. Heat a cast-iron skillet or frying pan over medium heat. Add the spices and toast until fragrant, 3 to 4 minutes. Immediately spoon the spices into a bowl to avoid burning them.

2. Add the toasted spices, stock, scallions, ginger, brown sugar, and fish sauce to a large pot and bring to a boil over high heat.

3. Reduce the heat to medium-low and simmer for 20 minutes, skimming the surface frequently.

4. Taste the broth and add more sugar or fish sauce if needed. Strain the broth and discard the solids. Add the kale and cook for 1 to 2 more minutes. Remove from the heat.

5. Add the turkey and noodles. Allow to sit for a few minutes while the noodles soften.

6. Ladle the broth into 2 bowls. Divide the kale, turkey, and noodles evenly between the bowls.

7. Sprinkle on the garnishes and add Sriracha to taste. Squeeze in lime juice to taste before eating.

TIPS AND TECHNIQUES

If you don't have leftover turkey on hand, WinnieAb wrote: "I see no reason why you couldn't use an uncooked turkey breast and cook it in the soup, then remove, shred, and add it back in."

ABOUT THE COOK

Winnie Abramson grew up in the kitchen of her parents' famed New York City restaurant The Quilted Giraffe. She currently lives in New Paltz, New York, and blogs about food and holistic nutrition at Healthy Green Kitchen (www.healthygreenkitchen.com). See her Smoky Minestrone with Tortellini and Parsley or Basil Pesto on page 387.

Her favorite recipe from a cookbook: "The Devil's Food Cake Cockaigne from *The Joy of Cooking*. It was the first recipe I ever baked completely on my own. I think I was thirteen or fourteen and made it as a surprise for my mom's birthday."

WHAT THE COMMUNITY SAID

Lastnightsdinner: "Oh my goodness, Winnie–we had this tonight with the last of our Thanksgiving heritage bird (thawed from the freezer) and it was phenomenal. We were silent through dinner except for '*mmm*' and 'wow' and lots of slurping. Such a great recipe–*thank you*."

Shrimp Biryani (Indian Shrimp and Rice)

BY AMREEN | SERVES 6

A&M: This biryani has the distinction of being both delicate and full of flavor. A bowl of this fragrant rice and shrimp would be equally suited to lunch or dinner, either enjoyed alone in private bliss or served for a dinner party. We love that the same mixture of garlic, ginger, cilantro, and chiles gets incorporated into both the rice and shrimp, the two parts of the dish mirroring each other aromatically. And amreen reminded us of the beauty and ease of baked rice!

---

2 cups basmati rice

1 pound medium shrimp, shelled and deveined

1 teaspoon salt

½ teaspoon ground turmeric

One 1-inch piece ginger

4 large garlic cloves

¼ bunch cilantro

2 serrano chiles

4 tablespoons neutral oil, such as vegetable or canola

1 teaspoon whole black peppercorns

One 1½-inch cinnamon stick

½ teaspoon whole cloves

10 whole green cardamom pods

2 bay leaves

1 large yellow onion, chopped

Salt

2 tablespoons unsalted butter

2 mint sprigs, chopped

---

1. Heat the oven to 350°F. Wash the rice and soak it in cold water until needed.

2. Wash the shrimp and drain it well. Add the salt and turmeric and mix. Refrigerate until ready to use.

3. Peel the ginger and garlic and use a food processor to blend it to a paste with the cilantro and chiles. You can add a little water if it's too dry.

4. In a large Dutch oven or oven-safe pot, heat the oil over medium heat. Add the peppercorns, cinnamon stick, cloves, cardamom, and 1 of the bay leaves. Sauté until fragrant, about 2 to 3 minutes.

5. Add the onion and sauté until light brown, stirring constantly.

6. Add half the ginger paste and sauté for another 1 or 2 minutes.

7. Add 3 cups water and salt (1 to 2 teaspoons, depending on taste) and bring the mixture to a boil.

8. Drain the rice and add it to the boiling water along with the butter and mint. Bring to a boil, cover, and put it in the oven. Bake for 20 minutes.

9. When the rice has been in the oven for about 10 minutes, heat some oil in a sauté pan and add the remainder of the ginger paste along with the remaining bay leaf. Sauté for 1 to 2 minutes and add the shrimp. Sauté the shrimp until done (they should be light pink), 2 to 3 minutes.

10. Remove the rice from the oven. Top it with the shrimp and serve.

TIPS AND TECHNIQUES

Some readers said they threw in additional vegetables, such as diced carrots or frozen peas, to make this an even more complete one-dish meal.

We cooked this in a shallow heatproof casserole dish, which worked well.

ABOUT THE COOK

Amreen Karmali is an educator living in Los Angeles. Here's her blog: Comida y Cultura (www.comidaycultura.wordpress.com).

Her favorite recipe from a cookbook: "It's from a small cookbook called *A Spicy Touch* by Noorbanu Nimji. This book is dear to my heart because it traces the culinary path of my people's history from India to East Africa. I love her recipe for bharazi, a pigeon pea and coconut curry. It's almost as good as my mom's."

WHAT THE COMMUNITY SAID

Bonnie59: "I just made this for the second time for my family and we all loved it. Even my fussy eater thirteen-year-old daughter gobbled it up and didn't pick out the onions. Quite a success for our household meals."

Lazy Mary's Lemon Tart

BY DYMNYNO | MAKES 1 TART

A&M: People who taste this smooth, fragrant tart won't believe that it contains a whole lemon, rind and all. Nor will they understand how you got it to be so fragrant and light and not at all gummy the way lemon curd tarts can sometimes be. In our view "Mary" wasn't lazy at all, she was brilliant. She has you whiz the filling together in a blender, then simply pour it into a blind-baked tart shell. Dymnyno, who lives in the Napa Valley, said, "Versions of this simple, quick dessert have circulated around the valley for years." She gave the tart her own touch—a Meyer lemon—which lends it fragrance and finesse and none of the intrusive acidity found in regular lemons. One catch: you'll need to use your own tart dough. If you don't have a favorite, we recommend *The Joy of Cooking*'s sweet pastry dough.

---

1 large Meyer lemon, cut into 8 pieces

1½ cups superfine sugar

8 tablespoons (1 stick) unsalted butter

1 teaspoon vanilla extract

4 large eggs

Your favorite 9-inch tart shell, blind-baked (see Tips and Techniques)

---

1. Heat the oven to 350°F. Put all the ingredients—except the tart shell—into a blender and whirl like crazy!

2. Pour into the tart shell.

3. Bake for 30 to 40 minutes. (Watch that the top does not burn.) Cool on a wire rack before serving.

TIPS AND TECHNIQUES

To blind bake the tart shell, we lined a 9-inch fluted tart pan with the pastry dough, pricked it with a fork, lined it with parchment, filled it with pie weights, and baked it at 375°F for 15 minutes, then removed the weights and baked it for another 10 minutes. Once the tart shell cooled, we added the lemon filling and sent it back for one last turn in the oven. Start checking it at 35 minutes.

Culinista Annouchka: "I actually put the mixture into ramekins and in a water bath–it was a superb crustless lemon tart!"

ABOUT THE COOK

Mary Fairbanks Constant owns Constant Winery in Napa Valley, California, where she also serves as the winery cook. See her Heart of Gold (panko-breaded artichoke hearts with a creamy cumin-lime dipping sauce) on page 374. Here's her blog: Current Vintage (www.current-vintage.com).

Her favorite recipe from a cookbook: "Chicken Fried Soft Shell Crabs from *Fish Without a Doubt* by Rick Moonen (an activist for sustainable fishery)."

WHAT THE COMMUNITY SAID

Aargersi: "Made this for a dinner party Saturday night and it was a *hit*! I used a pecan maple crust recipe that is super easy (Lazy Me! :-) and it all came together perfectly. Bless you, Lazy Mary! This appears to be one of the most popular recipes on Food52!!!"

BEHIND THE SCENES

It became clear with this recipe that we had a particular interest in techniques that would elevate accessible or already familiar recipes. Here are some of the other technique-driven recipes we've been moved by: Pink Greens (page 156), The (Not Barefoot) Contessa's Fish Pasta (page 61), and Classic Southern Buttermilk-Bathed Fried Chicken (page 86).

Cowboy Rubbed Rib-eye with Chocolate Stout Pan Sauce

BY ALIWAKS | SERVES 2

A&M: Ground coffee, smoked paprika, cumin, ancho chile, and brown sugar form an earthy, flinty rub that smells appealingly of wood smoke. "I started making this rub after reading about cowboy food," Aliwaks wrote. "They carried with them coffee, salt, pepper, and sugar . . . and they grilled their steaks in cast-iron pans. Since I do not often find myself on the open range, I have to make do with either my grill or, during wet yucky weather, my oven. I've added a couple of spices and few noncowboy-type extras . . . though I'm pretty sure if the cowboys had chocolate stout they would've enjoyed it, too." She also borrows a smart technique from Indian cooking and has you toast the spices over low heat before rubbing them on the steak. Then it's just a matter of searing the rib-eye in a very hot cast-iron pan and finishing the sauce with some chocolate brown stout, beef stock, and a lump of butter. We recommend some corn pudding on the side.

---

1 tablespoon ground coffee

2 tablespoons kosher salt

1 teaspoon smoked paprika (sweet or hot, depending on your taste)

1 tablespoon coarsely ground black pepper

1 teaspoon crushed red pepper flakes (preferably ancho chile)

1 teaspoon ground cumin

2 teaspoons dark brown sugar

1 nice, thick rib-eye, 1 to 1½ inches thick, big enough for two

1 tablespoon vegetable oil (if you are the type to save bacon fat, by all means use it)

1 thyme sprig

1 cup chocolate stout (you'll have to drink the rest!)

½ cup beef broth

1 tablespoon unsalted butter

I. Mix the coffee, salt, paprika, black pepper, red pepper flakes, and cumin together and toast lightly in a pan until fragrant. (Alternatively you can toast whole spices, then grind them.) Mix the spices with the sugar to make the rub.

2. Spread the rub all over the steak and let sit for a while. If you do it the night before you'll have stronger flavor, but if you do it right before cooking it'll be good, too. (If you prerub and set it in the fridge, be sure to bring it up to room temperature before searing.)

3. Heat a cast-iron pan until it's really really hot—a drop of water flicked into the pan should sizzle and bounce. Add the vegetable oil, wait a few seconds until it heats up, and place the steak in the pan. It should sizzle; leave it there, do not touch it at all for 3 to 4 minutes, or until it's browned on the bottom. Place the pan under a hot broiler and broil to medium-rare or desired doneness, 2 to 3 minutes.

4. Remove the steak and let it rest on a warm plate, covered with aluminum foil.

5. Add the thyme sprig to the pan and let it sauté a bit until it gets nice and fragrant. Pour in the chocolate stout and deglaze the pan. Add the broth, whisk together, and reduce by half over medium heat.

6. Remove the thyme sprig and whisk in the butter. Season to taste.

7. Slice the steak on the bias and drizzle the sauce over top. This is *yummy* with creamed spinach and hash browns or a baked potato and a nice big salad.

TIPS AND TECHNIQUES

Aliwaks added, "On the rare occasions when I've been forced to camp outdoors, I've brought prerubbed steaks with me to get a taste of the old West. If you have no chocolate stout available, any dark beer will do; you can also substitute red wine but it will be very different. I like to use a preheated cast-iron pan because it conducts the heat well . . . and you don't have to turn the meat over."

Lastnightsdinner said: "We've got a weird, very low-profile broiler underneath our oven that our iron skillet is too big to fit under, so when we had this over the weekend my husband seared it on the stovetop and then chucked the iron skillet into a 500°F oven just until the steak reached about 130°F to 135°F. He let it rest tented in foil while I made the pan sauce back on the stovetop, and our steak turned out perfectly medium-rare."

ABOUT THE COOK

Learn more about Aliwaks and check out her recipes for Smoky Fried Chickpeas on page 123 and Luciana's Porchetta (which went up against *Cook's Illustrated*'s best roasted pork shoulder–and almost won!) on page 329.

WHAT THE COMMUNITY SAID

Limonlemon: "I've made this twice, once with pork and another time with steak. The only downside of this recipe is that when you're toasting the spices, it 'seriously' makes you cough. *Everyone* does. Just turn on a fan, open a few windows, and it'll pass. Other than that, it's delicious, even three days later as a leftover sandwich. Definitely a keeper."

Andouille and Dijon Polenta

BY THE INTERNET COOKING PRINCESS | SERVES 4 AS A SIDE DISH OR 2 AS A MAIN COURSE

A&M: A one-dish meal that calls for nothing more than an accompanying green salad, The Internet Cooking Princess's polenta is as creamy and rich as it gets, but it's far from a one-note wonder. She came up with this by combining two of her favorite dishes. "I've borrowed the andouille sausage from dirty (or Cajun) rice, a go-to comfort food of mine, while also borrowing a Dijon lemon cream sauce that I like to use in scallop risotto," she wrote. There's a subtle tang from the Dijon, and it's studded with bits of spicy andouille and flecked with fresh spinach and tarragon—the latter managing to keep things just short of excessive. We'd never made polenta this way before (you build a base with the sausage and onions, then add chicken stock and polenta, cooking the ingredients all together), but we definitely will in the future. If you can't find raw andouille, you can just brown chopped precooked andouille in a bit of olive oil, as we did.

¾ pound andouille sausage, ground or casings removed

1 white onion, finely chopped

3 cups chicken broth

1 cup polenta

¼ cup white wine

½ cup heavy cream

1 tablespoon Dijon mustard

1 teaspoon garlic paste

1 teaspoon chopped tarragon

1 teaspoon lemon zest

½ cup chopped spinach

Kosher salt and freshly ground black pepper

1 tablespoon unsalted butter, broken into quarters (optional)

---

1. In a large sauté pan over medium-high heat, break up the sausage and cook all the way through, about 5 minutes.

2. Add the onion and cook in the fat from the sausage for 3 to 5 minutes, or until translucent.

3. Add the chicken broth to the pan and bring to a boil over high heat. Slowly whisk in the polenta.

4. Reduce the heat and stir the polenta to prevent clumping for about 10 minutes, or until the broth has been been absorbed by the polenta.

5. Meanwhile, make the Dijon sauce by adding the white wine and heavy cream to a smaller sauté pan over low heat. Whisk for about a minute, then add the mustard, garlic paste, tarragon, and lemon zest. Continue to whisk for another few minutes so that all the ingredients are properly incorporated and warmed through.

6. Stir the Dijon sauce and chopped spinach into the polenta, ensuring that all the ingredients are evenly distributed and heated through. Season with some hefty pinches of salt and pepper, pour into a serving dish, and top with a few pats of butter, if desired. Serve as a side or make it your main course with a simple salad.

TIPS AND TECHNIQUES
If you can't find andouille, use kielbasa or a mild chorizo.

ABOUT THE COOK
Meredith Shafer is a marketer living in Dallas, Texas, and writes the food blog The Internet Cooking Princess (www.internetcookingprincess.com). See her recipes for Norma's Eggnog on page 199 and Ricotta and Chive Gnocchi on page 263.

Her favorite entertaining tip: "Whenever I entertain, I require two things: a glass of wine and a wingman. The wine keeps me calm if I have a disaster in the kitchen, and the wingman keeps guests out of the kitchen in the event of said disaster."

WHAT THE COMMUNITY SAID
SBV: "I made this for friends this weekend, and they all wanted to know where I bought it (I've never been much of a cook). They were shocked when I said that I had made it myself. It was wonderful and so simple to make."

Sweet Potatoes Anna with Prunes

BY MRSP | SERVES 6 TO 10

A&M: This layered sweet potato gratin comes out of the oven caramelized on the edges and glistening with butter. The potatoes in the center are soft, their layers embedded with prunes; the ones around the edges are so crisp and sweet from the port, they taste candied. Slice the potatoes thinly—use a mandoline if you have one—and check the potatoes after 35 minutes in the oven. By 40 minutes, ours were perfect.

---

1 cup (2 sticks) unsalted butter

1 cup port

10 pitted prunes

5 to 6 small sweet potatoes, peeled and very thinly sliced

Salt and freshly ground black pepper

---

1. Clarify the butter: In a small saucepan set over low heat, melt the butter. Skim off any foam, then pour the clear liquid into a bowl, leaving behind the solids.

2. Heat the port to a simmer in a small saucepan over medium heat. Add the prunes, turn off the heat and let them soak until plumped, about 20 minutes. Drain and chop the prunes coarsely.

3. Heat the oven to 450°F.

4. Brush the clarified butter onto your favorite 8- or 9-inch round baking dish or ovenproof frying pan.

5. Arrange a layer of potatoes, overlapping in circles, in the dish. Brush with the clarified butter and season with salt and pepper. Arrange another layer of potatoes and sprinkle with about half the prune pieces. Season with salt and pepper. Brush with clarified butter. Repeat with one more layer of potatoes and prunes, then end with a layer of potatoes. Remember to brush each layer with clarified butter and salt and pepper. You can do four layers of potatoes or six; it's up to you. Pack the potatoes tightly by pressing down on them with your palms. If there's a little butter left at the end, it's no big deal.

6. Bake until crisp and tender, 35 to 45 minutes.

7. Remove from the oven and let cool in the pan for a few minutes. Then flip the cake onto a serving plate and cut into wedges.

TIPS AND TECHNIQUES

Mrsp: "This can be finished with a dusting of sugar and a couple of minutes of broiling, for a brûlée top. It can also be made using apples and prunes, or just apples."

If you can't find sweet potatoes, use yams.

ABOUT THE COOK

Mrsp is a writer living in New York City.

WHAT THE COMMUNITY SAID

Aliwaks: "I'm filing this away for the Seder—it's like tsimmes, but better."

thirschfeld: "I often add prunes to a potato galette à la *The French Laundry* and this held its own and then some in my book. I soaked the prunes in Cognac because I didn't have any port. This will go into the winter rotation."

Figgy Pudding Butter Cookies

Winter

Hot Spiced Drunken Apple Cider

BY CORDELIA | SERVES 8 TO 10

A&M: A more refined version of mulled cider, this punch also calls for an off-dry white wine and fresh cranberries. The cider is quickly steeped in spices—cloves, cinnamon, vanilla, and nutmeg—before you add the wine and cranberries, which give the punch a light rosy hue. Cordelia's concoction goes down easy, so sip slowly if you can restrain yourself!

½ gallon apple cider (I've used unfiltered)

4 cinnamon sticks

4 cloves

¼ teaspoon ground nutmeg

1 vanilla bean, split lengthwise

3 to 4 tablespoons honey (depending on the sweetness of the wine)

¾ bottle of Gewürztraminer

1 cup or so of fresh cranberrries (or cubed apple if not in cranberry season)

1. Put the cider, all the spices, and 3 tablespoons of honey into a medium saucepan and bring to a boil over medium-high heat.

2. Reduce the heat to low and simmer for about 10 minutes so that all of the flavors have a chance to blend.

3. Add the wine. Do not boil again, so the alcohol won't evaporate too much—just let it warm.

4. Add the cranberries and simmer for a few more minutes until they color the liquid a bit. Taste, adding more honey if needed.

TIPS AND TECHNIQUES

If you can't get Gewürztraminer, pick up a white wine that's not too dry—you can even use a semisweet one like Muscat.

ABOUT THE COOK

Learn more about Cordelia, and see her recipe for Moroccan Carrot Salad with Harissa on page 147.

TasteFood: "I love the idea of using white wine in a warm drink. I'll certainly try this recipe when we're skiing next week!"

Ancho Chile–Cinnamon Chocolate Bark

BY WANDERASH | MAKES ABOUT 3 GIFTS

A&M: Neither of us had ever made chocolate bark before we tried this recipe, and wanderash's version happens to be a great introduction. A carpet of smooth dark chocolate is spiced with smoky ancho, cinnamon, cloves, and black pepper and studded with dried cherries, cashews, and pistachios. The finished product looks lovely, packs easily, and takes a total of about 20 minutes to put together. We think it makes a great holiday gift. Wanderash said: "I often make this easy dessert when I have friends coming for dinner who love wine. I know we'll sit at the table well after the meal is over and continue talking and drinking for hours."

---

1 large ancho chile

1 whole star anise

½ teaspoon black peppercorns

3 cloves

One 2-inch cinnamon stick

⅔ cup shelled pistachio nuts

⅔ cup cashews, very lightly crushed

12 ounces bittersweet chocolate, cut into
  small pieces

½ cup dried cherries

Kosher salt or sea salt

---

1. To make the spice mix, heat the oven to 350°F. Spread the first 5 ingredients on a baking sheet and place in the oven. Toast until fragrant, about 10 minutes.

2. Remove the stems and the majority of the seeds from the toasted ancho. Place the ancho and the rest of the spices in a spice grinder or coffee grinder and pulverize. You may need to grind the spices in batches.

3. Toast the pistachios and cashews on a baking sheet in the oven. Check after 10 minutes. When they're nicely toasted, remove from the oven and let cool.

4. Place three-fourths of the chocolate in a bowl and slowly melt it, either in the microwave, checking and stirring it every 25 seconds, or over a double boiler on the stove.

5. When the chocolate is melted, take it off the heat and add the remaining chocolate. Stir until it is completely melted.

6. Add 1 teaspoon of the spice mix to the chocolate and taste; add more if you want it to be spicier. I like a subtle spice flavor; it keeps those eating it wondering what the secret spice could be.

7. Line the baking sheet with parchment paper or a Silpat. Spread the nuts and cherries close together in a single layer. Reserve a few of the nuts to decorate the top.

8. Sprinkle the salt over the nuts and cherries.

9. Slowly pour the chocolate onto the pan, covering the nuts and cherries in an even layer. Add any remaining nuts to the top of the chocolate and press them into the chocolate.

10. Cool the bark in the refrigerator for 45 minutes. Break into pieces and keep in a sealed container in the fridge.

TIPS AND TECHNIQUES

Wanderash said: "I serve this on one plate and put it in the middle of the table. It is a casual dessert, so easy to make and great with a good Cabernet."

Make sure to use good-quality chocolate, and feel free to substitute your favorite nuts and dried fruit.

ABOUT THE COOK

Ashley Hooker Jons is a caterer and writer living in Guadalajara, Mexico. She cowrites the blog Smash and Sniff (www.smashandsniff.blogspot.com) with her cousin Jiffer, who lives in Hamburg, Germany. (As childhood pen pals, Ashley's nickname was Smash; Jiffer's was Sniff.)

Her favorite recipe from a cookbook: "Sherry Yard's recipe for Master Lemon Curd in *The Secrets of Baking* is flawless. The curd has the perfect pucker and the soothing texture of a warm embrace."

WHAT THE COMMUNITY SAID

WinnieAb: "I made this today and just love it. I substituted pecans for the pistachios and crystallized ginger for the dried cherries. Simple to make and presents beautifully. Lovely recipe!"

BEHIND THE SCENES

Food gifts was a very popular theme, with dozens of submissions, ranging from Chocolate Swirl Cinnamon Marshmallows to Garlic-Infused Olive Oil to Homemade Bailey's.

Norma's Eggnog

BY THE INTERNET COOKING PRINCESS | SERVES 30

A&M: We loved The Internet Cooking Princess's story behind her recipe. "This is not my recipe, but I recognized that it was a gem worth sharing right away," she wrote. "It's my boyfriend's stepmother's former receptionist's eggnog. (Did you follow that?) My boyfriend swears this is the best eggnog you will ever imbibe during the yuletide season. I haven't tried it myself, but I was so tickled that this recipe was preserved for nineteen years that I had to post it." Well, *we* tried it, and we're so glad we did! This eggnog has a smooth, boozy base and mousselike cap, which encourages sipping. The ice cream is a completely unnecessary indulgence, and we highly recommend it.

---

24 large eggs, separated

2 cups sugar

1 quart bourbon

2 cups brandy

1 quart heavy cream

2 quarts milk

1 pint vanilla ice cream

Freshly grated nutmeg, for serving

---

1. In a large bowl, beat the egg yolks and sugar until thick. (Or make your life easier and do this in an electric mixer!)

2. Add the bourbon and brandy and stir to combine.

3. Add the cream and milk and continue to stir.

4. Break up the vanilla ice cream and add to the mixture in chunks.

5. In a separate bowl, whip the egg whites until stiff.

6. Fold the egg whites into the mixture and refrigerate for 30 minutes.

7. Sprinkle with nutmeg to serve.

ABOUT THE COOK

Learn more about The Internet Cooking Princess, and see her Andouille and Dijon Polenta on page 185 and her Ricotta and Chive Gnocchi on page 263.

WHAT THE COMMUNITY SAID

Camelotcook: "I am so happy to have found this recipe. Many many years ago my father-in-law Frank would instruct me to make this with him every Thanksgiving and Christmas. He never wrote a thing down, and he was a wonderful cook. This recipe is exactly what we did, and it was wonderful. Thank you so much for posting this. Hurry up, Thanksgiving, as this will be on my menu to surprise everyone."

Smoked Ham with Pomegranate Molasses, Black Pepper, and Mustard Glaze

BY TASTEFOOD | SERVES 6

A&M: Pomegranate molasses is something that wouldn't have occurred to us to slather on a baked ham, but it turns out it's genius. It's sweet but also tart—a great partner for spicy Dijon and black pepper—and highlights the smokiness of the ham rather than overpowering it. TasteFood's glaze yields a gorgeous, mahogany-slicked crust and tender meat. As always, it's essential to use good-quality pomegranate molasses. (We like the sort that comes out of the bottle chocolate brown rather than magenta!) TasteFood said to "serve the meat with Dijon mustard, cornichons, and extra glaze as condiments for a nice rustic presentation."

½ bone-in smoked ham, 5 to 6 pounds

¾ cup pomegranate molasses

¼ cup Dijon mustard, plus extra for serving

2 tablespoons whiskey

1 tablespoon coarsely ground black pepper

1 teaspoon ground allspice

1 teaspoon kosher salt

Cornichons

1. Let the ham come to room temperature 1 hour before cooking. Heat the oven to 325°F.

2. Make the glaze: Combine the pomegranate molasses, ¼ cup mustard, whiskey, pepper, allspice, and salt in a bowl, and mix to blend well.

3. Place the ham, fat side up, in a foil-lined roasting pan. Score the fat in a cross-hatch pattern at 1- to 2-inch intervals without incising the meat.

4. Generously baste the ham with the glaze. Bake in the oven, basting occasionally, until the internal

temperature of the ham is 120°F (about 10 minutes per pound). The ham should be deep golden brown and crusty at this time. If not, increase the heat to 450°F and continue to bake for a few minutes, keeping an eye on the ham so it doesn't burn.

5. Remove from the oven and transfer to a cutting board. Let rest 20 minutes before carving.

6. Transfer the remaining basting sauce to a small saucepan and simmer briefly, brushing down the sides, to heat through and burn off the alcohol.

7. Slice the ham and serve with the mustard, cornichons, and basting sauce as condiments on the side.

TIPS AND TECHNIQUES

TasteFood suggested crushing the peppercorns in a mortar and pestle so you get some larger pieces for greater bite.

ABOUT THE COOK

Learn more about TasteFood, and find her recipe for Southwestern Spiced Sweet Potato Fries with Chili-Cilantro Sour Cream, on page 159. You can also find her recipe for Whole Baked Fish in Sea Salt with Parsley Gremolata on page 224, and her Broccoli Rabe, Potato, and Rosemary Pizza recipe on page 371.

WHAT THE COMMUNITY SAID

lastnightsdinner: "The glaze was just delicious. We were out of pomegranate molasses (as was our local market), so my husband improvised and made a pomegranate-honey syrup to use instead. We both really loved it."

Figgy Pudding Butter Cookies

BY HELENTHENANNY | MAKES 3 DOZEN SMALL COOKIES

A&M: Like mince pies in cookie form, these delicate biscuits melt in your mouth, leaving a hit of sweet figs, a suggestion of orange zest, and a whisper of brandy on your tongue. Helenthenanny's rich, sophisticated cookies are not only delicious to eat but lovely to look at, drizzled as they are with a spiced brandy glaze. Make sure to squeeze as much liquid as possible from the softened figs, and do not be alarmed if the dough seems wet before you chill it—it will firm up in the fridge.

COOKIES

1½ cups all-purpose flour

1 teaspoon kosher salt

1 teaspoon freshly grated nutmeg

1 teaspoon ground cinnamon

8 to 10 large dried Turkish or Calimyrna figs (the light brown ones)

1 cup whole milk

12 tablespoons (1½ sticks) unsalted butter, softened

¾ cup confectioners' sugar

1 large egg

1 tablespoon orange zest (from 1 orange)

BRANDY-SUGAR GLAZE

1½ cups confectioners' sugar

½ cup unsalted butter, softened

2 tablespoons brandy

½ teaspoon vanilla extract

---

1. In a medium bowl, sift together the flour, salt, nutmeg, and cinnamon and set aside.

2. Cut the figs into small dice and put them in a small saucepan with the milk over low heat. Cook, stirring occasionally, for about 15 minutes, or until the figs are nice and soft. Don't be discouraged if the milk separates—you'll get rid of it later.

3. Put the butter into the bowl of an electric mixer fitted with the paddle attachment. Mix on medium-high until the butter is fluffy, about 2 minutes.

4. Sift the confectioners' sugar into the fluffy butter and mix until smooth.

5. Add the egg and reduce the speed to low.

6. Add the flour mixture and mix until just combined.

7. Strain the figs, discarding the milk. Fold the figs and orange zest into the dough until the ingredients are evenly distributed. Wrap the dough in plastic and refrigerate for 2 hours.

8. Heat the oven to 350°F. On a well-floured surface, roll out the dough until it is ⅛ inch thick. Using a 2-inch round cookie cutter, cut out the cookies and place them on parchment-lined cookie sheets, spaced 1 inch apart. Bake until the edges are golden brown, 10 to 12 minutes.

9. While the cookies are baking, combine all the ingredients for the brandy-sugar glaze in a saucepan over medium-low heat, stirring often until the sauce looks smooth. After the cookies have cooled, use a fork to drizzle the warm glaze on them.

10. Please enjoy and have the happiest of holidays!

TIPS AND TECHNIQUES

If you don't like figs, use prunes!

ABOUT THE COOK

Helen Allen is a theater education student (and nanny, of course) in Texas. Here's her blog: www .helenthenanny.blogspot.com.

Her favorite recipe from a cookbook: "Southern Fruit Dip: equal parts cream cheese and marshmallow fluff. 'Nuff said. (Set that cream cheese out so it's not too cold, then put 'em in a KitchenAid and whip 'em good. Serve with fruit or between two chocolate chip cookies.)"

WHAT THE COMMUNITY SAID

AntoniaJames: "Mmmm, very nice. Especially for those of us who adore figgy pudding but make it only once, for dinner on Christmas Eve or Christmas Day!"

Magical Coffee (aka Cafe Davio)

BY ERINH | SERVES 2 TO 4

A&M: One of those recipes that's a great concept rather than a precise formula, ErinH's iced coffee takes inspiration from both her local coffeehouse—Cafe Soleil in Madison, Wisconsin—and a recipe in the *New York Times*. At Cafe Soleil, she said, "they brew the coffee hot, but since it was summer and I am lazy, I wanted to use a cold-brewed coffee base." Adding a teaspoon of cinnamon and a few spoonfuls of dark brown sugar to the coffee as it cold-brews give it a lush sweetness and a hit of warmth. After it spends a night in the fridge, you strain the coffee and pour it over ice cubes. Then comes the cream. (Or milk, depending on your mood.) And then, as ErinH said, you "die of happiness." We loved this iteration and think her "Scandinavian version" (using almond extract and fennel) sounds like a winner too.

COFFEE BASE
⅔ cup coarsely ground coffee
1 teaspoon ground cinnamon
3 tablespoons dark brown sugar

FINISHED DRINK
Milk, half-and-half, or cream

---

1. Combine the coffee, cinnamon, and brown sugar in a 1-quart jar. Add 3 cups cold water and stir to dissolve the sugar. Cover and refrigerate overnight.

2. Pour the coffee base through a sieve or strainer into a bowl, then strain back into the jar for easy storage.

3. For each drink: Fill a tall glass halfway with ice. Pour in the coffee until the glass is about three-fourths full, and add milk, half-and-half, or cream to taste.

4. Die of happiness.

TIPS AND TECHNIQUES
Ted: "Delicious. I pour it back through a coffee filter to get rid of the sediment, but the powdered cinnamon clogs up the filter, so I use 2 cinnamon sticks instead."

ABOUT THE COOK

Erin Hanusa is a writer and editor in Madison, Wisconsin.

Her favorite kitchen tip: "Whenever you dice onions, dice some extra to keep in the fridge. It makes starting dinner on another night super-easy, and may even prevent takeout from happening."

Her best entertaining tip: "When bringing food to an event, everyone from kids to the snobbiest food snobs love homemade chocolate chip cookies. You can't lose."

WHAT THE COMMUNITY SAID

Sandy Castle: "I made this for my daughters (seventeen and fourteen) and they loved it so much that they're now making it themselves every evening so they can have it in the morning. They prefer it over the coffeehouse drinks! Thank you."

Kitchen Butterfly: "Made this, drank it, enjoyed it . . . thoroughly, and I'm not a coffee drinker. Wow, magically good coffee! I'm going to make it again with crushed cardamom seeds and maple syrup! Thank you for introducing me to the world of cold brew—which I didn't know existed."

Caramel Rice Pudding with Brown Butter and Crème Fraîche

BY MERRILL | SERVES 6 TO 8

Merrill: For this dessert, I began with the idea of using brown butter and Arborio rice to make a risotto-style rice pudding. But my first attempt wasn't that exciting. That's when the idea of starting with a brown butter caramel worked its way into the pudding, along with the addition of crème fraîche, which I thought would cut the sweetness nicely. After a few more test runs, I also decided that the rice had a nicer texture when it was simmered with all the liquid than it did when I cooked it like risotto, adding the liquid bit by bit. The bonus is that this also means less work!

2 tablespoons unsalted butter	6 cups whole milk
¼ cup plus 3 tablespoons sugar	Seeds from ½ vanilla bean
2 tablespoons crème fraîche, plus more for serving	¼ teaspoon sea salt
	¾ cup Arborio rice

1. Melt the butter in a 3-quart heavy saucepan over medium heat. Once the butter stops foaming, and you see orangey-brown specks start to appear, stir gently with a wooden spoon. After a minute or two, when the specks are nut brown and the butter smells nice and toasty, sprinkle ¼ cup of sugar over the butter and stir to combine. (It will clump up a little, but don't worry!)

2. Switch to a whisk and cook the butter and sugar, whisking constantly, until the sugar has melted and the mixture becomes a smooth, rich brown caramel, about 5 minutes. (Early on, the butter and sugar will separate, and the butter will pool around the edges of the sugar, but never fear! Once the sugar has fully melted, the two will start to come together again, and you'll have a nice smooth caramel.)

3. When the caramel is a rich nut brown and starts to smoke, remove the pan from the heat and quickly and carefully whisk in the crème fraîche and about ½ cup of the milk. Don't worry if the mixture bubbles up when you do this—it'll settle down again quickly. (This step cools off the caramel and keeps it from

cooking further.) Return the pan to the heat and whisk in the rest of the milk, the remaining 3 tablespoons sugar, the vanilla seeds, and the salt. If the caramel seizes a little, just keep whisking until the mixture becomes smooth again.

4. Switch back to the wooden spoon and stir in the rice. Turn up the heat and bring the mixture to a boil. Reduce the heat so that the milk is simmering steadily. Cook the rice pudding, uncovered, for about 25 minutes, stirring frequently to make sure nothing sticks to the bottom of the pan, especially toward the end. The rice should be tender but not mushy, and the pudding should thicken but still be quite loose— remember that it will thicken a lot more as it cools. Transfer the pudding to a container, cover, and refrigerate until cold. Serve in individual bowls with a dollop of crème fraîche.

ABOUT THE COOK

Merrill Stubbs is a cofounder of Food52.

Her favorite food group: cheese, followed closely by crème fraîche.

She loves: beating Amanda in cooking contests.

WHAT THE COMMUNITY SAID

cheese1227: "Merrill, I made this recipe this weekend and it was fabulous. I want to thank you for all of the parenthetical notes within the recipe that pretty much predicted right where I would say 'uh, oh,' thinking it was all going wrong. The notes told me where to expect the rough spots and to keep working through them to the finished product. This one is a keeper."

BEHIND THE SCENES

This was a special week at Food52: we faced off against each other to see who could come up with the best rice pudding! Amanda took her defeat in stride, although there was that one incident of Gordon Ramsay–like pot throwing.

Roasted Cauliflower Soup with Chimichurri and Poblano Crème Fraîche

BY CHEZSUZANNE | SERVES 6 AS A FIRST COURSE OR 4 AS A LUNCH ENTRÉE

A&M: ChezSuzanne's technique of roasting cauliflower before simmering it gives this soup a caramel undertone, and the touch of cream and Parmesan lends just the right amount of richness to the velvety cauliflower and leek puree. The chimichurri sauce and poblano crème fraîche require a bit of extra time (and blender cleanup), but it's worth the effort; this is a perfect weekend project for when you have an hour or two to lose yourself in a recipe. We recommend using a small head of cauliflower for the right texture.

ROASTED CAULIFLOWER SOUP

1 cauliflower head, quartered and sliced thinly, including the core

3 tablespoons unsalted butter

1 tablespoon olive oil

½ medium yellow onion, diced

1 leek, white and light green parts only, diced

½ teaspoon chopped garlic

2 celery ribs, diced

1 teaspoon salt

1 cup chicken broth

1 tablespoon freshly grated Parmesan

2 tablespoons heavy cream

CHIMICHURRI SAUCE

1 serrano chile, seeded and coarsely chopped

2 garlic cloves, peeled and coarsely chopped or smashed

2 cups lightly packed cilantro leaves

2 tablespoons mint leaves

5 to 6 tablespoons olive oil

½ tablespoon fresh lemon juice

½ teaspoon kosher salt

POBLANO CRÈME FRAÎCHE

1 poblano or pasilla pepper, roasted, peeled, and seeded

2 garlic cloves, peeled

⅛ teaspoon kosher salt

1 tablespoon olive oil

2 tablespoons heavy cream

2 tablespoons crème fraîche

Sugar, to taste

1. Heat the oven to 350°F. Place the slices of cauliflower on a dry cookie sheet and roast until tender, 15 to 20 minutes.

2. In a large, heavy pot, heat the butter and olive oil over medium heat until the butter melts. Sauté the onion, leek, garlic, and celery in the butter-oil mixture until soft and very aromatic, 5 to 7 minutes. Season with the salt. Add the roasted cauliflower and toss with a large spoon until the cauliflower is completely covered with the onion mixture. Cook for another 2 minutes.

3. Add the broth and 2 ½ cups water (you can add a bit more water if the cauliflower isn't quite covered). Bring to a boil over high heat, then lower the heat and simmer for 5 minutes, or until the cauliflower is tender.

4. While the soup cools for a few minutes, make the chimichurri sauce and poblano crème fraîche. Place the chimichurri ingredients in a blender or food processor and process until finely chopped. This is a very versatile chimichurri—I've used it on pork, in omelets with Spanish Manchego cheese, and in this soup.

5. Combine all the poblano crème fraîche ingredients in a blender and puree until very smooth. I put it into a squirt bottle that allows for different pipe tips, and squeeze the crème fraîche on the soup.

6.   Working in batches, purée the soup in a blender until fairly smooth. If you want the soup to be completely smooth, you'll need to use a food mill, but having some texture to it adds to the rustic nature of the roasted flavor. Pour back into the pot and bring to a simmer. Stir in the Parmesan and cream, then the chimichurri sauce, until well incorporated. Serve hot in soup bowls. Drizzle some poblano crème fraîche over the soup.

TIPS AND TECHNIQUES

ChezSuzanne said: "I keep the poblano crème fraîche in a squirt container in the fridge and put it on all kinds of things to add a little softened heat. This crème fraîche also works well as a sandwich spread."

ABOUT THE COOK

Susan Pridmore is a cooking teacher in the San Francisco Bay area.

Her favorite cooking tip: "When I make soup and am balancing my flavors at the end, I always finish the soup with a squeeze of lemon juice to freshen and sharpen the flavors. It's always amazing to me the difference a little lemon juice can make. The exception is if I'm adding a sauce (like a chimichurri) to the soup that has lemon already in it. If it's a vegetable-based soup using peas, I also always add a splash of sherry. Amazing combination!"

For Susan's recipe for Rosemary Ciabatta with Stout Beer, turn to page 341.

Lentil and Sausage Soup for a Cold Winter's Night

BY ANTONIAJAMES | SERVES 4 ADULTS WITH PLENTY OF LEFTOVERS

A&M: The beauty of this soup is that it manages to be soul-warming but not overly heavy. The broth is light and aromatic with wine and marjoram, and you feel as if you've won the lottery each time you come across a piece of garlicky sausage. AntoniaJames has you simmer the lentils and veggies until they're just cooked through, so that they retain a bit of a bite and the soup, while filling, seems fresh rather than leaden. A sprinkle of red wine vinegar adds a bright hit of acidity. AntoniaJames added, "You'll see that the primary herb is marjoram. That's not an herb that you see often in recipes, but to my mind, it's what makes this soup so tasty."

---

3 tablespoons bacon fat or olive oil

2 bay leaves

3 to 4 sausages made with herbs and/or garlic

1½ cups French green lentils

4 cups chicken or beef stock (preferably homemade)

1 large yellow or white onion, cut into ½-inch dice

4 garlic cloves, chopped

½ cup sturdy red wine

3 celery stalks, diced small, and their leaves if possible, chopped

1 tablespoon dried marjoram or 2 tablespoons minced fresh marjoram

4 to 5 carrots, depending on their size, cut into bite-size chunks

Salt and freshly ground black pepper

3 tablespoons organic ketchup

2 cups chopped spinach (frozen is fine, if you don't have fresh; just use 1 ½ cups instead)

¼ cup chopped flat-leaf parsley

Red wine vinegar

---

1. Fill a teakettle with water and put it on the stove to boil.

2. Meanwhile, heat 2 tablespoons of the bacon fat or oil with one of the bay leaves and gently sauté the sausages, if they are not already cooked. Cut the cooked sausages into ¾-inch slices and brown them in the bacon fat or oil. Remove the sausage slices with a slotted spoon and set them aside. Reserve the pan; do not wash it!

3. Rinse the lentils in cold water two or three times, pick out any stones or other debris, and put the lentils on the stove in a saucepan with at least 3 cups of hot water from the kettle. If it hasn't boiled at this point, don't worry about it. Stir the lentils and cook them over medium heat, stirring occasionally, until almost tender, about 20 minutes. If they start to look dry, add more hot water as they cook.

4. Heat the stock in the microwave or a medium saucepan over low heat.

5. Add the remaining bacon fat or oil, the onion, and garlic to the pan in which the sausages were browned and cook over medium heat, stirring occasionally. When the onions start to look translucent, push them aside with a spoon and add the wine. Cook for 1 to 2 minutes to deglaze the pan.

6. Stir in the lentils, their cooking water, and the hot stock. Add the celery, marjoram, carrots, sausages, second bay leaf and salt and pepper to taste, and stir well.

7. Simmer the soup until the carrots are tender, at least 10 minutes, adding more water as needed and stirring occasionally to prevent the lentils from sticking.

8. Add the ketchup and stir well. Add the spinach and parsley. Taste and correct the seasonings. Heat until the soup is very hot before serving.

9. Pass the red wine vinegar separately for people to add to taste. Enjoy!

TIPS AND TECHNIQUES

Serve this with a hearty whole grain bread and follow it with fruit and cheese for a lovely, easy dinner at home.

AntoniaJames said: "This soup holds really well and, in fact, improves a bit if eaten the next day, but—and this is important—don't chop and add the spinach until right before eating. The greens will cook up nicely in just the time it takes to heat the soup through."

ABOUT THE COOK

Helen Leah Conroy is a transaction lawyer living in Piedmont, California.

Her favorite recipe from a cookbook: "The banana bread recipe from *The Tassajara Bread Book* by Edward Espe Brown (Shambhala 1986). It's easy, it's flexible, and everyone loves it."

Her best cooking tip: "If you like to cook (and especially, make preserves) using local produce in season, keep a separate calendar for remembering—and planning—projects in upcoming seasons. When you run across a recipe that appeals to you but requires produce that's not in season, make a note on the appropriate calendar month of the recipe and where you found or have stored it. For clipped or other hard-copy recipes, use an accordion file, such as one designed for sorting recipes by month, or a notebook with pocket dividers labeled for each month, solely for 'want to try' or 'plan to do' projects using seasonal produce. If working digitally, put the month in the file name for easy retrieval."

WHAT THE COMMUNITY SAID

monkeymom: "I've made this soup now twice, using different sausages and veggies depending on what I could find or what I had in the fridge. The first time was with a chicken Italian sausage and the spinach. I fell in love; it was so warm and satisfying without being heavy. The second time I did it with Aidell's garlic and Gruyère and cabbage. Very different, but still hit the spot. The little bit of vinegar added is genius!"

Maria Teresa Jorge: "Brilliant recipe; the addition of the red wine vinegar is a great idea. Just waiting for the snow to melt so I can buy some more lentils!"

One-Pot Kale and Quinoa Pilaf

BY DEENSIEBAT | SERVES 2 TO 4

A&M: Deensiebat's pilaf breathes new life into a familiar classic. The quinoa and hearty strips of lacinato kale (you can use chard or standard kale) crunch lightly between your teeth, and Meyer lemon juice and zest keep blandness at bay. Fresh goat cheese and walnut oil just barely coat the warm pilaf, giving it a creamy, tangy finish, and toasted pine nuts lend some crunch. We love the technique of layering the quinoa and the kale. Deensiebat said, "It's one-pot easy, making it a simple way to incorporate healthy eating into a worknight rotation."

1 cup quinoa

1 bunch lacinato (or regular) kale, washed and chopped into 1-inch lengths

1 Meyer lemon, zested and juiced

2 scallions, minced

1 tablespoon toasted walnut oil (or olive oil)

3 tablespoons toasted pine nuts

¼ cup crumbled soft goat cheese

Salt and freshly ground black pepper

1. Bring 2 cups salted water to a boil over high heat in a large pot with a cover. Add the quinoa, cover, and lower the heat until it is just high enough to maintain a simmer. Cook for 10 minutes, then top the quinoa with the kale and re-cover. Simmer another 5 minutes, then turn off the heat and allow the quinoa and kale to steam for 5 more minutes.

2. While the quinoa is cooking, take a large serving bowl and combine the lemon zest, half the lemon juice, the scallions, walnut oil, pine nuts, and goat cheese.

3. Check the quinoa and kale—the water should have absorbed, and the quinoa will be tender but firm, and the kale tender and bright green. If the quinoa still has a hard white center, you can steam it a bit longer,

adding more water if needed. When the quinoa and kale are done, fluff the pilaf and tip it into the waiting bowl with the remaining ingredients. As the hot quinoa hits the scallions and lemon, it should smell lovely. Toss to combine, seasoning with salt and pepper and the remaining lemon juice if needed.

TIPS AND TECHNIQUES

EarlyToBed: "I've now made this delicious recipe several times, with variations. Variation 1: I use half white and half brown quinoa, toasted (until popping) before cooking. Variation 2: I increased the kale-to-quinoa proportion, and then used it as the filling for a frittata (or quiche). Six eggs plus a bit of cream, mix in the kale and quinoa, pour into an 8 × 8-inch dish or pie plate or pie crust, bake at 350°F until set, and then serve and enjoy."

ABOUT THE COOK

Deena Prichep produces stories for print and public radio and writes the blog Mostly Foodstuffs (www.mostlyfoodstuffs.blogspot.com) from her home in Portland, Oregon.

Her best entertaining tip: "Sangria can be cheaper than a six-pack."

Her favorite recipe from a cookbook: "The herb jam from Paula Wolfert's *The Slow Mediterranean Kitchen*—I've made it scads of times, and there's really nothing quite like it."

WHAT THE COMMUNITY SAID

Rolando74: "You're probably getting bored with people telling you how good this is. I substituted feta for the goat cheese and it was great. I'm sending it to my vegetarian sister right now."

Lacerise: "This is one of my new favorite recipes! It's destined to become a staple in my cooking repertoire. Healthy, bright and flavorful, easy, and picnic or dinner party worthy. The lemonyness from the juice and zest and the walnut oil's nuttiness are terrific!"

Thistlepie: "This is a wonderful recipe! I have now made it three times in the past month! Yum! I am a huge fan of quinoa and vowed to try to find some new kale recipes to convert me to a kale enthusiast. This one recipe did it. Thank you!"

Savory Grapefruit Sabayon

BY BERNA | SERVES 2

A&M: As Berna notes, this frothy, creamy sauce would be great with shellfish. It's tangy, sweet, and savory all at once, with just a suggestion of bitterness from the grapefruit zest. It's a sauce we'd double or triple and serve with shrimp or scallops for a dinner party.

¼ cup chicken stock

1½ tablespoons grapefruit-flavored vodka (or vermouth)

½ cup grapefruit juice

2 teaspoons grapefruit zest

1 teaspoon honey

2 egg yolks

¼ teaspoon salt

1. In a small saucepan, simmer the stock and vodka over medium heat until reduced by half. Let cool.

2. Combine the grapefruit juice, zest, and honey in a small bowl. Stir into the cooled stock mixture.

3. Make a double boiler by bringing some water to boil in a saucepan. Place the egg yolks in a small bowl, preferably metal, and set over the saucepan (the bowl should not touch the water). Slowly begin to add the stock mixture to the eggs, whisking constantly. You may need to take the bowl on and off the hot water so as not to overcook the eggs. The sabayon will start off frothy and then become thick and creamy.

4. Cook until an instant read thermometer reads 160°F. Whisk in the salt.

5. Serve immediately with grilled shrimp or scallops.

Berna Bader is a life enrichment director in an assisted living community in northern New Jersey.

Her favorite recipe from a cookbook: "Although *Joy of Cooking* became my culinary bible (pre-Internet) I always return to the *McCall's Cookbook* for one simple recipe: Deluxe Popovers for Two. This recipe is quite simple and I should know the correct proportions by now but I still check it each time I make popovers."

gluttonforlife: "I'm going to try this over steamed asparagus and as a dipping sauce for artichokes!"

mrslarkin: "This looks so good, I think I might take a bath in it!"

Whole Baked Fish in Sea Salt with Parsley Gremolata

BY TASTEFOOD | SERVES 6

A&M: "The first time I tasted Pesce al Sale was at a restaurant in Milan," TasteFood wrote. "I remember the dramatic presentation of the baked fish encrusted in salt and cracked open tableside, revealing a steaming, aromatic, and succulent fish." This method for cooking a whole fish has the dual benefit of being effective and fun—an opportunity to play with your food. Another plus is flexibility, as it's the method that really counts here: cooking a whole fish in a salt crust keeps it incredibly tender and moist. TasteFood calls for a 5-pound fish, but we used a 2½-pound red snapper, halved the rest of the ingredients, and decreased the cooking time to roughly 25 minutes. The simple gremolata is a bright, refreshing adornment for an otherwise gorgeously simple piece of fish.

FISH
1 lemon, thinly sliced

1 small bunch flat-leaf parsley sprigs

Fronds from 1 medium fennel bulb (reserve the bulb for another use)

1 whole fish, approximately 5 pounds, such as snapper or sea bass

2 egg whites

4 pounds coarse sea salt or kosher salt

Extra virgin olive oil

Lemon wedges

PARSLEY GREMOLATA
½ cup finely chopped parsley

1 garlic clove, minced

Finely grated zest from 1 organic lemon

Sea salt

Freshly ground black pepper

1. Heat the oven to 450°F.

2. Place the lemon slices, parsley, and fennel in the cavity of the fish. Do not overstuff.

3. Combine the egg whites and sea salt in a bowl. Mix well to moisten the salt.

4. Spread one-third of the salt on the bottom of a large baking dish or pan. Lay the fish on top. Pour the remaining salt over the fish, covering completely. If needed, the tail can be exposed.

5. Bake for 45 minutes (test with a fork if you're nervous). Remove from the oven and let rest 10 minutes.

6. While the fish bakes, make the gremolata: Combine the parsley, garlic, and lemon zest in a small bowl. Season to taste with a pinch of salt and pepper.

7. Crack open the crust with a small hammer or knife. Remove and discard the crust. Fillet the fish.

8. Arrange the fish on warm plates. Drizzle with olive oil and freshly squeezed lemon juice from the lemon wedges. Serve with the parsley gremolata.

TIPS AND TECHNIQUES

TasteFood: "Have your fishmonger clean and scale your fish for you. Note that since the fish cavity is stuffed, the cooking time will run about 10 minutes longer than unstuffed."

ABOUT THE COOK

For more information on TasteFood, and to see her recipe for Southwestern Spiced Sweet Potato Fries with Chili-Cilantro Sour Cream, turn to page 159. You can also find her recipe for Smoked Ham with Pomegranate Molasses, Black Pepper, and Mustard Glaze on page 201 and Broccoli Rabe, Potato, and Rosemary Pizza on page 371.

WHAT THE COMMUNITY SAID

Rivka: "I made this last night for a dinner party, and it totally blew my guests out of the water. The look on their faces as I took a hammer and hacked away at the top crust was priceless. Midway through the meal, we all looked up at each other and laughed as we realized that we couldn't stop the moans of "mmm!" Thanks for bringing this dramatic dish within reach of the home cook. Two notes: first, I made a 6.5-pound red snapper, which easily fed 6 with leftovers. I needed 6 pounds of salt to cover the fish, and the tip of the tail was still sticking out. Second, as delicious as the fillets are, the cheeks are by far the best part—don't miss them!"

Fregola Sarda with Caramelized Squash and Charmoula

BY PORKTOPURSLANE | SERVES 6 TO 8

A&M: Fregola, a Sardinian pasta resembling Israeli couscous, lends a hearty feel to this dish. We loved how the rich flavors of caramelized butternut squash and toasted pine nuts are balanced by the musky charmoula (made with cilantro, cumin, garlic, parsley, lemon zest, spicy and sweet smoked paprika, and cayenne)—which, as porktopurslane noted, "can turn even the prissiest dish into certified man-food." There's a lot going on here and all of it is good. Add the lemon juice to taste, and if pine nuts are too expensive, feel free to substitute toasted walnuts or almonds. Roast a chicken, grill some shoulder lamb chops, or just make a nice big salad with some goat cheese, and a fine dinner will be yours.

---

1 medium butternut squash, peeled, seeded, and cut into 1 ½-inch dice

Extra virgin olive oil

Sea salt

1 pound fregola sarda or Israeli couscous

1 cup toasted pine nuts

CHARMOULA

2 tablespoons cumin seeds

2 medium garlic cloves

3 cups roughly chopped fresh cilantro

1 cup roughly chopped fresh parsley

1 teaspoon hot paprika

2 teaspoons sweet smoked paprika

½ teaspoon cayenne pepper

Zest of 1 lemon

Juice of 2 lemons

---

1. Heat the oven to 475°F. Bring a large pot of salted water to a boil. On a large sheet pan, toss the butternut squash with about 2 tablespoons olive oil and a generous pinch of sea salt (make sure not to overcrowd the pan; use 2 pans if necessary). Roast the squash for 20 to 25 minutes, or until tender and caramelized. Remove from the oven and allow to cool slightly.

2. Cook the fregola sarda in boiling water for 10 to 11 minutes, or until al dente. Drain and return to the pot; set aside and keep warm.

3. For the charmoula: In a small skillet over medium heat, toast the cumin seeds for 1 to 2 minutes—or until they release a fantastic smell and start to make a popping sound (keep an eye on them, so they don't burn). Transfer the toasted cumin seeds to a mortar; add the garlic and a big pinch of sea salt. Pound the cumin and garlic into a paste. Add the chopped herbs in batches, and continue to pound until a chunky paste forms. Add the hot and smoked paprikas, cayenne, lemon zest, and ¼ cup olive oil; stir to combine and set aside. (Alternatively, you could process all the ingredients in a food processor.)

4. To the pot with the fregola, add the butternut squash, lemon juice, charmoula, and the toasted nuts. With a wooden spoon, toss gently to combine (avoid mashing the squash). Serve warm or at room temperature.

TIPS AND TECHNIQUES

Porktopurslane: "Charmoula can be used as a marinade for meat and fish or as a dressing for any number of grain and vegetable dishes (try it on potatoes!)."

ABOUT THE COOK

Michelle McKenzie Waltman is a private chef and culinary instructor in San Francisco, California. Here's her blog: Pork to Purslane (www.porktopurslane.com).

Her favorite recipe from a cookbook: "Braised Chicken with Saffron, Onions, Italian Couscous and Dates from *Sunday Suppers at Lucques*."

Her best kitchen tip: "Learn to listen to your intuition and senses above all else. Close the book and open your eyes, nose, and ears. When you're fully present in the kitchen, the end product will taste better and you'll have had more fun!"

WHAT THE COMMUNITY SAID

mtrelaun: "I've had my eye on this recipe since it first appeared, and I finally made it tonight for dinner. Talk about rock 'em, sock 'em flavor! It's terrific."

Moroccan Merguez Ragout with Poached Eggs

BY EPICUREANODYSSEY | SERVES 4

A&M: We ate this for lunch and agreed it was the perfect meal for the middle of the day—or the beginning of the day, or the end of the day. The spicy merguez (you can use hot Italian sausage if you can't find merguez or chorizo) is bathed in a lush, smoky sauce of tomatoes, onion, garlic, and spices; when you cut into the soft eggs on top, poached right in the sauce, the buttery yolk streams into the rest of the dish and enriches the sauce. We found that we didn't need all of the oil, as the sausage gave off a lot of its own fat, so we just spooned off some of the extra oil before poaching the eggs.

½ cup extra virgin olive oil

1 large onion, cut into small dice

4 large garlic cloves, minced

1 pound merguez sausage, cut into ½-inch-thick-slices (see Tips and Techniques for how to make your own)

1 tablespoon ras el hanout (see Tips and Techniques)

1 teaspoon sweet smoked paprika

1 teaspoon kosher salt

Two 15-ounce cans fire-roasted diced tomatoes, preferably Muir Glen

8 extra-large eggs

½ cup roughly chopped cilantro, stems included

2 tablespoons harissa (see Tips and Techniques)

Warm crusty bread, for serving

---

1. Heat the olive oil in a large frying pan over medium heat. Add the onion and sauté until golden. Toss in the garlic and cook another 2 minutes. Add the merguez and sauté until almost cooked through, about 3 minutes.

2. Lower the heat to medium-low and add the ras el hanout, paprika, and salt. Stir to combine and cook for a minute to lightly toast the spices. Add the tomatoes. Turn up the heat to medium and cook until the mixture has thickened slightly, about 5 minutes.

3. Crack the eggs over the mixture, cover, and cook until the whites set but the yolks are still soft.

4. Spoon the ragout into 4 warm bowls and top each portion with 2 of the eggs, a sprinkling of cilantro, and a teaspoon of harissa.

5. Serve immediately with crusty bread.

TIPS AND TECHNIQUES

ecswantner: "If you cannot find merguez in your area, use whatever sausage suits your taste, but I particularly like Spanish chorizo. Harissa is a fiery condiment found on most North African tables and is used to spice up dishes to suit your palate. Ras el hanout translates to 'top of the shop' and refers to the top combination of spices a Moroccan spice vendor can sell. You can find both harissa and ras el hanout at www.gourmetfoodstore.com, or you can make your own."

epicureanodyssey noted: "A really fine commercial blend of ras el hanout and smoked paprika can be ordered at wholespice.com." She also gave this tip for making your own merguez: "Merguez is really easy to make. If you have a few minutes, mix 1 pound ground lamb with ¼ cup finely minced cilantro stems, 1½ tablespoons ras el hanout, 2 minced garlic cloves, 1 tablespoon harissa, 1 tablespoon extra virgin olive oil, and kosher salt to taste. Roll into sausagelike cylinders, store in plastic wrap, and refrigerate until ready to use. Voilà, merguez."

ABOUT THE COOK

Emily C. Swantner is a chef living in Santa Fe, New Mexico.

Her favorite cooking tip: "When planning a menu, prepare only one complicated dish. The accompanying recipes can be simple with just a few ingredients or easily made ahead."

Her favorite entertaining tip: "Keep a well-stocked pantry, meaning the cupboard, freezer, and refrigerator, as it makes spur-of-the-moment entertaining easy."

WHAT THE COMMUNITY SAID

nasreenSeattle: "I fell in love with the recipe the first time I read it and I knew I had to make it right away. I bought merguez at Uli's and spices from Pike Place Market here in Seattle. This recipe is quick, easy, and delicious, and also a real crowd pleaser. The recipe can be scaled up pretty easily if the eggs are poached separately and then served over the ragout. Served this with a baguette and white wine with Looza apricot nectar."

ChezSuzanne: "I made this wonderful recipe this week and it was a big hit at my house. The great thing for me, besides the wonderful blend of flavors, was that I put it together in about 30 minutes!"

Mussels for One (or Two)

BY LASTNIGHTSDINNER | SERVES 1 TO 2

A&M: Here you have all the flavors that go so well with mussels—fennel, saffron, thyme, tomatoes, vermouth, and of course (something we love!), Pernod. You do a little chopping, then add the ingredients a few at a time to the pot. In a few short minutes, you have a fragrant and delicious mussel stew, a dinner for one that underlines the importance of treating yourself well, even when alone. And you can quadruple the recipe for a party.

Lastnightsdinner said she "learned to love mussels in college, when I spent many an evening with my beau at the Cadieux Café, located on the east side of Detroit, where I grew up. The place had an amazing jukebox and a stellar array of Belgian beers, and it served mussels in a multitude of ways: stuffed, steamed, on the half shell, or bathed in flavorful broths. There was a preparation for just about anyone. I love mussels to this day and indulge in them often, as they're inexpensive, sustainable, and versatile, but this is probably my favorite way to eat them. The rule of thumb for an entrée portion of mussels is one pound per person, but I never seem to be able to finish a whole pound on my own—especially when you factor in the crusty bread that is an essential accompaniment to this dish. Your mileage may vary."

---

1 pound mussels, scrubbed and debearded

1 tablespoon unsalted butter

1 tablespoon extra virgin olive oil

1½ cups thinly sliced leeks, white and pale green parts only

1 small fennel bulb, cored and chopped or thinly sliced (about 1 cup), plus a few fronds for garnish

Kosher or sea salt

1 to 2 pinches saffron threads

2 (or more, if you're solo) fat garlic cloves, peeled and smashed

1 tablespoon fresh thyme leaves

½ ounce (1 tablespoon) Pernod or other anise liqueur

4 ounces (½ cup) white vermouth or dry white wine

1 cup crushed tomatoes with juice

¼ cup heavy cream

1. Look over your mussels and discard any that have cracked or broken shells. They all should be tightly closed, but if any open mussels don't close when you squeeze them gently with your fingers, discard those as well.

2. In a deep, heavy-bottomed pot with a lid, melt the butter in the olive oil over medium heat.

3. Add the leeks and fennel, season with a pinch or two of salt, and cook until softened, about 5 minutes.

4. Clear a space in the bottom of the pot and add the saffron, crumbling it with your fingers as you do, and lightly toast it before stirring it through the vegetables. Add the garlic and thyme, stir, and cook just until you can smell the garlic, about a minute or so.

5. Add the Pernod and vermouth or wine, stir, and let cook for 2 to 3 minutes, then add the tomatoes. Reduce the heat to low, cover the pot, and simmer for 20 minutes.

6. Add the mussels, stir, re-cover the pot, and cook for another 5 to 8 minutes or so, just until the mussels open (the timing will vary depending on the size of your mussels). Discard any mussels that don't open.

7. Off the heat, stir in the cream and taste for seasoning. Spoon the mussels, vegetables, and sauce into a big, wide bowl—two, if you're sharing. Sprinkle the fennel fronds on top and serve with plenty of crusty bread.

ABOUT THE COOK

To learn more about lastnightsdinner, and to see her recipe for Smoky Pork Burgers with Fennel and Red Cabbage Slaw, turn to page 66. You can also find her recipe for Seared Scallops with Spring Onion and Tarragon Cream on page 349 and her Beef Chopped Salad on page 94.

WHAT THE COMMUNITY SAID

mrslarkin: "Made these today. Simple recipe, delicious results! The sauce is so tasty—even without the cream. Definitely a keeper, this one."

Roasted Bagna Cauda Broccoli

BY MARIARAYNAL | SERVES 4

A&M: For a dish that's packed with assertive flavors—garlic and anchovy—this also contains a whole lot of subtlety. Roasting the broccoli caramelizes the tips, giving it both a little crispness and nuttiness. The nut flavor is echoed in the toasted almonds, and a squeeze of Meyer lemon perks up the whole. This is a dish that's easy enough for a weeknight meal and impressive enough for a dinner party.

---

1 broccoli head, cut into bite-size florets

Salt and freshly ground black pepper

2 tablespoons olive oil

3 tablespoons unsalted butter

2 garlic cloves, minced

2 anchovy fillets

A splash of white wine

A big squeeze of lemon, preferably Meyer

¼ cup sliced or slivered almonds

Grated Parmesan, for dusting

---

1. Heat the oven to 425°F. Arrange the broccoli florets on a Silpat or parchment-lined cookie sheet. Season with salt and pepper and drizzle with 1 tablespoon of the olive oil. Roast until toasted on the tips and still crisp-tender, 20 to 25 minutes.

2. In a small skillet, melt the butter and remaining 1 tablespoon olive oil over medium heat. Add the garlic and anchovies and sauté for about 3 minutes. Add the wine and lemon and allow to reduce for a minute or two. Season with black pepper, if desired.

3. Meanwhile, in another small skillet over medium heat, toast the almonds until they are lightly browned, taking care not to burn them.

4. Drizzle the sauce and sprinkle the almonds and Parmesan over the broccoli, then serve. Or, dip the broccoli in the sauce at the table. Enjoy!

Maria Raynal is an executive speechwriter, food writer, and blogger living near Detroit, Michigan.

Her favorite cooking tip: "When making meatballs or meat loaf, I combine the wet and dry ingredients together before adding to the ground meat, assuring the meat remains tender." Here's her blog: Fresh Eats (www.fresheats.blogspot.com).

WHAT THE COMMUNITY SAID

roryrabbitfield: "I made this again tonight, using steamed lacinato kale instead of broccoli. I ate a huge bowlful, it is so yummy."

Littlepots: "I make this dish fairly often in our house. I generally substitute bread crumbs (panko works well here) for nuts, which I add in at the end to soak up any last bits of goodness from the sauce. Aleppo pepper adds a nice heat element to this as well."

dinnerthyme: "I made this dish last night but with pine nuts instead of almonds. It was delicious! My family loved it. I will make this again for friends."

Barbacoa Beef Cheek Tacos

BY AARGERSI | SERVES 6 TO 8 (DEPENDING ON HOW MANY TACOS EACH PERSON CAN EAT!)

A&M: When we asked for "nose to tail" recipes, we didn't expect to see many universal crowd-pleasers, but aargersi's tacos are just that. The beef cheeks, marbled and melting after more than three hours in the oven, absorb the spices, coffee, chile, and peanut butter from the marinade and sing with the freshness of the lime juice in which they're braised. Add a warm corn tortilla, some addictive pink pickled onions, a slab of avocado, and a fistful of cilantro leaves, and you've got an epic taco. Make sure to save any leftover onions! We've used them on toasts with smoked salmon, in watercress salads, and on top of burgers.

PICKLED ONION

1 red onion, peeled

¼ beet, scrubbed well

1 handful cilantro leaves

1 tablespoon salt

2 tablespoons sugar

Cider vinegar

BARBACOA BEEF CHEEKS

2½ pounds beef cheeks or short ribs

1 dried ancho chile

4 garlic cloves, chopped

1 tablespoon natural peanut butter

1 teaspoon instant espresso powder

4 tablespoons olive oil

1 tablespoon honey

2 teaspoons ground cumin

1 teaspoon smoked sweet paprika

1 handful fresh cilantro, plus more for serving

1 teaspoon salt

1 cup chicken broth (you can use beef too; I just had chicken on hand)

3 limes

Corn tortillas

1 avocado, sliced

1. Make the pickled onion. Slice the onion very thinly and put it in a microwaveable container. Add the beet, cilantro, salt, and sugar. Cover everything with 1 part water to 2 parts vinegar.

2. Microwave for 1 minute, stir, and microwave for another minute. Cool, then refrigerate overnight. The beet will turn the onion a really pretty hot pink color. Remove the beet before serving.

3. Prepare the cheeks. Clean and trim the beef cheeks. Put them in a container in which you can marinate them.

4. Remove the stem and seeds from the ancho chile, cut it into chunks, and rehydrate it in a little hot water (I stick it in a ramekin and microwave for 30 seconds).

5. Combine the ancho chile and soaking water, garlic, peanut butter, espresso powder, 2 tablespoons of the olive oil, the honey, cumin, paprika, cilantro, and salt in a food processor and blend into a paste. Toss the paste with the cheeks, cover, and marinate in the refrigerator for several hours or, better yet, overnight.

6. When it is time to cook, heat the oven to 275°F and heat the remaining 2 tablespoons olive oil in a Dutch oven over medium heat. Brown the cheeks on both sides. Use the broth to rinse the rest of the marinade into the Dutch oven, then squeeze the juice of the limes in.

7. Braise for 3 ½ hours, turning the cheeks over once or twice while they cook. If the liquid dries up, add a bit more broth.

8. When the cheeks are fall-apart tender, use two forks to pull the meat apart in the pan so that it mixes in with all the fatty juicy goodness.

9. To serve: Heat 2 tortillas (I like to double-wrap the tacos, as they are juicy). Fill with the barbacoa, a slice of avocado, some of the pickled onions, and some fresh cilantro. Serve and enjoy!

TIPS AND TECHNIQUES

"I couldn't face a whole cow head . . . so I made this with cheeks," aargersi said. Well, we've also made it with short ribs, and they work beautifully, too!

ABOUT THE COOK

Abbie Argersinger is a marketing database manager in Austin, Texas.

Her favorite recipe from a cookbook: "I am going to say Tagine of Chicken with Preserved Lemons and Artichokes from Kitty Morse's *Cooking at the Kasbah*—it got me on the road to Moroccan food and is the first thing I ever cooked in my tagine."

WHAT THE COMMUNITY SAID

JKohler: "Substituted brisket and it was great. Onions were yummy, too. Leftovers will make for a nice salad tomorrow."

Jennie's Homemade Manicotti

BY JENNIFER PERILLO | SERVES 4

A&M: A unique take on baked pasta, this recipe requires a little faith, but not all that much work considering the results. If you have a well-seasoned crepe pan, this is the perfect excuse to put it to work. You just whizz the batter up in a blender, and then all you need to do is crank out 10 or so crepes to roll around a simple mixture of ricotta, eggs, parsley, and Parmesan. Jennifer Perillo provides a recipe for fresh ricotta, but if you're pressed for time a good store-bought ricotta is just fine.

CREAMY HOMEMADE RICOTTA
4 cups whole milk
1 cup heavy cream
¾ cup buttermilk
½ teaspoon salt

PASTA
1 large egg
1 cup all-purpose flour
¼ teaspoon salt
¾ cup whole milk, plus more as needed to thin the batter
Canola oil, to lightly grease the pan (see Tips and Techniques)

FILLING
16 ounces fresh ricotta cheese (use Creamy Homemade Ricotta, if desired)
1 large egg, lightly beaten
1 teaspoon fresh chopped flat-leaf parsley, plus more for garnish
¼ cup freshly grated Parmesan
Salt and freshly ground black pepper

ASSEMBLY
2 cups good-quality marinara sauce, preferably homemade (see Eggplant Parmesan on page 89 for a recipe)
¼ cup freshly grated Parmesan

1. Make the ricotta (optional). Add the ricotta ingredients to a 4-quart pot and warm over medium heat. Meanwhile, line a sieve or fine-mesh strainer with a few layers of cheesecloth and place it over a deep bowl or pot.

2. Once the curds begin to separate from the whey (the liquid temperature will be between 175°F and 200°F), remove from the heat. Gently spoon or ladle the curds into the cheesecloth-lined strainer. You may need to gently gather the cheesecloth at the top to help the curds drain.

3. Let the curds drain for 15 to 30 minutes, depending on how creamy you'd like your ricotta. Store in the refrigerator for up to 2 days.

4. Make the pasta. Add the pasta ingredients to the bowl of a blender. Blend, adding more milk, 1 teaspoon at a time, until the batter is a thin, almost runny consistency. Heat a nonstick 8-inch skillet over medium-low heat. Brush the pan lightly with oil, if needed. Hold the pan at an angle and swirl it as you pour in enough batter to coat the bottom of the skillet. Cook 30 to 45 seconds, flip carefully using a thin spatula, and cook for 15 more seconds. And don't forget, the first one or two pasta crepes might end up being sacrificial until you get the hang of swirling the pan. Transfer to a flat dish or tray. Repeat with the remaining batter. You should have 8 to 10 crepes by the end.

5. Heat the oven to 350°F. Combine all the filling ingredients in a medium bowl and mix well. Spread ½ cup of the marinara sauce on the bottom of a 9 × 13-inch casserole dish. Lay the pasta crepes on a flat surface and spoon an even amount of filling in a long strip down the center of each one. Roll the crepes closed and place, seam side down, in the casserole dish. Evenly pour the remaining sauce over the filled crepes. Sprinkle the Parmesan over the top and bake for 20 minutes, or until golden and bubbly. Garnish with parsley and serve immediately.

TIPS AND TECHNIQUES

Jennifer Perillo: "I decided to buy a skillet exclusively for making manicotti and crepes, so it wipes clean with a cloth to preserve the coating, eliminating the need to grease the pan."

Don't skimp on the ricotta or on the marinara sauce—you'll be doing these delicate, creamy manicotti (and yourself) a huge disservice.

ABOUT THE COOK

To read about Jennifer Perillo, and to see her recipe for Sweet and Savory Tomato Jam, turn to page 80. You can also find her Wildcard-winning recipe for Seriously Delicious Ribs on page 84.

WHAT THE COMMUNITY SAID

lastnightsdinner: "I made these last night, subbing in our favorite local ricotta for homemade, and topping them with a little fresh mozzarella. We practically licked the baking dish clean. What a fabulous dish, and thank you for sharing it."

AntoniaJames: "Gorgeous! Very nice of you include the fresh ricotta instructions, too. This looks just like the food I remember eating every day when I lived in Italy . . . visually appealing, not heavy, and thoughtfully made. Brava!"

Leek, Lemon, and Feta Quiche

BY FEEDING THE SAINTS (A. C. PARKER) | MAKES 1 LARGE QUICHE OR 4 INDIVIDUAL QUICHES

A&M: Feeding the Saints aptly describes these individual little quiches as "light and cheerful." We love the delicate flavor of leeks, and the crisp, airy puff pastry is a nice change from a more traditional, and sadly often leaden, short crust; lemon zest and ouzo lend just the right mix of lift and fragrance. We especially like the slabs of feta that, instead of being crumbled into the egg mixture, are laid gently across the top of each quiche. Chilling the quiches for about 20 minutes before baking will help the pastry puff handsomely and crisp.

---

1 sheet frozen puff pastry

1 pound leeks

2 tablespoons extra virgin olive oil

1 cup half-and-half

3 large eggs

1 teaspoon freshly grated lemon zest

1 teaspoon kosher salt

Freshly ground black pepper

2 teaspoons ouzo (optional)

2½ ounces feta, cut into 4 (approximately ½-inch) slices

---

1. Heat the oven to 375°F. Thaw the puff pastry according to package directions.

2. Prepare the leeks. Rinse off any visible dirt and slice off the roots. Remove the dark green tops, leaving a couple inches of light green with the white portion of the leeks. (The dark trimmings can be reserved for another use—in a vegetable or chicken stock, for example.) Halve the leeks lengthwise, then cut them crosswise in ½-inch slices. Dump the slices in a colander or salad spinner and rinse thoroughly; if you don't, you risk having a gritty, sandy quiche, as leeks often hide dirt deep in their layers. Let the leeks drain well, or spin dry.

3. Heat the olive oil in a large skillet over medium heat until it shimmers. Add the leeks and cook until they are wilted, about 3 minutes; don't cook them so much that they give off liquid. Turn off the heat and let sit.

4. In a mixing bowl or large measuring cup, using a whisk or fork, beat together the half-and-half, eggs, lemon zest, salt, and pepper to taste. Add the ouzo, if using.

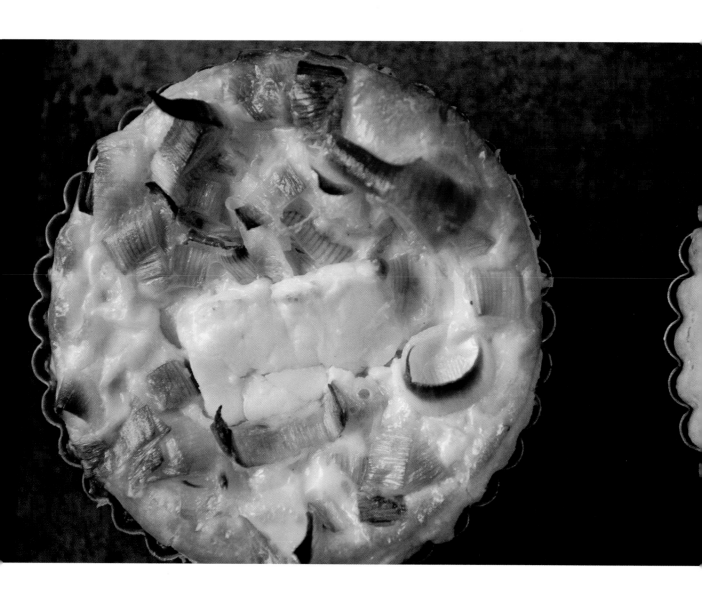

5. Prepare the pastry crust(s). On a lightly floured surface, or between two layers of plastic wrap or parchment paper, roll out the thawed puff pastry to a thickness of about ¼ inch. Line a shallow pie plate or cut the pastry into 4 circles to fill individual baking dishes. Press the pastry up the sides to make a nice edge.

6. Fill the quiche(s). Distribute the leeks evenly across the bottom of the dish(es). Pour the milk mixture over the leeks. Top the quiche(s) with the slices of feta. (If you have feta that crumbles apart, don't worry, just sprinkle it on top.)

7. Bake 30 to 40 minutes, depending on the size of the quiche(s). The center should be solid and the crust and top nicely browned. Let the quiche(s) cool for at least 10 minutes before serving. These taste great hot, at room temperature, and even cold.

8. Enjoy with a simple green salad and a glass of chilled Assyrtiko from award-winning Domaine Sigalas (Santorini).

TIPS AND TECHNIQUES

Feeding The Saints: "The ouzo is optional, but highly recommended. In a small dose, it brings a subtle sweet anise flavor that balances the sharp saltiness of the feta." If you can't get ouzo, use any other anise-flavored liqueur.

If you're cooking just for one, make individual-size quiches and freeze some, baked, for later; you'll be glad to have them on hand.

A variation for omnivores: Dice 1 package of Canadian bacon (about 8 slices) and add it to the quiche(s) at the same time as the sautéed leeks.

ABOUT THE COOK

Allison Cay Parker is a freelance writer, editor, recipe developer, and tester. She lives in New York City and writes the blog Feeding the Saints (www.feedingthesaints.com).

Her favorite baking tips: First, use unflavored dental floss to cut through delicate or sticky cake layers. Second, to keep cookies soft, place in a bag with a slice of soft bread—the bread will dry out but the cookies will stay wonderfully moist.

Chocolate Bundt Cake

BY KELSEYTHENAPTIMECHEF | MAKES 1 BUNDT CAKE

A&M: If Betty Crocker had a seductive cousin, this would be her signature cake: it's pure deep, dark, fudgy goodness. Because KelseyTheNaptimeChef's cake calls for oil instead of butter, plus a fair amount of coffee, it emerges from the oven heroically tender and moist. In fact, we noted that it has a texture similar to that of a British steamed pudding. The best part is that you can throw this together in 15 minutes, and it will be out of the oven in another 45—making your total time to greatness about an hour.

¾ cup Dutch-process cocoa powder, plus more for dusting

2 cups sugar

1¾ cups all-purpose flour

½ teaspoon salt

1 teaspoon baking powder

2 teaspoons baking soda

1 cup sour milk (see Tips and Techniques)

1 cup freshly brewed strong black coffee

½ cup vegetable oil

2 large eggs

1 teaspoon vanilla extract

Confectioners' sugar, for dusting

---

1. Heat the oven to 350°F. Butter a Bundt pan and dust the inside with cocoa powder; set aside.

2. In a medium bowl, sift together the sugar, flour, ¾ cup cocoa powder, salt, baking powder, and baking soda. Set aside.

3. Add the sour milk and coffee to the bowl of a standing mixer. With the speed on low, gradually add the vegetable oil, eggs, and vanilla. Mix until everything is incorporated. Then, with the mixer still on low speed, slowly add the dry ingredients. Once all of the flour mixture is added, mix the batter for a full 4 minutes on medium speed.

4. Pour the batter into the prepared pan and bake for 45 minutes, or until a cake tester comes out clean. Allow to cool to room temperature on a wire rack, then dust with confectioners' sugar and serve.

TIPS AND TECHNIQUES

To make sour milk, combine 1 cup milk with 1 teaspoon vinegar and let sit for 5 minutes.

Mtrelaun: "My Bundt pan (which has two parts) leaks during the initial 10 minutes of baking, as the batter is very liquidy. I recommend placing a cookie sheet on the lower rack to catch the drips."

ABOUT THE COOK

Learn more about KelseyTheNaptimeChef, and find her recipe for Zucchini-Lemon Cookies on page 52. You can also find a recipe for her Double Chocolate Espresso Cookies on page 138.

WHAT THE COMMUNITY SAID

nannydeb: "I made this into cupcakes with butterflies . . . and they were a huge hit. The recipe worked well made into cupcakes baking them for about 12 to 15 minutes."

CarynCooks: "I was so excited to see this recipe that I went out and bought a Bundt pan so I could make it. A Valentine's day present to myself! I do plan on sharing the cake, however."

Grilled (or Broiled) Oysters with a Sriracha Lime Butter

BY MELISSAV | MAKES AT LEAST 2 DOZEN OYSTERS AND SERVES 4 TO 6 AS A FIRST COURSE

A&M: We wish more people would grill or broil oysters—it's so easy, and the quick blast of heat concentrates the oysters' brine and browns their edges without drying them out. Here you mash up butter with Sriracha, shallots, lime juice, and cilantro, and as the oysters cook (we broiled them) the flavorful butter melts and poaches the plump little bivalves. We think the spicy butter would also be pretty great on clams, fish, shrimp, crab, and even corn. One detail to keep in mind: the lime juice will not fully mash into the butter, so just spoon the juices over the oysters after dabbing them with the butter.

---

4 tablespoons (½ stick) butter, softened

2 teaspoons finely minced shallot

1 teaspoon Sriracha

1 tablespoon lime juice

¼ teaspoon kosher salt

2 teaspoons minced cilantro

2 dozen oysters on the half shell

---

1. In a small bowl, mix the butter with the shallot, Sriracha, lime juice, salt, and cilantro. Let it set up in the fridge. It doesn't have to set up completely, but it should be more solid than liquid—give it at least an hour.

2. Meanwhile, heat the grill (or broiler) until very hot.

3. Top each oyster with a dollop of the flavored butter.

4. Grill (or broil) until the oysters plump up and their edges begin to curl, 3 to 4 minutes.

5. Enjoy! But be careful, as the shells will be very hot.

TIPS AND TECHNIQUES

Melissav: "Shucking is a task. If you aren't up for it, most fish stores will shuck oysters for you. If I pick them up late enough in the day, I have them shuck them and leave them on the half shell. If there's a bit of time between the trip to the fish store and dinner time, you can have them shuck the oysters and put the oysters and the oyster liquor in a small container with the shells on the side. When it's time to prepare the oysters, just place an oyster in each shell along with a small spoonful of the liquor. Not as ideal as a freshly shucked oyster, but a great time saver."

ABOUT THE COOK

To learn more about Melissav, and to see her recipe for Ciabatta Stuffing with Chorizo, Sweet Potato, and Mushrooms, turn to page 150.

WHAT THE COMMUNITY SAID

Rhonda35: "Really looking forward to trying this tonight. Making Valentine's Day dinner—think we'll start with some bubbly and these delightful-sounding morsels, move on to lobster risotto with a lemony green salad, and finish with something dark and chocolatey."

Rhonda35 (follow-up!): "I usually prefer my oysters raw with just a squeeze of lemon, but this recipe is so unbelievably fabulous that I just might have a new preference!"

Autumn Olive Medley (Braised Lamb Shanks with Fennel, Celery Root, and Olives)

BY ABRA BENNETT | SERVES 4

A&M: If you're in the mood for a rich, comforting stew but want something with a bit of flair, this dish is for you. Abra Bennett has you simmer lamb shanks in a heady broth of red wine, stock, fennel, celery root, and aromatics until the meat falls from the bone, adding sun-dried tomatoes and green olives two-thirds of the way through. The resulting dish is brilliant: the fennel and shallots melt into the sauce, the olives leach some of their brine and become almost artichokelike in flavor, the sun-dried tomatoes soften and mellow, and a finishing splash of Pernod and a shower of freshly grated lemon zest cut through the fattiness of the lamb.

Salt and freshly ground black pepper	1 teaspoon dried bouquet garni
4 lamb shanks	2 cups young red wine
3 tablespoons olive oil	2 cups veal or beef broth
1 fennel bulb, diced small	1 cup green olives, pits in
1 softball-size celery root (celeriac), peeled and diced small	½ cup sun-dried tomatoes in oil
	1 splash Ricard or Pernod (optional)
2 large shallots, chopped	Finely grated zest of 1 lemon (use a Microplane if you have one)
3 garlic cloves, chopped	
1 bay leaf	

---

1. Salt and pepper the lamb shanks liberally. Heat the olive oil over medium-high heat in a large, heavy pan with a tight-fitting lid. Brown the lamb shanks all over. Take your time with this and get them really nice and brown. Remove the lamb from the pan and set aside.

2. Lightly brown the fennel, celery root, shallots, and garlic in the pan used for the meat, about 5 minutes. Add the meat back to the pan. Add the bay leaf, bouquet garni, wine, and broth. Cover the pot and simmer over medium-low heat for 1 hour.

3. Add the olives and sun-dried tomatoes to the pot. If necessary, add a little more wine or broth. Simmer, covered, an additional 30 minutes, or until the meat is nearly falling off the bone.

4. If you'd like to emphasize the fennel flavor and bring out the mellowness of the olives, add a splash of Ricard or Pernod. This really does enhance the dish and is very Mediterranean. Taste the sauce and add additional salt and/or pepper to taste. Just before serving, sprinkle the lamb with the lemon zest.

5. You can gently pull the meat off the bone and serve it as a stew, or as a sauce over pasta. You can also serve these on the bone as is, or over polenta. Be sure to mention to your diners that the olives contain pits!

TIPS AND TECHNIQUES

Abra Bennett: "Like most stews and braises, this tastes even better the next day, so make it ahead if you have the chance."

You may want to drain some of the oil in the pan after browning the lamb (we kept 3 tablespoons). We also reduced the sauce by simmering it for a bit after the meat was cooked.

ABOUT THE COOK

Abra Bennett is a food and wine writer living in Bainbridge Island, Washington.

Her favorite recipe from a cookbook: "Anything from Paula Wolfert's *Cooking of Southwest France,* but if I have to pick just one recipe, her Ragout of Veal with Orange. It's astoundingly delicious."

You can find her Wildcard-winning Risotto Rosso recipe on page 347.

Here's her blog: French Letters (www.frenchletters.wordpress.com).

WHAT THE COMMUNITY SAID

aargersi: "Okay, I had this last night and I think it may be the best lamb shank I have ever had . . . I have never cooked celeriac before, and I am hooked! Also on Pernod . . . I confess to having a little sip or two before dinner as well."

Secret Ingredient Beef Stew

BY SMALLKITCHCARA | SERVES 8 TO 10

A&M: This savory, rich stew may be named after one ingredient, but it's because of a mix of components that it succeeds so well. Tomatoes and tomato paste give it a sunny sweetness, diced veggies lend texture, and red wine and vinegar brighten everything. Anchovies, the "secret ingredient," are briny and buttery, giving the sauce a smooth, complex finish. We recommend using beef with generous marbling for the best results. SmallKitchCara serves this "over buttery, parslied orzo and accompanied by crusty bread."

---

5 to 5½ pounds beef stewing meat, cut into 2- to 3-inch pieces

Salt and freshly ground black pepper

⅓ cup mixed olive and canola oil

2 leeks, washed well and sliced thinly

1 large onion, diced

8 garlic cloves, minced

2 carrots, diced

4 celery ribs, diced

4 ounces white mushrooms, roughly chopped

¼ cup tomato paste

2 anchovies

1 cup red wine

½ cup red wine vinegar

1 cup canned whole tomatoes with juice

3 to 3½ cups beef broth

3 bay leaves

¾ teaspoon dried thyme

⅓ cup chopped parsley

---

1. Season the beef with salt and pepper on both sides. Heat the oil in a 5- to 6-quart Dutch oven over high heat and brown the meat in batches, adding more oil as needed. Remove the meat to a plate.

2. Lower the heat and add the leeks, onion, garlic, carrots, celery, and mushrooms. Cook until softened, 5 to 10 minutes. Stir in the tomato paste and the anchovies and cook for 1 or 2 minutes to melt and distribute the anchovies.

3. Add the beef and its juices back to the pot. Add the wine, vinegar, and tomatoes with juice (breaking them up against the side of the pot as you go) and raise the heat to bring to a boil. Pour in the broth to cover (you may need a bit more than 3 cups). Add 1 ½ teaspoons salt, the bay leaves, and the thyme and bring to a boil. Simmer, partially covered, until the meat is tender, 2 to 3 hours. Cool to room temperature. Refrigerate for several hours.

4. When cool, skim off most of the fat from the top. Reheat over low heat, letting the stew simmer for 30 to 45 minutes before serving.

5. Mix in half the parsley and garnish with the rest.

TIPS AND TECHNIQUES

Make this a day ahead—its flavor will improve and you can enjoy the stew without thinking of all the dishes you have to wash.

ABOUT THE COOK

Cara Eisenpress is the co-author of the blog Big Girls, Small Kitchen and the book *In the Small Kitchen* (her co-author, Phoebe Lapine, or BigGirlPhoebz as we know her at Food52, can be found on page 135 with a recipe for Prosciutto and Fontina Panini with Arugula Pesto). Cara lives in New York City.

Her favorite recipe from a cookbook: "The dill tofu from Peter Berley's *Modern Vegetarian Cookbook*."

WHAT THE COMMUNITY SAID

pierino: "I'm absolutely down with the anchovy part. It adds a bottom flavor that even anchovy haters (like my sister) can't detect. It's one of our secret weapons."

lastnightsdinner: "I love this. I've been playing with adding things like anchovies and fish sauce to beefy dishes for a few months myself, and it really does boost the meaty flavor!"

Mashed Potatoes with Caramelized Onions and Goat Cheese

BY SONALI | SERVES 6 TO 8

A&M: With a generous hit of half-and-half and butter (infused with bay leaf and garlic) and a dollop—or four—of fresh goat cheese, Sonali's potatoes are creamy and ethereal with the lightest tang. She has tried many varieties of potato, but russets remain her favorite. "Their high starch content and low moisture make them ideal for creating fluffy, creamy mashed potatoes," she said. Caramelized onions, which are both folded into the potatoes and piled on top before serving, thread their mellow sweetness throughout. We agree that the use of a ricer (which we usually loathe) is key in order to achieve just the right silken texture for this bowl of mash.

4 tablespoons (½ stick) unsalted butter

1 tablespoon olive oil

1½ pounds yellow onions (approximately 2 large onions), thinly sliced

Kosher salt

¼ teaspoon sugar

3 pounds russet potatoes, peeled and cut into 1-inch pieces

1½ cups half-and-half

1 garlic clove, smashed

1 bay leaf

3 ounces goat cheese

Freshly ground black pepper

1. To make the caramelized onions, heat 2 tablespoons of the butter with the olive oil in a large sauté pan over medium heat. Add the onions and stir to coat with the fat. Add ¼ teaspoon salt and the sugar and cook, stirring frequently, until the onions are golden brown and caramelized, 30 to 40 minutes. If the onions get too dry, add a small amount of water to deglaze the pan. Set aside.

2. Place the potatoes in a large pot of cold, salted water. Bring to a boil and cook until fork-tender, about 20 minutes.

3. While the potatoes are cooking, heat the half-and-half, garlic, bay leaf, and the remaining 2 tablespoons butter in a small saucepan over medium heat.

4. Drain the potatoes and return them to the hot, dry pot. Stir them over low heat for 2 minutes, or until they are dry. Pass the potatoes through a ricer into a large bowl. Gently stir in the hot cream mixture, a little at a time, until the potatoes are smooth and creamy (discard the garlic and bay leaf). You may not need to use all of the liquid. Set aside a small amount of the caramelized onions for garnish and stir the remaining onions into the mashed potatoes. Crumble the goat cheese into the potatoes and stir to combine well. Season with salt and pepper to taste.

5. Spoon the mashed potatoes into a serving bowl and garnish with the remaining caramelized onions. Serve hot.

ABOUT THE COOK

To learn more about Sonali, and to see her recipe for Braised Moroccan Chicken and Olives, turn to page 125. You can also find her recipe for Autumn Celeriac (Celery Root) Puree on page 133.

WHAT THE COMMUNITY SAID

kemanche: "Just made these mashed potatoes to serve with Pork Tenderloin and Merlot reduction sauce. Absolutely a great side. Will make it again!"

lacerise: "Made these this afternoon and, though a bit labor intensive for mashed potatoes, they were worth the effort. Creamy, buttery, with the tang of the goat cheese and the sweet onions. They are dee-lish!"

Ricotta and Chive Gnocchi

BY THE INTERNET COOKING PRINCESS | SERVES 4 TO 6

A&M: In this gnocchi recipe, The Internet Cooking Princess has reimagined the classic sour-cream-and-chive-topped baked potato in the most ingenious way: she swaps in ricotta for the sour cream, lightening the dough and lending it a faint sweetness, and sautés the gnocchi in olive oil and butter for a golden crust. We sprinkled some chives and grated Parmesan on top and helped ourselves to bowl after bowl. After making them, The Internet Cooking Princess wrote, "For a Millennial of Spanish, Turkish, German, and English descent, I felt like a total Italian grandmother from the Old World."

---

3 medium russet potatoes

2 large eggs

1 cup ricotta

½ cup freshly grated Parmesan

⅓ cup thinly sliced chives

2 cups all-purpose flour, plus more for rolling out the dough

6 tablespoons olive oil

6 tablespoons (¾ stick) unsalted butter

Kosher salt and freshly ground black pepper

Chopped parsley or chives, for serving (optional)

---

1. Bring a large pot of water to boil and add the potatoes. Simmer for 45 minutes, drain them in a colander, and let cool.

2. Once the potatoes are cool, remove and discard the skins. In a large bowl, mash the potatoes. The mixture needs to be as smooth as possible. Stir the eggs into the mixture, then the ricotta, Parmesan, and chives.

3. At this point, the mixture should be thick, but it needs to be as thick and malleable as dough. Add the flour and stir until you get a doughy consistency. The mixture will still be a little sticky, but that's okay. Take a handful or two of flour and scatter it on a clean work surface. Place the dough on the flour and roll it around until it's more doughlike and doesn't stick to everything in sight.

4. Begin rolling the dough with your hands as if you're forming a large snake. When the dough tube is about 2 feet long, cut it into quarters. Continue rolling each of the individual segments until you have rolls that are no bigger than a quarter in circumference. (Any bigger and you'll have difficulty cooking the gnocchi.)

5. Cut or pinch off ¾-inch sections from the rolls and roll them around in the palm of your hand to make the gnocchi. You may need to continue dredging them in a little flour as you go, which is fine. Set all the finished gnocchi on a large plate to the side.

6. Once all the gnocchi have been formed, bring a large pot of salted water to a boil. Dump the gnocchi into the water and boil for 5 minutes to ensure that their centers are nice and tender. (They will automatically start popping up to the top of the pot once they're cooking, but make sure you give them a little extra time in the water.) Drain the gnocchi in a colander.

7. In a very large sauté pan over medium-high heat, put 2 tablespoons each of the oil and the butter. Add the gnocchi in batches so that they have enough space to get a light, brown crust around them. Add more oil, butter, and gnocchi when the first batch is done (you may not need to use all the butter and oil). Lightly season the gnocchi with a little kosher salt, parsley, if desired, or extra chives.

TIPS AND TECHNIQUES

We scored an "X" onto each end of the potatoes before boiling so they were easier to peel afterward; used a ricer to mash the potatoes to ensure that they were perfectly smooth; and shaped the gnocchi by rolling them down the back of a fork, because we're fancy.

ABOUT THE COOK

To learn more about The Internet Cooking Princess, and to see her recipe for Norma's Eggnog, turn to page 199, and for Andouille and Dijon Polenta, turn to page 185.

WHAT THE COMMUNITY SAID

pierino: "I like this recipe because the American kitchen tends to deploy chives more as a garnish rather than for their distinct flavor."

monkeymom: "Finally had a chance to make these just now. They were addictive . . . light and slightly chewy with that crispy fried exterior. Fun to make, too!"

Overnight Steel-Cut Oats with Almond Butter and Honey

BY YING | SERVES 2 TO 3

A&M: We'll admit that before this contest, we were somewhat bemused by the recent slow-cooker revival. Ying's porridge helped change our minds. We love her idea of using a slow-cooker as a bain-marie, and what better way to be greeted on a chilly morning than with a steaming batch of steel-cut oats, ready for a dollop of rich, toasty almond butter and a swirl of honey. (If you don't have almond butter, any nut butter will do.) We'll take this over Wheaties any day.

---

1 cup whole milk

½ cup steel-cut oatmeal

Pinch of salt

¼ cup almond butter

2 to 3 tablespoons flavorful honey

---

1. In a 4-cup glass measuring jug, stir together 2 cups water, the milk, oatmeal, and salt. Place the jug in a large slow-cooker, add enough water to come halfway up the side of the jug, switch the slow-cooker to "low," and go to bed.

2. In the morning, stir in the almond butter and honey. There will be a tablespoon's worth of grain clumped together at the bottom of the glass jug; it needs only to be mixed in. Serve. You'll have a halo of warmth around you for the rest of the morning.

TIPS AND TECHNIQUES

Lindachoi said: "You can also do this without the slow-cooker—I use a regular pan, put the oats into boiling water, boil for a minute, and turn off and just leave it sitting out overnight. It's done in the A.M. If you're skittish about leaving food out, you can also refrigerate."

ABOUT THE COOK

Ying S. Lee is a writer in Kingston, Ontario.

Her favorite recipe from a cookbook: "Beef Rendang from James Oseland's *Cradle of Flavor*. Better than my mother's."

Her top entertaining tips:

"Start cooking earlier than you think you'll need to!"

"Do a make-ahead dessert. At that point in the meal, you want to be at the table with your friends, not flambéing something in the kitchen."

Here's her website: www.yslee.com.

WHAT THE COMMUNITY SAID

freshparsley: "I use my rice cooker to make oatmeal. Simply set it up as you would for rice. In the time it takes me to shower, the oats are ready. The Irish steel-cut oats are the best tasting. Nice thing about the rice cooker is that it keeps the oats warm once they are cooked."

KelseyTheNaptimeChef: "What a delicious recipe! I love the slow-cooker, such a great solution to many things. I am particularly taken with your use of almond butter and honey in the oats—that just might be my favorite combination for oatmeal yet! Perfect timing too; my maple syrup and cream is getting a little repetitive."

Olive all'Ascolana

BY ARIELLECLEMENTINE | MAKES 24

A&M: This high-low treat can work just as easily for a movie snack as it can for a dinner party hors d'oeuvre. These crunchy little flavor bombs come out of the hot oil looking like hedgehogs with a shaggy brown coating of panko. Inside is a layer of tangy olive and then rosemary-and-dried-chile-scented goat cheese. The olives hold up well, so you can fry them up to an hour in advance; just keep them warm in a low oven. And chill some Prosecco.

½ cup soft goat cheese

1 teaspoon mustard seeds

1 teaspoon finely chopped rosemary

¼ teaspoon crushed red pepper flakes

1 garlic clove, minced

24 large green olives, pitted

1 cup vegetable oil

1 cup all-purpose flour

1 large egg, beaten

1 cup bread crumbs (fresh or panko)

⅓ cup freshly grated Parmesan or similar cheese, plus more for sprinkling

Zest and juice of 1 lemon, for sprinkling

---

1. In a small bowl, mix together the goat cheese, mustard seeds, rosemary, red pepper flakes, and garlic. Stuff the olives with this goat cheese mixture (I like to use my fingers, but you could use a piping bag if you're really classy). Put the stuffed olives on a plate and refrigerate for 20 minutes, to let the cheese firm up.

2. While the olives are chilling, gently heat the oil in a heavy-bottomed frying pan to 375°F.

3. Set up three plates for your breading station. Put the flour on one plate, the beaten egg on the next, and mix the bread crumbs and Parmesan on the last.

4. Roll half the chilled olives in the flour, then in the egg, then in the bread crumbs, and carefully drop them into the heated oil. Fry until golden brown, about 1 minute per side. Transfer to a plate lined with paper towels to drain, and repeat with the remaining olives.

5. Pile on a plate and finish with a shower of freshly grated Parmesan and lemon zest and a spritz of lemon.

ABOUT THE COOK

Arielle Arizpe is an education specialist in Austin, Texas.

Her favorite recipe from a cookbook: "Quiche Lorraine, from the *New Best Recipe* (from the editors of *Cook's Illustrated*). I didn't know what quiche was until I made this recipe. Now I make it at least once a month (with varied fillings)."

Her top entertaining tip: "If at all possible, get Helenthenanny to make an appearance at your fête, because that girl knows how to get a party started."

Now for a bit of Food52 trivia: arielleclementine, a self-described "olive fiend," is the sister of Helenthenanny, another recipe winner–see her Figgy Pudding Butter Cookies on page 205.

See Arielle Clementine's recipe for Griddled Polenta Cakes with Caramelized Onions, Goat Cheese, and Honey on page 289.

Here's her blog: www.arielleclementine.blogspot.com.

WHAT THE COMMUNITY SAID

Naked Beet: "These look absolutely sinful. I'm afraid if I made them for a movie snack and not a dinner party I would never share my plate!"

Lemon Posset

BY MRSLARKIN | SERVES 4

A&M: This recipe is the perfect thing for anyone who may be fearful of making custard but harbors a weakness—as we do—for this sort of milky, comforting, nursery food. "In Ye Olde English days of yore," mrslarkin explained, "it was a milk drink thickened with wine. My posset recipe is so simple, as they all are, really. Using just three ingredients, it seems almost magical, setting up immediately. The wonders of food science in front of your very eyes. Curdled milk never tasted so good." In flavor, this posset is like a creamier, less aggressive version of lemon curd, and it's rich enough that a small amount goes a long way. Do be careful that the cream doesn't boil over—we watched it like a hawk, but it still managed to catch us by surprise!

2 cups heavy cream

⅔ cup sugar

5 tablespoons lemon juice

Unsweetened whipped cream or shortbread cookies, for serving

1. In a small saucepan, heat the cream and sugar to boiling, stirring to dissolve the sugar. Continue boiling for 5 minutes. Watch the heat—don't let the cream boil over.

2. Remove the pan from the heat and stir in the lemon juice. Let cool, about 15 minutes.

3. Pour even amounts into 4 ramekins. Refrigerate until set, at least 2 hours.

4. Serve with unsweetened whipped cream or shortbread cookies to dunk.

TIPS AND TECHNIQUES

Use the best-quality cream you can find—if you have access to cream straight from a farm, this is the moment to buy it!

Liz Larkin, aka the Pound Ridge Scone Lady, is a baker living in Pound Ridge, New York.

Her favorite recipe from a cookbook: "Hungarian Shortbread in *Cooking with Julia* by Dorie Greenspan."

Her favorite cooking tip: "When making scones or biscuits, make the dough ahead, form the dough and cut into wedges or rounds, and freeze on a cookie sheet until solid. Place in freezer zipper bags. Then, you can bake as many or as few as needed at a moment's notice."

See her recipe for Chewy Sugar Cookies #2, which heroically represented Food52 in our smackdown with *Cook's Illustrated*, on page 333.

WHAT THE COMMUNITY SAID

jhagye: "This is one of my favorite go-to desserts. I serve it in stemmed crystal wineglasses with a dab of whipped cream and a few berries and mint. Looks as elegant as it tastes."

gabrielaskitchen: "This lemon posset is stand-alone delicious but also so versatile! I baked some lemon cupcakes, cut a little well out of the middle of each baked cake, filled them with the chilled posset, and then topped each one with lightly sweetened whipped cream and a berry. They were sooooooo good!"

Airy Rosemary Citrus Pignole Bread Pudding

BY GABRIELASKITCHEN | SERVES 8

A&M: We nicknamed this "restaurant" bread pudding—not because it's difficult to make, but because it seems like restaurant fare. Gabrielaskitchen brought together her love for chiffon cakes, flan, and lemon pignoli cookies. The herbs, vanilla, and a trio of citrus zests infuse the milk, and honey adds a rich, musky sweetness that sugar simply cannot. The sweetness of the custard is offset by lemon juice and butter-soaked bread cubes, and whipped egg whites lighten the pudding. The resulting dessert miraculously separates into a rich, custardy base and a puffy, tender top layer studded with toasted pine nuts.

---

1 large loaf Italian or French bread

1½ cups whole milk

2 fresh rosemary sprigs or ½ teaspoon dried rosemary, pulverized

1 teaspoon lemon zest

1 teaspoon grapefruit zest

1 teaspoon orange zest

½ teaspoon vanilla extract or ½ vanilla bean, scraped

¾ cup honey

Juice of 1 small lemon

8 tablespoons unsalted butter, melted, plus some for the pan

4 large eggs, separated

½ cup toasted pine nuts

1 cup heavy cream

2 tablespoons sugar

---

1. Heat the oven to 300°F. Cut or tear the loaf of bread into approximately 1-inch cubes. Spread 3 cups of the bread cubes in one layer on baking sheets. Toast for about 10 minutes, or until the bread is slightly crisp on the outside but still spongy on the inside. Remove from the oven, then increase the oven temperature to 350°F.

2. Place the milk, rosemary, citrus zests, and vanilla in a saucepan over medium heat. Bring to a gentle boil, then promptly remove from the heat and cover. Let rest for 15 minutes. If you used fresh rosemary, remove and discard the sprigs and leaves. Add the honey to the milk mixture and stir until completely incorporated.

3. In a large bowl, combine the bread cubes, lemon juice, and melted butter.

4. Lightly grease the bottom and sides of an 8-inch square pan with butter. Place the bread mixture in the pan.

5. In another bowl, beat the egg yolks until lemon colored. Whisk the warm milk mixture into the eggs a little at a time.

6. In yet another bowl, beat the egg whites to just under stiff peaks. Fold into the milk and egg mixture.

7. Pour the final puddinglike mixture over the bread, coating it evenly. Top with the toasted pine nuts.

8. Place the baking pan in a larger pan or roasting pan. Pour enough hot water into the outer pan to come halfway up the sides of the pan containing the bread pudding.

9. Bake until just springy in the center, about 45 minutes. Meanwhile, whip the cream, gradually adding the sugar, until it holds soft peaks. Serve the bread pudding with the fresh whipped cream.

ABOUT THE COOK

Gabrielle Marie Lopez works in arts administration and special events and writes the blog Gabriela's Kitchen (www.gabrielaskitchen.com) in New York City.

Something she'd like a chance to eat or cook: "Traditional southeastern Chinese home cooking (my sous chef and boyfriend is one-half Chinese)."

WHAT THE COMMUNITY SAID

ZiggyPiecrust: "I made a Strawberry Rhubarb pie *and* this fabulous amazing bread pudding for my husband's birthday party last night to rave reviews from all. How can you not love something covered in pignole?"

ENunn: "Oh, my God: I have just had a bread pudding conversion. I will never compare bread pudding to Joe Lieberman again. Lovely!"

French Onion Soup

BY WCFOODIES | SERVES 4 TO 6

A&M: This is almost, but not quite, the traditional French onion soup we all know. It starts with a full 3 pounds of onions and some smashed garlic, which you caramelize slowly and thoroughly in butter and olive oil. You add thyme and bay leaf and some rich veal stock (homemade is highly recommended both by wcfoodies and by us), and then it's time for the crowning glory: 2 full cups of wine or beer. We used a dark ale and really liked the bit of kick that the finished soup still had after two-plus hours on the stove.

3 pounds onions

3 tablespoons unsalted butter

2 tablespoons olive oil

4 to 6 garlic cloves

Generous pinch of salt and a few grinds of fresh pepper

4 fresh thyme sprigs, plus more for garnish

1 bay leaf

4 to 6 cups beef, veal, and/or vegetable stock, preferably homemade

2 cups red wine, preferably a Burgundy, or 2 cups beer, preferably a brown ale or stout (not chocolate)

1 baguette or other crusty bread, sliced (stale bread is fine)

4 to 6 deli slices of cheese, or ½ cup each of Gouda, Gruyère, Parmesan, and pecorino

1. Halve and slice the onions.

2. Melt together the butter and olive oil over medium-low heat in a large stockpot.

3. Crush and peel the garlic. You don't have to mince it; it will caramelize and turn soft and sweet as it cooks. Caramelize the garlic in the olive oil and butter, 5 to 7 minutes.

4. Add the onions, season with salt and pepper, and stir around just until all the onions are coated in the olive oil and butter.

5. Add the thyme and bay leaf and cook until the onions are caramelized and cooked down, about 40 minutes.

6. Pour in the stock, 4 to 6 cups depending on whether you prefer your soup more oniony or more soupy. Add the wine or beer and simmer, uncovered, for at least 1 hour (you can cook it as long as 3 hours if you want really developed flavors, but add more liquid as needed), tasting occasionally to adjust the seasoning.

7. If you're using stale bread, heat it up a bit in a warm (250°F) oven first to soften it. Toast the bread; you can rub both sides with a cut clove of garlic, if you like. You'll want 2 pieces of toast per person; one for the bottom of the bowl, and one for the top.

8. Heat the broiler. Remove the thyme sprigs and bay leaf from the soup.

9. Arrange oven-safe individual serving bowls on a rimmed cookie sheet.

10. To serve, drop a piece of the toast in the bottom of each bowl. Ladle in the soup and cover with a second slice of toast. Cover the toast with a mix of the grated cheese or a slice of cheese. Be generous! You want the cheese to seal in the soup and drape over the edge of the bowl.

11. Broil for a few minutes until the cheese is browned and bubbling. Garnish with a little fresh thyme and serve.

TIPS AND TECHNIQUES
Take your time with the onions, and use the three-cheese combo instead of a deli slice for best results. And don't forget to put a piece of toast in the bottom of each bowl—it makes for a lovely surprise.

ABOUT THE COOK
Rebecca Lando is the writer, producer, and host of the show Working Class Foodies.

Her favorite recipe from a cookbook: "Thomas Keller's Mon Poulet Roti from *Bouchon*. A small, well-raised chicken, a hot pan, and salt and pepper are all you need to make this truly failproof recipe, and Keller's recipe reads like a love letter to the art of cooking."

WHAT THE COMMUNITY SAID
Naked Beet: "I've always made French onion soup with sherry, but I love this beer variation, and the three-cheese combo is a nice touch!"

Creamy Sausage Stuffed Mushrooms

BY ADRIENE | SERVES 15 TO 20

A&M: Adriene's stuffed mushrooms are the kind of coveted hors d'oeuvre that vanish at a party—so it's a good thing this recipe makes enough for a crowd. The splash of balsamic that cloaks the mushrooms prior to their first go-round in the oven infuses them with a touch of sweetness and acidity that acts as a wonderful counterpoint to the burly sausage-and-cream-cheese stuffing. We chose an aged Asiago and, though it didn't melt as well as a young one would, we loved the earthy, piquant pulse it gave to these delicious little 'shrooms.

---

5 pints button mushrooms

7 tablespoons olive oil

3 tablespoons balsamic vinegar

Salt and freshly ground black pepper

4 Italian sausages

2 medium yellow onions, minced

5 garlic cloves, minced

8 ounces cream cheese (at room temperature)

5 ounces Asiago, shredded

---

1. Heat the oven to 350°F. Wipe the mushrooms clean with a damp cloth. Pull out the stems and discard. Toss the cleaned, destemmed mushrooms with 5 tablespoons of the olive oil, the balsamic vinegar, and salt and pepper to taste. Spread on a sheet pan and bake for 30 minutes. Set aside and cool.

2. Slit the sausages and remove them from their casings. Crumble the sausage into a skillet set over medium-high heat and sauté until golden brown. Break the sausage up into small pieces as it cooks. Remove the sausage from the pan and set aside to cool.

3. Heat the remaining 2 tablespoons olive oil in the skillet over medium heat and add the onions. Cook, stirring occasionally, until dark and caramelized, 15 to 20 minutes. Add the garlic and cook for 1 minute.

4. Add the sausage, onions and garlic, cream cheese, salt and pepper, and 3 ounces of the shredded Asiago to a bowl and mix well with your hands. Break apart any large pieces of sausage.

5. Heat the oven to 375°F. Line up the mushrooms in a large greased baking dish with the hollows facing up. Stuff each mushroom with a generous portion of the creamy sausage mixture. Top the mushrooms with the remaining Asiago.

6. Bake for 20 to 30 minutes, or until the cheese on top is golden brown.

TIPS AND TECHNIQUES

Instead of just discarding the unused mushroom stems, use them to fortify a vegetable stock, or create a mushroom stock as a base for Creamy Mushroom Soup (page 119).

Adriene: "This dish can be made up to 3 days ahead of time, covered and refrigerated until you are ready to put it in the oven."

ABOUT THE COOK

Adriene Goldstein manages sales for a large bakery in Chicago, Illinois.

Her favorite entertaining tip: "While planning a menu for entertaining, have three-quarters of the items be food that can be prepared one or two days prior and just finished off before your guests come so you have some time to enjoy your party as well."

WHAT THE COMMUNITY SAID

dymnyno: "I made these last night for pupus and everyone loved them! I chopped up the leftovers and made a frittata this morning."

Wishbone Roast Chicken with Herb Butter

BY MONKEYMOM | SERVES 4 TO 6

A&M: This recipe, with its unassuming five ingredients, caught our eye for its use of simple techniques to achieve a flavorful bird with crisp skin. Monkeymom has thought a lot about roasting chicken: she has you tuck shallots and butter under the skin, season the bird, and then let it rest in the fridge, uncovered, for 8 hours. The butter keeps the meat moist and the air-drying in the fridge ensures a crackly skin. She also came up with an ingenious way to replicate the vertical roasting of "beer can chicken," in which the chicken sits on top of a beer can while it grills: she sets the chicken on the tube part of a tube pan. The vertical positioning allows the fat to drip off the bird while it cooks, and we think it does a great job of helping to cook the chicken evenly, as every part is equally exposed to the oven heat. And did we mention that the finished bird is then served with an herb butter? Herb butter gets us every time.

WISHBONE CHICKEN
One 3- to 4-pound chicken
2 tablespoons softened unsalted butter
1 shallot, sliced thin
Freshly ground black pepper and salt

HERB BUTTER
4 tablespoons (½ stick) softened unsalted butter
½ teaspoon kosher salt
1 teaspoon finely minced flat-leaf parsley
1 teaspoon finely minced chives

---

1. Wash and dry the chicken. Using your hands, spread the softened butter under the skin on the chicken breasts, especially the part near the neck. Tuck the shallots under the skin all around. Sprinkle with pepper, then salt the bird very generously all over. The key to a crispy skin is a dry bird, plenty of salt, and a hot oven. Place in the refrigerator, uncovered, for 8 hours or overnight.

2. For the herb butter: In a bowl, combine the butter with the salt, parsley, and chives. Mash with a fork to mix thoroughly, then scrape onto a piece of plastic wrap. Wrap the butter up to form a tube and chill in the refrigerator.

3. To roast the chicken, heat the oven to 400°F. Use only one rack, placed in the bottom slot of your oven.

4. Place the chicken, leg side down, on the tube insert of a 9-inch cake pan. This forms a stable base that will catch the drippings without leaking out. Tuck the wing tips behind the neck and pull the legs out to separate them from the breast. This helps them cook a little faster so the breast won't dry out. If the skin has torn or is short, you can use a toothpick and pin it to the bottom end of the breast. Roast the chicken until the juices are no longer pink when you pierce the thickest part of the leg with a sharp knife. (My chicken was a little under 4 pounds and was cooked perfectly at 55 minutes.) Remove the nicely browned chicken from the oven. Let it rest on the tube while preparing the rest of your dinner.

5. Slice the legs from the bird, then carve the breasts from the bones. Be careful not to cut the wishbone, which is near the neck cavity on the front top of the breast! I've disappointed my kids many times by accidentally breaking the wishbone prematurely.

6. Slice the herb butter and serve with the carved chicken. A little dab of butter on the chicken goes a long way.

7. Play the wishbone game.

TIPS AND TECHNIQUES

monkeymom: "You can vary the herbs and use what you prefer: chervil, thyme, lemon zest, cayenne, etc. One bird, many options for flavoring."

ABOUT THE COOK

Diana Chu is a scientist living in the San Francisco Bay area.

Her favorite recipe from a cookbook: "Carrot Cake Cupcakes from *Barefoot Contessa Parties!* An amazing treat. I make an unfrosted 'muffin' version by reducing the sugar by ⅓ cup, and substituting half the flour for white whole wheat flour. These are great bake sale and birthday treats for kids (no dairy, no nuts!)."

See her recipe for Caramelized Pork Bánh Mì on page 397.

WHAT THE COMMUNITY SAID

nannydeb: "You have just changed my life! We usually cook the chicken on a beer can (Pollo Boracho) inside a roasting pan. The can is always falling over with the chicken. I can't wait to try it on my tube pan. Thanks!"

French "Peasant" Beets

BY AMY N-B | SERVES 2 AS AN ENTRÉE, 4 AS A SIDE DISH

A&M: When Amy N-B told her husband that she came up with this dish as an homage to a simple French peasant dinner, he teased her: "What peasants eat Bucheron cheese and drink Muscadet with their beets?" "Um, French ones?" Well, in our next life, we'd like to be French peasants, or at least eat like them. We have a soft spot for beet recipes that utilize both the sweet root and minerally tops. Here, Amy N-B has you caramelize slices of yellow and red beets (we used four large beets total; might do three next time) and then add a mix of beet tops and Swiss chard, cooking them just enough to wilt. You'll love the dish at this point, but you'll be riveted if you serve it with a soft Bucheron and good country bread.

---

4 to 6 beets with greens (I like a mixture of golden and red beets)

1 bunch Swiss chard, rinsed and dried

3 tablespoons unsalted butter

1 shallot, minced

Salt and freshly ground black pepper

2 tablespoons white wine (Muscadet is my preference)

½ pound Bucheron (at room temperature), cut into 4 wedges

Crusty peasant-style bread (warmed in the oven)

---

1. Scrub and peel the beets. Remove the greens, wash and dry them, and chop coarsely. Set the greens aside in a large prep bowl. Slice the beets into ¼-inch rounds.

2. Remove the ribs from the Swiss chard and coarsely chop the ribs. Toss the leaves and ribs into the bowl with the beet greens.

3. In a large sauté pan, melt the butter and sauté the shallot over medium heat until softened.

4. Add the beet rounds to the shallot-butter mixture. Toss in a pinch of salt and crack some pepper over the beets. Reduce the heat and sauté the beets, turning to ensure even cooking, until the beets are beginning to glaze and become tender, about 15 minutes.

5. Add the beet greens, chard, and chard ribs and sauté for about 5 minutes, then add the wine and cover. Cook until the greens are wilted, adding 2 tablespoons water if necessary. Allow the liquid to be mostly absorbed into the greens. Adjust the seasonings.

6. Scoop the greens and beets into a shallow bowl. Serve with a generous wedge of Bucheron and some crusty bread. Crack a little bit of pepper over the entire dish.

TIPS AND TECHNIQUES

To find the right cheese, Amy N-B said: "Nice grocery stores (such as Wegmans and Whole Foods) usually have it, and any good cheese counter should have it. It can be spelled Boucheron, Bucherondin, or Boucherondin. All will do the trick."

ABOUT THE COOK

Amy Nichols-Belo is a cultural anthropologist from Richmond, Virginia.

Her favorite entertaining tip: "When hosting an event where guests will be contributing dishes or beverages, provide a theme (tapas, sixties hors d'oeuvre, Latin) to avoid a meal that's more 'church basement potluck' than party."

Here's her blog: Amy Cooks and Brad Does the Dishes (www.amycooksbraddoesthedishes .blogspot.com).

WHAT THE COMMUNITY SAID

deensiebat: "Made this last night and loved it. I had fallen into a rut of always making beets the same way—wedges parboiled, then roasted, greens reserved for later. Nice to have a new all-in-one method, with a sweet result."

romanolikethecheese: "Droplets of good balsamic vinegar on top set this dish up from good to really good!!"

Griddled Polenta Cakes with Caramelized Onions, Goat Cheese, and Honey

BY ARIELLECLEMENTINE | SERVES 8

A&M: As we tasted this polenta—crisped in a pan and topped with caramelized onions, goat cheese, and a sprinkling of honey—we thought aloud that it would make a great first course. No, a small lunch! Or how about breakfast! We'd happily eat it all day long, and we think you would, too. You can make arielleclementine's polenta and onions ahead of time, then just crisp the polenta and assemble the dish when you're ready.

POLENTA

2 cups whole milk

1 teaspoon kosher salt

1 cup polenta

Extra virgin olive oil

TOPPING

1 tablespoon unsalted butter

1 tablespoon extra virgin olive oil

1 medium yellow onion, halved and cut into ¼-inch slices

Kosher salt

2 ounces goat cheese, crumbled

Honey, to drizzle

---

1. In a medium saucepan over medium-high heat, bring 2 cups water, the milk, and the salt to a boil. Slowly whisk in the polenta. Turn heat to low and continue whisking for 5 minutes, or until the polenta is smooth and creamy. Spread the polenta into a 9-inch square baking dish and set aside to cool.

2. For the topping: While the polenta is setting up, add the butter and olive oil to a heavy-bottomed skillet set over medium-low heat. Add the onion and a sprinkle of salt and cook, stirring occasionally, until soft, golden, and caramelized, 20 to 25 minutes.

3. Pour 1 tablespoon of olive oil into another skillet set over medium heat. Using a 3-inch round cookie or biscuit cutter, cut out circles of the firm polenta and place in the hot skillet. Cook until slightly browned

and crusty on one side, about 2 minutes, then flip and cook the other side, another 2 minutes. Work in batches, adding more oil as needed.

4. To assemble the polenta cakes, arrange them on a plate, top with 1 tablespoon of caramelized onions and about a teaspoon of crumbled goat cheese, and drizzle with honey. Enjoy!

TIPS AND TECHNIQUES

arielleclementine: "I would recommend following the directions on your polenta packaging, since there are so many varieties. Some may need to cook for 20 to 25 minutes before they get thicker and porridge-y."

ABOUT THE COOK

To learn more about arielleclementine, and to read her recipe for Olive all'Ascolana, turn to page 268.

WHAT THE COMMUNITY SAID

Davilchick: "I know I'm six months late, but *this is the best appetizer evah!* I make it all the time now for company. It's a fail-safe for me. I can caramelize the onions ahead of time, so the only time I have to be away from guests is when I heat the polenta."

student epicure: "This looks wonderful—I'm making it tonight! My mom's family is Mennonite, and for breakfast at our reunions, we always eat fried mush, a.k.a. polenta cakes, with tomatoes and maple syrup. I'm excited to try it with the onions, goat cheese, and honey!"

Zesty Herbed Chicken Broth

BY LECHEF | MAKES 3 QUARTS

A&M: Zesty is the perfect adjective to describe this rich, savory broth. We were initially skeptical of lechef's direction to add two entire dried chipotles to the stock, but the resulting spice is balanced and leaves you wanting another spoonful rather than mopping your brow. The broth takes on a russet hue from the dried chiles, and the veggies and herbs add layers to the intense chicken flavor. Lechef says to use a teaspoon or two of black pepper—rather than grinding a pile of pepper, we used a teaspoon of whole peppercorns, which worked nicely.

2 roast chicken carcasses

4 celery ribs, roughly chopped

2 carrots, roughly chopped

1 large white onion, quartered

1 tablespoon chopped cilantro

8 to 10 fresh thyme sprigs

2 fresh rosemary sprigs

2 dried chipotle chile peppers

Salt and freshly ground black pepper

1. Place the chicken carcasses in a 2-gallon stockpot and cover with 4 quarts water.

2. Bring nearly to a boil over high heat, and add the celery, carrots, onion, cilantro, herbs, chiles, 1 tablespoon salt, and 1 teaspoon black pepper. Cover, reduce the heat to low, and simmer for at least 45 minutes. Be sure to add water as needed to keep the chicken covered.

3. Strain the broth, return it to the pot, and taste. Adjust the salt and pepper (you will probably need at least 1 more tablespoon of salt but your taste buds will tell you).

4. Use the broth in your favorite dish, or boil to reduce by half and freeze (this helps to save freezer space). To use, defrost and dilute with an equal part of water.

TIPS AND TECHNIQUES

Lechef: "This broth can be made into an easy chicken noodle soup or can be frozen and stored for later use in risottos, soups, and polentas."

ABOUT THE COOK

Drew Lambert is a furniture designer and amateur chef from New York City.

His favorite recipe from a cookbook: "Pig's Head Torchon from David Chang's *Momofuku.*"

See his recipe for Pasta with Prosciutto, Snap Peas, Mint, and Cream on page 352.

Here's his blog: Le Chef's Kitchen (www.lechefsblog.com).

Feta Frozen Yogurt with Blood Orange and Mint Granita

BY HELENTHENANNY | SERVES 4

A&M: It's rare to come across a recipe that's both sophisticated and economical. Just four ingredients and three simple stages and you have a dessert that's easy enough to whip up for your kids and impressive enough for a dinner party. The granita offers a balanced sprinkling of bitterness and sweetness. And the frozen yogurt (which, by the way, gets very hard in the freezer; leave it out for a bit before scooping) is tangy with lashings of salt and honey. Make sure you use full-fat yogurt, and if you can't find honey-flavored, just buy plain and sweeten it with honey (we did it both ways and each worked out fine). And get ready for a grown-up, faintly subversive dessert. As Helenthenanny wrote, "Greek yogurt and Greek feta were meant to be friends, and served along with the blood orange and mint granita, it's an orgy of ingredient love." We agree wholeheartedly!

FETA FROZEN YOGURT
½ cup soft feta, preferably fresh and packed in water

9 ounces honey-flavored Greek yogurt

BLOOD ORANGE AND MINT GRANITA
2 big, fat, juicy blood oranges

1 handful mint leaves

---

1. Tune your iPod or Pandora Radio to Sarah Vaughan. Or Dinah Washington. Or just play Nancy Wilson's "Peel Me a Grape" on a loop.

2. For the feta frozen yogurt: Get out your immersion blender, or beaters, or your whisk and gumption, and put the feta and 6 ounces of the yogurt into a freezer-safe bowl. Now beat or blend those fellas till they are smooth. Don't worry if there are some tiny chunks of feta; they are going to be little salty bursts of flavor in this sweet dessert.

3. Stir in the remaining 3 ounces yogurt, cover with plastic wrap, and put in the freezer for a few hours or until frozen.

4. For the blood orange and mint granita: Cut the blood oranges in half, run a knife around the inside rim, and gut them with a spoon. Put the guts into a bowl. Don't worry if a bit of rind goes in, we just want as much pulp and juice as possible.

5. Squeeze any leftover juice from the orange peels. Zest the orange peels into the bowl. Throw in the mint leaves and immersion-blend or food-process the mixture till it is quite pulpy. Strain through a fine-mesh sieve. Compost the pulpy remains, or something—we're only using the beautiful blood orange juice infused with mint.

6. Pour the liquid into a freezer-safe baking dish (I used a round cake pan, and it was gangbusters). Freeze for 2 to 3 hours, but do check on it frequently and rake through it with a fork every time it looks like the liquid is freezing, maybe every 30 minutes? Keep an eye out and a fork handy, as it depends how cold your freezer is and which pan you used. My granita looked like glittery flakes of blood orange ice after only 1½ hours or so.

7. Scoop the feta fro-yo into a pretty dish, top with the granita, and turn your music machine to Ella Fitzgerald's version of "Goody Goody," then eat your little treat standing up in the kitchen. And I hope you're satisfied, you rascal you!

TIPS AND TECHNIQUES

Helenthenanny suggests having "a small lemon on hand in case your blood oranges are crazy sweet and you'd prefer a bit more acidity."

If you like a sweeter dessert, add a drizzle of honey on top when serving.

ABOUT THE COOK

For more on Helenthenanny, and to read her recipe for Figgy Pudding Butter Cookies, turn to page 205.

Sweet and Spicy Horseradish Dressing

BY LINZARELLA | MAKES ABOUT ¾ CUP

A&M: It's hard not to love a recipe where the only instructions are essentially zest, scoop, and shake. As written, this dressing comes out nicely positioned between zippy, sweet, and savory, but then linzarella encourages us to customize—a dash more horseradish for the spice fiends, a dollop more crème fraîche for the indulgent—and shake again. The two types of dairy—equal parts tart yogurt and mellow, rich crème fraîche—are an especially smart touch, bringing a tempered zing to the dressing. We think it would be lovely tossed with some chilled poached shrimp and watercress or alongside some crudités.

1 lemon

3 tablespoons crème fraîche

3 tablespoons plain whole-milk yogurt

1 tablespoon honey

2 tablespoons prepared horseradish

2 tablespoons Dijon mustard

Salt and freshly ground black pepper

Zest the lemon, then juice half of it. In a jar, combine the juice and zest with the remaining ingredients and a pinch each of salt and pepper. Stir, then cover the jar and shake. Taste and adjust to make it spicier, creamier, or sweeter to your preference.

ABOUT THE COOK

Lindsay Meisel lives in Oakland, California.

Her favorite recipe from a cookbook: "Winter Squash Soup with Red Chili and Mint from *The Greens Cookbook* by Deborah Madison."

Here's her blog: Different Kind of Human (www.differentkindofhuman.blogspot.com).

WHAT THE COMMUNITY SAID

ChezSuzanne: "I used this in a potato, bean, and radish salad. It was fabulous! Just the right balance of flavors. It's amazing how the honey makes this a real standout."

Rhonda35: "Made this last night and used it to make coleslaw. Delicious! Then, today, I put it on rye bread with thinly sliced pastrami and it was so yummy!"

Meat Loaf with Blackberry Barbecue Sauce

BY DAX PHILLIPS | SERVES 6

A&M: Dax Phillips's meat loaf hews closely to tradition, relying on the classic triumvirate of ground veal, beef, and pork; a little bread and milk; garlic, onion, and Worcestershire sauce. All are thoughtfully fused, producing a savory, light-textured loaf. Dax said, "If you're truly looking for comfort, then come on in." The standout here is the sauce, whose garlic, ginger, and cayenne make sparks fly around the berries. You'll want to eat the sauce by the spoonful—enjoy the snap of the blackberry seeds!

BLACKBERRY BARBECUE SAUCE
2 small onions, peeled and quartered
2 garlic cloves, roughly chopped
2 cups blackberries, fresh or thawed frozen
½ cup light brown sugar
1 tablespoon ground ginger
1 teaspoon cayenne pepper
Salt and freshly ground black pepper

MEAT LOAF
½ pound ground beef
½ pound ground pork

½ pound ground veal
½ cup diced yellow onion
½ teaspoon dried basil
½ teaspoon kosher salt
½ teaspoon cracked black pepper
3 garlic cloves, finely chopped
1 tablespoon Worcestershire sauce
1 large egg, beaten
¾ cup whole milk
3 pieces white bread, crusts removed, torn into small pieces

1. To make the sauce: Put all the ingredients in a blender or food processor and puree until nice and smooth. Add the sauce to a small saucepan and cook over medium-low heat for about 20 minutes, until dark and thick. Stir and remove from the heat.

2. Heat the oven to 350°F. In a large bowl, use clean hands to combine all the meat loaf ingredients. Get in there, and get dirty and greasy from the meat. Place the meat loaf mixture in a 5 × 9-inch or other desired pan and shape it into a loaf. Pour about ½ cup of the barbecue sauce over the top. Bake the meat loaf for 1 to 1½ hours until just cooked through.

3. Let the meat loaf cool for roughly 5 minutes. Meanwhile, warm up the rest of the barbecue sauce. Remove the loaf to a serving dish and drizzle some sauce on the top. Spread more sauce on each plate before slicing and serving.

TIPS AND TECHNIQUES

We halved the spices in the sauce because we're wimps. Start with half and adjust to your taste. And don't opt for lean meats unless you want a dry loaf.

Kevin Purdy: "I gave it a go, and the results were dee-licious. I would consider, next time, letting the sauce reduce more before applying it as a kind of top glaze to the meat loaf, because it tends to break apart in the oven if it's still carrying much blackberry liquid."

ABOUT THE COOK

Dax Phillips is a director of technology in New Berlin, Wisconsin.

His top entertaining tip: "Make sure you have a great appetizer to start, and offer a few bottles of nice wine to loosen things up."

Here's his blog: Simple Comfort Food (www.simplecomfortfood.com).

Yogurt and Spinach Dip "Borani Esfanaaj," in the Persian Manner

BY SHAYMA | SERVES 2 TO 4

A&M: Don't let a little blanching stop you from making this wonderful dip. While it's true that blanching spinach is a pain in the neck, once the water comes to a boil, the whole process is over in a minute, and then you're well on your way to culinary goodness. Shayma smartly heats the blanched and chopped spinach in a little garlic-scented oil and then adds more fresh garlic to the creamy, tangy dip. We love Shayma's backstory, too: "It has been said that Poorandokht, the daughter of the Sassanian Persian King Khosrow Paravaiz, loved cold yogurt-based dishes. When she was proclaimed Queen, the name Poorani was given to yogurt-based dishes. Later on Poorani turned into Borani. I so do like to believe this story."

Two 6-ounce packets baby or regular spinach

1 garlic clove, minced and divided

2 tablespoons olive oil (not extra virgin)

Salt

Two 5.3-ounce tubs very thick, drained yogurt (I use Total Fage Greek yogurt)

Dried mint (please do use dried not fresh mint; the beauty of this dish is in the use of a woodsy, earthy, dried herb)

1 handful crushed walnuts

Your best extra virgin olive oil

Lavash or whole wheat pita bread, for serving

1. Blanch the spinach briefly in a pot of boiling water.

2. Drain well, making sure to get all the liquid out. Chop fine.

3. Sauté half the minced garlic in the 2 tablespoons olive oil. Add the spinach and a pinch of salt. Stir for a few minutes.

4. Set the spinach aside to cool, then squeeze out any excess liquid.

5. In a bowl, gently stir together the yogurt, the remaining garlic, and the spinach. Add salt to taste.

6. Transfer to the serving bowl (I use a shallow, round bowl) and sprinkle with dried mint, the crushed walnuts, and a lazy trail of your best olive oil.

7. Serve with lavash or whole wheat pita.

TIPS AND TECHNIQUES

Don't worry about squeezing the spinach in Step 4, unless it looks particularly soppy. Do use whole-milk Greek yogurt–the low-fat stuff will be watery and joyless. Use a wide, shallow dish so you have room to spread out the dip, making a broad landing pad for the oil, mint, and walnuts. And reach for your best olive oil for sprinkling over the top.

Shayma said: "This creamy appetizer is lovely with some lavash (flatbread from Iran) or some crisped-up-in-the-oven whole wheat pita bread. The combination of spinach, garlic, thick and creamy yogurt, walnuts, and mint begs for a Pinot Gris from Alsace."

ABOUT THE COOK

Shayma Owaise Saadat is an economist living in Toronto, Canada. She writes about the foods of "Pakistan, Afghanistan, Iran and beyond" on her blog (see below).

Her favorite recipe from a cookbook: "I can't say that I have a favorite recipe, but my favorite cookbook is Claudia Roden's *The New Book of Middle Eastern Food.* It is my go-to book for entertaining–everything from kibbeh to batoursh to ma'moul."

Her favorite cooking tip: "Always soak your basmati rice for at least an hour to ensure–in the words of the women in my family–that 'each cooked grain is like the eyelashes of a young girl: elongated, separated, curved, and slender.'"

Her favorite entertaining tip: "In the words of Ami, my mother, 'For a dinner party, always cook for double the amount of people you have invited; this will make your neighbors happy the following day.'"

Here's her blog: The Spice Spoon (www.thespicespoon.com).

WHAT THE COMMUNITY SAID

arielleclementine: "We had this last night and all agreed it was the best spinach dip we'd ever had. I love, loved it! Thank you so much for sharing the recipe. I'll make it for years to come."

Couscous with Roasted Fennel and Toasted Almonds

BY JENNIFER ANN | SERVES 4

A&M: This is a dish whose simplicity belies its depth of flavor. Its success is dependent on little touches like plumping the raisins in fresh orange juice, incorporating chopped fennel fronds as well as roasted wedges of the bulb itself, and using loads of minced shallot to add sweetness and bite to a basic sherry vinaigrette. Jennifer Ann has you fold all of the ingredients except for the roasted fennel and toasted almonds into the delicate, springy couscous, and then arrange the fennel and almonds over the top for a lovely presentation.

⅓ cup black raisins

Juice of 1 orange (about ½ cup)

1 fennel bulb, trimmed and cored and cut into about 16 slim wedges

3 tablespoons good-quality olive oil

Salt and freshly ground black pepper

¼ cup whole almonds

1¼ cups chicken stock

1 cup couscous

1 large shallot (or 2 small), minced

1 tablespoon sherry vinegar

1 to 2 tablespoons chopped fennel fronds

Coarse sea salt, such as Maldon

---

1. Soak the raisins in the orange juice until they plump up, 1 to 2 hours; strain and set aside.

2. Heat the oven to 350°F. Toss the fennel wedges in 1 tablespoon of the olive oil and season with salt and pepper to taste. Spread on a baking sheet lined with parchment paper or aluminum foil and roast for 12 to 15 minutes, until the fennel wedges are softening but still have a little bite and the edges are beginning to brown.

3. Toast the almonds in a separate pan in the oven until lightly browned, 5 to 7 minutes; cool, coarsely chop, and set aside.

4. Meanwhile, bring the chicken stock to a boil in a small saucepan over high heat; add the couscous, stir, cover, and remove from the heat. Let rest for about 15 minutes until all of the stock is absorbed.

5. In a separate bowl, whisk together the shallot and vinegar, then whisk in the remaining 2 tablespoons olive oil; add salt and pepper to taste.

6. Transfer the couscous to a serving bowl and fluff with a fork. Stir in the orange-soaked raisins and the fennel fronds and toss with enough of the vinaigrette to lightly coat everything—be sure to include all of the shallot bits.

7. Top with the roasted fennel and almonds; finish with a sprinkling of ground pepper and a pinch of coarse sea salt.

TIPS AND TECHNIQUES

Jennifer Ann recommends serving this with roast chicken, and we agree. She also says you can use vegetable stock or water to lighten the couscous.

AntoniaJames says: "Bet this would be great with pine nuts."

ABOUT THE COOK

Jennifer Vandenplas does international patent research in Milwaukee, Wisconsin.

Her favorite recipe from a cookbook: "Lamb Skewers with Lima Bean Puree and French Feta Salsa Verde from Suzanne Goin's *Sunday Suppers at Lucques.*"

Her favorite entertaining tip: "Always be ready to set a few more places at the table for any last-minute guests."

WHAT THE COMMUNITY SAID

1devo: "I have started making this on practically a biweekly basis. Easy, and so delish! Best way to eat the next day: cold, with a fried egg or two on top!"

Bell-less, Whistle-less, Damn Good French Toast

Spring

Preserved Lemon and Spring Vegetable Risotto with Grilled Pernod Shrimp

BY THE DOG'S BREAKFAST | SERVES 6 TO 8

A&M: We'll never turn down a spring risotto that's flush with asparagus and peas, but we've come to expect a rich and buttery dish that tamps down the seasonal embellishments. Not so here—The Dog's Breakfast, who described this risotto as a "celebration of the verdant flavors of asparagus, pea, fennel and mint," uses anise-scented Pernod and lemon juice to brighten the rice and broiled sweet shrimp to underscore the clean flavors in the asparagus and peas. Plan this dish for your next dinner party (and save the shrimp portion of the recipe to grill for weeknight dinners).

SHRIMP

24 to 32 large deveined shrimp, shell on

3 tablespoons olive oil

2 tablespoons Pernod, or other anise apéritif

3 garlic cloves, minced (about 1 tablespoon)

Zest of ½ large lemon

2 teaspoons finely chopped rosemary leaves

1 teaspoon kosher salt

½ teaspoon freshly ground black pepper

RISOTTO

1 bunch asparagus, woody stems removed, cut into 2-inch lengths

6 to 8 cups chicken stock

¼ cup olive oil

2 medium onions, chopped

1 small fennel bulb, chopped

4 garlic cloves, minced (about 1 tablespoon)

Fine sea salt

2 cups Arborio rice

½ cup Pernod, or other anise apéritif

½ cup lemon juice

3 tablespoons unsalted butter

½ cup mascarpone

2 tablespoons rinsed and finely diced preserved lemon rind

¼ cup coarsely chopped mint leaves

2 cups peas (frozen are fine)

Freshly ground white pepper

---

1. In a shallow dish just large enough to hold the shrimp, mix the shrimp with the olive oil, Pernod, garlic, lemon zest, rosemary, and salt and pepper. Let the shrimp marinate at room temperature while you make the risotto.

2. Prepare all the risotto ingredients: Blanch the asparagus for 1 minute in salted, boiling water and set aside. Heat the stock in a medium saucepan over low heat. Have everything measured and close at hand by the stove. Once you start stirring risotto, there's no stopping.

3. Heat the olive oil in a large Dutch oven. Add the onions, fennel, and garlic and sweat over low heat for about 10 minutes until soft and translucent. Season with salt to taste, about halfway through.

4. Add the rice and raise the heat to medium-high. Stir to coat and slightly toast the rice, about 3 minutes. You should hear a lively crackling in the pot. The rice will take on a shiny, translucent coat.

5. Add the Pernod and lemon juice to the rice and continue stirring until the liquid is almost completely absorbed.

6. Add a ladleful of hot stock to the rice and continue stirring. It's important to regulate the heat at this point. The rice should neither boil vigorously nor cook too slowly. You're looking for an even, medium heat that gives the rice a billowy loft and brings some bubbles to the surface.

7. As the stock is absorbed, continue adding it by ladlefuls and stirring. If you watch carefully, you'll see that toward the end the rice really gives itself over to the liquid, releasing its starch to make a kind of cream. Stop incorporating stock once the rice is creamy but still al dente, cooked but not too soft. This should take between 20 and 30 minutes, and between 6 and 8 cups of stock.

8. Remove the risotto from the heat and immediately fold in the butter, mascarpone, preserved lemon rind, most of the

mint (save some for garnish), the peas, and several grinds of white pepper. The heat of the risotto will cook the peas. Stir slowly to blend, check a final time for seasoning, and carefully fold in the asparagus. Put a lid on the risotto and let it rest while you prepare the shrimp. The risotto will expand slightly in volume, and take on a marvelous sheen.

9. Grill or broil the shrimp for about 60 seconds on each side, or until the flesh is completely opaque.

10. Top each serving of the risotto with 4 shrimp, garnish with the remaining mint and a flourish of pepper, and serve.

TIPS AND TECHNIQUES

The Dog's Breakfast said: "We love this with grilled shrimp, but well-seared scallops or fillets of black cod or sea bass will also do very well. Depending on the saltiness of both your stock and the preserved lemons, you may need to use up to a tablespoon of salt in this recipe. It's best to add a little at a time throughout the process, tasting as you go, and seasoning one last time if necessary before serving. You can replace the preserved lemon rind with the zest of a large lemon, but reduce the amount of lemon juice by half if you do. Following the ban on absinthe in 1915, anise-based liqueur became the favorite long-drink of French gourmands from Paris to Marseille. Pour one-fifth liqueur to four-fifths water over ice, and serve little picholine olives on the side. Sunshine in a glass."

How to preserve lemons, by The Dog's Breakfast: "Cut 4 or 5 medium lemons almost in half lengthwise, then make a second cut perpendicular to the first, exposing four 'quarters' of flesh. Sprinkle the flesh of each lemon with a generous tablespoon of kosher salt, and then stuff them into a jar just large enough to hold them. Really squish them in. Let the jar sit overnight on the counter. In the morning, if the lemons aren't covered with exuded juice, add enough fresh lemon juice to cover them. Put a lid on the jar and put the jar in the fridge. Shake it well once a day, and after about two weeks you'll have preserved lemons. You can add things to the lemons—coriander or fennel seeds, Old Bay spice, fresh bay leaves, and so on. Works really well with limes, too."

ABOUT THE COOK

David Rollins and Robert Lee live in Montreal. Together, they produce the blog The Dog's Breakfast (www.the-dogs-breakfast.com)—Rollins writes and Lee takes care of the visuals.

Their favorite recipe from a cookbook: "Bob Blumer's Caesar salad dressing from *The Surreal Gourmet*. We've been making this at least once a month for the past eight years. Could make it blindfolded, and still can't believe how good it is."

Their favorite cooking tip: "Learn to salt. We use three different salts in day-to-day cooking: a kosher salt, a fine sea salt, and fleur de sel. Feeling, seeing, tasting, and eventually knowing which salt to use, in what amount, at what moment, has taught us a lot about how to build flavor into a dish."

WHAT THE COMMUNITY SAID

BrooklynBridget: "I just have to say, this recipe just keeps on giving! Last night, used same flavor combination with green beans, kale, and pasta. So so lovely and light."

The Obsessive Cook: "This was wonderful! A great excuse to finally use the preserved lemons I made a month ago. For a little decoration I sprinkled some of the wispy leaves from the fennel on top. Worked nicely and tasted good."

Saffron Semifreddo with Cherry-Cardamom Syrup and Salted Honey Hazelnuts

BY BRENNA | SERVES 6

A&M: Brenna knows her way around a pastry kitchen. "This recipe," she wrote, "was inspired by my final project in culinary school, placing saffron in dessert and letting it shine by sweet deliverance." While this isn't the quickest recipe, no one part is difficult and every little step contributes exponentially to its flavor. You'll love the semifreddo alone, but the cardamom-infused cherries toss in bursts of acidity and the salted nuts add woodsiness and crunch. Don't change a thing about the recipe, except maybe to double it.

SAFFRON SEMIFREDDO
5 egg yolks
½ cup sugar
¼ teaspoon saffron threads
1 tablespoon sweet vermouth
1 cup heavy cream

CHERRY-CARDAMOM SYRUP AND SALTED
HONEY HAZELNUTS
½ cup dried, unsweetened cherries
¼ cup sugar

1 teaspoon ground cardamom, toasted
½ cup dry white wine
¼ cup fresh lemon juice
½ cup hazelnuts
1 teaspoon extra virgin olive oil
1 teaspoon sea salt
2 teaspoons honey

---

1. Prepare a small saucepan of boiling water or a double boiler and bring the water to a gentle simmer. Have ready an ice water bath big enough for the base of the double boiler or mixing bowl.

2. In a medium mixing bowl or the pan of the double boiler, combine the egg yolks, sugar, and saffron threads. Place the bowl over the gently simmering water and whisk constantly until the mixture is thick and doubled, 5 to 6 minutes.

3. Remove the bowl from the heat and place it in the ice water bath, continuing to stir to bring down the temperature. (If the mixture gets too cold and is sticking to the bottom of the pan, it will release easily if you run hot water on the outside of the bowl.)

4. In the bowl of an electric mixer and using the paddle attachment, whip the egg yolk mixture with the sweet vermouth until it becomes thick and pale in color, 4 to 5 minutes.

5. As the mixer is going, whip the heavy cream in a separate bowl until soft peaks form (this can also be done ahead of time).

6. With a spatula, add a third of the whipped cream to the egg mixture and stir together gently to lift the base. Fold the remaining whipped cream into the egg mixture. When this is done, you can spoon the mixture into 6 individual ramekins or leave it in the mixing bowl. Cover the ramekins or bowl with plastic wrap and freeze until firm, at least 6 hours.

7. For the cherry-cardamom syrup: Combine the cherries, sugar, cardamom, wine, lemon juice, and ¼ cup water in a small saucepan and bring to a boil over medium-high heat. Reduce the heat and simmer until the mixture has reduced by half and coats the back of a spoon. Set the syrup aside to cool.

8. For the salted honey hazelnuts: Heat the oven to 350°F.

9. Place the hazelnuts in a small mixing bowl and toss with the olive oil and sea salt. Add the honey and toss once more to coat.

10. Transfer the nuts to a baking sheet lined with parchment paper and toast, stirring at least once, until the nuts are golden, about 10 minutes. Remove from the oven, let cool completely, and roughly chop.

11. To serve, run a butter knife under hot water and cut around the edge of the ramekin to invert the semifreddo onto individual plates. Or, if you prefer, use a hot spoon to scoop the semifreddo from the mixing bowl. Serve with the Cherry-Cardamom Syrup and Salted Honey Hazelnuts.

TIPS AND TECHNIQUES

Brenna said: "My favorite part about making this is that you can make the semifreddo (the diligent part) first and simply finish the other two components while the custard freezes. I prefer to serve mine scooped straight from the bowl for a rustic presentation. A bonus to this recipe is you can use the leftover egg whites for macaroons or for making an omelet for lunch."

amanda: "Another great thing about this semifreddo is that if you leave it out to soften a little bit before serving, and then forget about it until it's almost room temperature, like I did tonight, it's still terrific. It becomes mousselike and very delicate. I'd happily serve it either way."

ABOUT THE COOK

Brenna is a private chef based in Reno, Nevada.

Her favorite entertaining tip: "The invitation seems to be an overlooked detail for simple get-togethers. Nothing says "Come eat at my home" like the personal touch of the host's penmanship on an envelope, or delivery by mail. Did I mention how much fun selecting or creating your own invitations can be?"

Here's her blog: Honey + Fig (www.honeyandfig.com).

WHAT THE COMMUNITY SAID

cheese1227: "I made this for Easter dinner dessert. It was fabulous for me because I could make all of the different bits of this recipe on Saturday and just assemble it once we'd digested our lamb a bit on Sunday afternoon. Rave reviews from everyone at the table (it was an 18–0 vote, with one abstention for health reasons), even the three-year-old who passed up the sugar cookies in favor of the the 'yellow ice cream'! The flavors in this combination are exceptional."

Leg of Lamb with Garlic Sauce

BY CHEFJUNE | SERVES 8 GENEROUSLY

A&M: A classic leg of lamb at first glance, this recipe by ChefJune has several details that make it exceptional—as she noted, "it's the highlight of one of the most requested classes I have ever taught." The leg is larded not only with garlic, but with pieces of anchovy, too, which infuse the meat with a rich brininess. A generous crust of herbs renders it fragrant, while a simple sauce of sautéed garlic (24 cloves!) and red wine, mixed with pan drippings, makes the lamb even more juicy and robust.

LAMB

One 5-pound leg of lamb, bone in (I especially like a long shinbone for presentation)

6 large garlic cloves, slivered

12 anchovy fillets, coarsely chopped

1 tablespoon finely chopped fresh rosemary

1 tablespoon finely chopped fresh thyme

Sea salt and freshly ground black pepper

2 tablespoons extra virgin olive oil

GARLIC SAUCE

2 tablespoons olive oil

24 garlic cloves, peeled, left whole

1 cup dry red wine (such as Côtes-du-Rhône)

Sea salt and freshly ground black pepper

2 tablespoons finely chopped parsley (preferably flat-leaf)

---

1. Have your butcher prepare the meat by removing most of the fat and skin from the leg, and by removing most of the bare bone that protrudes from the leg. If you want a slightly smaller leg, have him (or her!) shorten it from the hip end. When you're ready to roast it, trim the lamb of any excess fat. Make many slits all over the lamb and insert a sliver of garlic and a piece of anchovy into each incision. Mix the herbs with sea salt and pepper to taste in a small bowl. Rub the lamb with the olive oil and the herb mixture. Let it stand at room temperature for 1 to 2 hours.

2. Heat the oven to 425°F. Place the meat on a rack in a roasting pan and cook, uncovered, for 20 minutes. Reduce the heat to 350°F and cook for 40 to 45 minutes longer for medium-rare (how it's supposed to be!). The temperature on an instant-read thermometer should register 130°F.

3. Meanwhile, to make the sauce, heat the olive oil in a heavy skillet and cook the garlic cloves slowly for about 10 minutes, or until they are soft (don't let the edges get crisp or brown). Set the sauce aside in a small bowl to finish once the lamb is cooked.

4. Remove the lamb to a warmed platter and turn off the oven. Cover with an aluminum foil tent and set it in a warm place while you finish the sauce. On top of the stove, pour the wine into the roasting pan, scraping the bottom well to loosen any brown bits or caramelized juices, and cook the wine over a high flame to reduce it by about one-third. Add the reduced liquid to the garlic cloves. Mash well with a fork and mix in sea salt and pepper to taste.

5. Slice the lamb and grind some fresh black pepper over it. Spoon on the sauce and sprinkle it all with freshly chopped parsley.

TIPS AND TECHNIQUES

Make sure to test the temperature frequently toward the end—the last thing you want is 5 pounds of overcooked lamb!

ChefJune: "There are two wines that pair magnificently with this dish. Not surprisingly, they both come from Provence: Châteauneuf-du-Pape (my favorite is Clos des Papes) and Bandol Rouge (I love those from Domaine Tempier inordinately!). If you are on a budget, a Côtes-du-Rhône will do admirably."

ABOUT THE COOK

June Jacobs, CCP, is a food and wine educator, consultant, and writer living in New York.

Her blog is Feastivals (www.feastivals.com).

Her favorite recipe from a cookbook: "This week it's Sausage Sauce from *Cremaldi Cookbook* by Catherine Cremaldi."

Her favorite entertaining tip: "When serving a meal to guests, don't invite too many people. It's another case of less is more."

WHAT THE COMMUNITY SAID

Furey and the Feast: "I love that underneath the herbed crust, there's a world of garlic. This sounds outrageous, in a good way."

Meyer Lemon Macarons

BY DOLCETTOCONFECTIONS | MAKES 20

A&M: An excellent recipe in every way. DolcettoConfections demystifies French *macarons*, and you'll discover just how easy they are to make. To get the confectioners' sugar and almonds ground finely enough, we had to use the blender, which required a fair amount of shaking and scraping and digging—between whirring!—to make sure the almonds close to the blade didn't turn to paste. But it's worth it for the fine texture. And while the curd takes vigorous whisking over the stove, it turns out as light as whipped cream and just as tempting to eat by the spoonful. Not that we did. Ahem.

MEYER LEMON CURD
2 large eggs
2 egg yolks
⅓ cup sugar
⅓ cup Meyer lemon juice
1 tablespoon Meyer lemon zest (packed)
¼ teaspoon kosher salt
6 tablespoons unsalted butter, cubed

MACARONS
3 large egg whites, aged at room temperature for 24 hours (see Tips and Techniques)
2½ tablespoons sugar
⅔ cup blanched almonds
1 cup plus 2 tablespoons unsifted confectioners' sugar

1. In a medium metal bowl, whisk the eggs, egg yolks, sugar, lemon juice, zest, and salt to blend well.

2. Set the bowl over a saucepan of simmering water (do not allow the bottom of the bowl to touch the water).

3. Whisk constantly until the mixture thickens and an instant-read thermometer inserted into the mixture registers 170°F to 172°F, 5 to 6 minutes. Do not allow the mixture to boil.

4. Remove the bowl from the water. Whisk the butter into the curd, 2 or 3 cubes at a time, allowing it to melt before adding more and whisking until the curd is smooth.

5. Press plastic wrap directly onto the surface of the curd and refrigerate overnight or for several hours.

6. Make the macarons: Put the egg whites in the bowl of a standing mixer. Whisk on low to medium speed until frothy. Add the sugar, a little bit at a time. Allow the sugar to incorporate fully before making the next addition.

7. When all of the sugar has been added, increase the speed to medium and allow the meringue to form stiff peaks. To test, remove the bowl from the mixer and turn it upside down. There should be no movement in the meringue.

8. Combine the blanched almonds and confectioners' sugar in a food processor. Process until you cannot distinguish the almonds from the sugar, about 30 seconds, scraping down the sides of the bowl as necessary.

9. Add half of the almond-sugar mixture to the meringue. Using a strong spatula, begin combining the two elements. During this first combination, you actually want to combine them rather vigorously. Do not be gentle—you have to reduce the air in the meringue somewhat or your macarons will be too puffy. Continue for 10 to 15 turns.

10. Add half of the remaining almond-sugar mixture and incorporate for 15 to 20 turns. Fold the remaining almond-sugar mixture gently into the meringue, for no more than 10 turns, or until you can no longer distinguish between the two.

11. Fit a pastry bag with a #806 tip (½-inch diameter). Pipe 1-inch rounds onto a baking sheet lined with parchment paper or a Silpat. Leave plenty of room between the macarons—they will expand! Allow the macarons to sit 30 minutes to 1 hour to develop a shell.

12. Heat the oven to 300°F. Bake the macarons for 10 to 12 minutes until the shells are just slightly golden. Cool on the baking sheet on a wire rack.

13. When the shells are completely cool, pipe or spread the Meyer lemon curd on the flat side of one macaron and sandwich with another.

TIPS AND TECHNIQUES

DolcettoConfections says: "The egg whites should age, outside the shell, for about 24 hours prior to making the macarons. I usually separate the egg whites into a small plastic container, cover, and place in the coolest part of my kitchen. If you place them in a bowl, just be sure to loosely cover the whites with plastic wrap. Aging the whites for 24 hours helps extract the moisture, which in turn helps create a "foot" (the base of the macaron) the same width as the shell. It also helps reduce cracking in the shell when they are baking."

ABOUT THE COOK

Alison M. Veinote is a pastry cook and blogger living in New York.

Her favorite recipe from a cookbook: "Roasted Potato Leek Soup from Ina Garten's *Back to Basics*—an absolutely perfect soup to warm you thoroughly on a cold winter's night."

Here's her blog: Dolcetto Confections (www.dolcettoconfections.blogspot.com).

WHAT THE COMMUNITY SAID

Chef Michael: "Creamy, light, elegant, and perfectly sized. Try to eat just one, I dare you."

Luciana's Porchetta

BY ALIWAKS | SERVES 6 TO 8

A&M: We think porchetta should become a staple in everyone's kitchen. It's inexpensive, requires little but marinating and oven time, and produces a roast that's robustly flavored and goes with most anything. Aliwaks's version is brilliant: she has you toast the spices and combine them with fresh rosemary, garlic, and orange zest. By the time the roast emerges from the oven, your entire neighborhood smells like an Italian trattoria. The first time around, make the porchetta with ½ tablespoon red pepper flakes and if that doesn't do it for you, then feel free to increase it to a full tablespoon.

1½ tablespoons black peppercorns

1 tablespoon fennel seeds

1 tablespoon coriander seeds

½ to 1 tablespoon crushed red pepper flakes

1½ tablespoons coarse salt

1 tablespoon chopped fresh rosemary

1 tablespoon finely grated orange zest

5 garlic cloves, mashed with a fork

3 tablespoons olive oil

6 pounds butterflied pork shoulder

3 bay leaves

1 piece pork skin, large enough to cover the shoulder like a pashmina shawl, or 9 thin slices pancetta

½ cup good red wine vinegar

---

1. Toast the spices and the salt in small, heavy-bottomed pan until fragrant, then crush with a mortar and pestle or in a mini chopper. The spices should be rather coarse, not powdered. (I am not ashamed to admit I use a Magic Bullet blender that I bought on TV; it grinds beautifully and makes smoothies.)

2. Mix the spices with the rosemary, orange zest, and garlic. Add olive oil till it makes a paste.

3. Slather the pork in the spice paste and place in a large plastic bag with the bay leaves; put it in the refrigerator overnight or for up to 3 days. Remember to smoosh it around whenever you happen to go into the refrigerator.

4. Heat the oven to 325°F; bring the pork to room temperature.

5. Take the pork out of the bag, turn it inside out, and rub some spice paste over the inside of the pork skin.

6. Roll the pork into a cylindrical shape and tie it with butcher twine at 1-inch intervals. Stick the bay leaves under the middle strings, and lay the skin over the top. (If using pancetta, lay the slices across the top, overlapping like fish scales.)

7. Place the pork in a roasting pan with a rack and roast until the internal temperature reaches 150°F, 1½ to 2½ hours. Depending on your oven, you may need to rotate it every so often. Remove and let sit until the temperature gets to about 160°F.

8. Remove the skin, scraping off the fat (if you like), and cut it into strips with a sharp set of shears (say that four times fast!) to serve. (The pancetta will crisp, so simply break it into small pieces for serving alongside the porchetta.)

9. Deglaze the roasting pan with the vinegar. Don't reduce too much—just enough to get rid of some of the sharpness (this is more like a porky vinaigrette).

10. To serve: Slice the porchetta into ¼-inch slices, add a strip of skin (or pancetta) to each plate (or pile atop if serving en masse on a platter), and drizzle with the sauce.

11. Serve with garlicky bitter greens and roasted or mashed potatoes or escarole and white beans.

TIPS AND TECHNIQUES

Aliwaks said: "This is definitely one of the those get to know your butcher times (though I think you should always get to know your butcher; they offer a world of knowledge, and they're often supernice and flirty in a good way)."

ABOUT THE COOK

Learn more about Aliwaks, and read her winning recipe for Smoky Fried Chickpeas, on page 123. You can also find her recipe for Cowboy Rubbed Rib-eye with Chocolate Stout Pan Sauce on page 182.

WHAT THE COMMUNITY SAID

Midge: "Made this last night: foolproof and *de*lish. Thanks, Aliwaks, you've got my vote."

BEHIND THE SCENES

This recipe, along with the next one, Chewy Sugar Cookies #2, faced off against *Cook's Illustrated* in a smackdown on Slate.com.

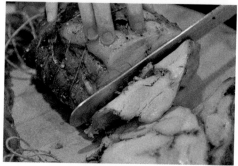

Chewy Sugar Cookies #2

BY MRSLARKIN | MAKES ABOUT 2 DOZEN

A&M: Mrslarkin's classic sugar cookie makes use of three sugars: granulated, light brown, and turbinado. The granulated sugar gives the cookie a foundation of sweetness, the light brown adds caramel notes, and the turbinado's there for a little snap. The cookies are crisp and buttery on the edges and chewy through the center. Mrslarkin added, "One of the things I like best about this sugar cookie is that it's not tooth-achingly sweet. It's got a nice proportion of crunch-to-chew. The inspiration behind this cookie came from the *New York Times*'s chocolate chip cookie recipe, printed March 1, 2000, one of the best chewy cookies I've ever tasted." Perfect for dunking and ice cream sandwiches, we think!

8 tablespoons (1 stick) unsalted butter, at room temperature

½ cup granulated sugar

¼ cup light brown sugar

2 teaspoons vanilla extract

1 large egg

1½ cups unbleached all-purpose flour (I use King Arthur)

½ teaspoon sea salt

¼ teaspoon baking soda

1 cup turbinado or coarse sugar, for rolling

1. Heat the oven to 375°F. Line 2 large sheet pans with parchment paper.

2. Using a standing or handheld mixer, beat the butter, granulated sugar, and light brown sugar for 1 minute. Scrape the sides of the bowl. Continue beating for another minute. Scrape the bowl again.

3. Add the vanilla and beat for 1 minute. Scrape the sides of the bowl.

4. Add the egg and beat for 1 minute. Scrape the sides of the bowl.

5. Add the flour, salt, and baking soda, and beat for 1 minute. Scrape the sides of the bowl and beat for another minute.

6. Put the turbinado sugar in a small, shallow bowl. Using a small cookie/ice cream scoop (mine is 1½ inches in diameter), scoop balls of dough and drop a few at a time in the turbinado sugar and gently roll them around. Place the balls of dough on the parchment-lined sheet pans, leaving about 1½ inches of space around each. My pans fit 12 cookies very comfortably. Do not press the balls down. This will ensure a chewy middle.

7. Bake for 8 to 10 minutes, turning and reversing the pans midway through baking. Resist the urge to bake your cookies longer, or they won't be chewy. The tops don't get much color, but the bottoms do.

8. Place the pans on cooling racks, removing the cookies to the racks after a few minutes. When cool, store the cookies in airtight containers.

TIPS AND TECHNIQUES

If you use a dark, nonstick baking sheet, reduce the oven temperature by 25°F (this is a good general rule for all baking).

Mrslarkin: "I've made these into ice cream sandwiches using coffee ice cream, and rolling the sides in more turbinado—so good!"

ABOUT THE COOK

To learn more about Mrslarkin, and to read her recipe for Lemon Posset, turn to page 271.

WHAT THE COMMUNITY SAID

mcs3000: "Made these again—can't thank you enough. The turbinado sugar is like icing on the cake. Your recipe actually replaced an old family recipe as my fave."

mdm: "YUM! My three-year-old, Simone, and I had such fun making and eating these together over the weekend—thank you! I don't have much of a sweet tooth but I have gobbled these up—perfect level of sweetness for my taste."

Tuscan Chicken Liver Pâté

BY GLUTTONFORLIFE | MAKES ABOUT 2 DOZEN CROSTINI

A&M: "An old boyfriend, obsessed with all things Italian, taught me to make this deliciously intense spread that rivals anything your Jewish grandmother served," said gluttonforlife. Her Tuscan Chicken Liver Pâté is a rich dose of umami spread on grilled country bread. Unlike typical French versions, this Italian-inspired pâté gets its seasoning from anchovy, capers, and Parmesan—giving it a well-rounded, nuanced salting—in addition to aromatic sage, shallot, and garlic. And cooking the wine down in two stages helps draw in every bit of flavor from the deep brown chicken liver sauce.

---

1 pound organic chicken livers

2 tablespoons unsalted butter

2 tablespoons extra virgin olive oil

2 large shallots, thinly sliced

1 large garlic clove, smashed

3 anchovy fillets (or 1 tablespoon anchovy paste)

1 tablespoon capers, minced

4 to 6 sage leaves

Salt and freshly ground black pepper

⅔ cup dry white wine

½ teaspoon grated lemon zest

½ cup grated Parmesan

Grilled country bread, for serving

---

1. Trim any sinew from the livers and dry them well with paper towels.

2. In a large skillet, melt the butter and olive oil over medium-high heat. Sauté the shallots, garlic, anchovies, capers, and sage until the shallots are lightly browned, 6 minutes or so.

3. Season the chicken livers with salt and pepper and add them to the pan. Cook over high heat until browned, then add ⅓ cup of the wine and keep stirring with a wooden spoon, breaking up the livers as they start to cook through. When the wine is absorbed, add the remaining ⅓ cup and repeat the process.

4. Remove from the heat and transfer the mixture to a food processor. Process until quite smooth, then add the lemon zest and Parmesan and process again. Taste and add salt or pepper as needed. Serve warm or at room temperature; spread on grilled country bread.

TIPS AND TECHNIQUES

Be sure to dry the livers well, and wear an apron—they spatter and pop like mad when sautéing.

For a looser, more mousselike spread, we recommend that you don't let all of the liquid evaporate from the pan, but you can always adjust the consistency as you buzz it in the food processor by drizzling in olive oil, water, or even wine (depending on how unctuous or boozy you like your pâté).

Gluttonforlife added: "Serve this with traditionally thin crostini or thicker grilled country bread, and maybe even a garnish of fried sage leaves."

ABOUT THE COOK

Laura Chávez Silverman is a writer and blogger living in Eldred, New York.

Her favorite recipe from a cookbook: "Green Wrapped Flavor Bundles from *Hot Sour Salty Sweet* by Jeffrey Alford and Naomi Duguid."

Here's her blog: Glutton for Life (www.gluttonforlife.com).

WHAT THE COMMUNITY SAID

humblecook: "I made this last night and it was so sensational my husband and I sat down and ate it warm straight from the food processor. This is a fabulous recipe, so simple, yet such rich flavors—thank you for sharing it."

thirschfeld: "Just finished making this and I am eating it for breakfast right now. I am afraid I won't be able to stop. This is going to the top of my liver pâté list."

Absurdly Addictive Asparagus

BY KAYKAY | SERVES 4

A&M: The title pretty much says it all. With her recipe, kaykay takes an already promising set of ingredients and artfully combines them in such a way that the resulting dish exceeds the sum of its parts. Two-inch lengths of asparagus, crisp-tender to the bite, take center stage in a savory tangle of leeks, pancetta, garlic, orange zest, parsley, and pine nuts. The rendered fat from the pancetta (we love kaykay's assertion that "bacon may rule, but its Italian cousin, pancetta, is also a contender for the crown"), along with a knob of butter, is just enough to save the vegetables from being dry without smothering the fresh flavors. The recipe is supposed to serve four, but we could easily imagine polishing off an entire pan by ourselves.

---

4 ounces pancetta, cut into 3/8-inch to ¼-inch dice

1 tablespoon unsalted butter

1 pound asparagus, woody ends trimmed, sliced into 2-inch pieces on the bias

1¼ cups thinly sliced leeks (white and pale green parts only)

2 garlic cloves, minced

Zest of 1 lemon

1 teaspoon orange zest

2 tablespoons toasted pine nuts

1 to 2 tablespoons chopped flat-leaf parsley

Salt and freshly ground black pepper

---

1. In a large nonstick pan, sauté the pancetta over medium heat, stirring frequently, until crisp and lightly golden.

2. Add the butter to the pan. Add the asparagus and leeks and sauté until the asparagus is tender-crisp, 3 to 4 minutes.

3. Add the garlic, lemon and orange zests, pine nuts, and parsley and sauté until fragrant, about 1 minute. Season to taste with salt and freshly ground pepper and serve immediately.

TIPS AND TECHNIQUES

Kaykay: "I think this dish is pretty versatile. It could easily go with a roast chicken, herb-roasted pork, or even a steak. It can go with anything where the flavors are simple—for example, a steak seasoned with salt and pepper and finished with some herbs and garlic would be great. Or perhaps a special roast chicken like the Wishbone Roast Chicken with Herb Butter recipe created by monkeymom" (page 283).

She also advised: "I tried adding Parmigiano Reggiano at the end, but it overpowered the citrus."

ABOUT THE COOK

Karen Kwan is a creative director living in the San Francisco Bay area.

Her top cooking tips: "Use aluminum-free baking powder for more delicately flavored baked goods. If you like thin, crispy cookies, cream the butter and sugar longer. (The air bubbles cause the cookies to rise and since they aren't contained, they spread out more.)"

WHAT THE COMMUNITY SAID

WinnieAb: "My mom made a double batch of this recipe over the weekend and I happily ate all of the leftovers . . . delicious!"

Rosemary Ciabatta with Stout Beer

BY CHEZSUZANNE | MAKES 2 BOULES

A&M: ChezSuzanne recalled: "One of my big surprises when I was in school was that I discovered I *loved* making bread. This is a flavorful dough that I created then and have continued to tweak." As she notes, using a poolish (pre-ferment) makes for an extra crisp crust and a lovely, air pocket–filled crumb. The bread is a gorgeous caramel color from the combination of stout, malt syrup, and honey, and the resulting loaf is chewy with a pleasant tang from the beer. The sea salt on top lends a savory crunch, and there's plenty of rosemary to go around (if you prefer a subtler flavor, you can decrease the amount by half—we liked it woodsy!).

POOLISH (PRE-FERMENT)
¼ teaspoon instant yeast (⅜ teaspoon if using active dry yeast)
7½ ounces (1½ cups) bread flour (I recommend King Arthur bread flour)

ROSEMARY CIABATTA WITH STOUT BEER
15 ounces (3 cups) bread flour (I recommend King Arthur bread flour)
¼ teaspoon instant yeast (⅜ teaspoon if using active dry yeast)

1 tablespoon kosher salt
10 ounces poolish (see recipe on this page)
1 cup stout beer (other beers can be used as well)
2 teaspoons malt syrup
1 tablespoon olive oil, plus more for the bowl
1 tablespoon honey
2½ tablespoons minced fresh rosemary
Fleur de sel

---

1. Make the poolish. Mix the yeast and 1 cup of 70°F water together in a small bowl. Add the flour and mix well with a spoon. Cover and let rest at room temperature at least 12 hours, ideally overnight.

2. Before using, check to make sure the yeast has grown, as evidenced by many air bubbles on the surface of the dough and enhanced dough mass.

3. Now make the dough: Combine the flour, yeast, and salt in the bowl of a standing mixer and mix with a whisk. Add the poolish, beer, malt syrup, olive oil, and honey. (If using active dry yeast, add it at this

time with the wet ingredients.) Using the hook attachment, mix for 5 to 7 minutes at the lowest speed. The dough should be wet and sticky to the touch. If it is too wet, add a little bread flour; if it's too dry, add a little more beer. It should be a fairly smooth dough at this stage.

4. Sprinkle the rosemary over the dough. Increase the mixer speed to the next speed and mix for 2 minutes. There are two ways to check if the dough is ready for its first rising: (1) Detach the dough hook and pull up on the dough with the hook to see if the dough is very elastic and moves with the hook, or if the dough breaks or tears; (2) take a piece of dough the size of 2 large marbles and with your fingers carefully stretch it out, pulling on 4 corners of the dough to see if it stretches or tears as you pull on it. If the dough tears fairly easily in either test, more kneading is necessary. What you're doing in this stage is developing the gluten, or elasticity, of the dough.

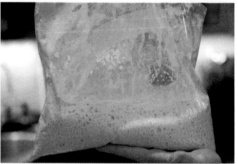

5. For the first rising: Put the dough in a lightly oiled bowl, cover it, and put it someplace warm until it doubles in size. This can take 3 to 3½ hours. During this stage of rising, uncover the dough each hour and pull up one side of the dough and fold it over on itself to essentially fold the dough in half. This is done to help build structure in the bread. (If you can't find a warm place for the dough to rise, heat a cup of water in the microwave oven to really hot. Turn the microwave off and put the covered bowl of dough in the microwave with the cup of water. Or place the covered bowl near the stove if you're cooking—be careful that it doesn't get too hot!)

6. Weigh the dough so that you can divide it in equal halves to form 2 boules, or loaves. Loosely preshape each boule

and place the loaves on a large, parchment-lined baking sheet. Cover each loaf with a towel and plastic wrap and let rest for 10 to 20 minutes.

7. Perform the final shaping of the boules on a lightly floured board. Return to the parchment-lined baking sheet for the second rising. Re-cover with a towel and plastic wrap and let rise for 1 to 1½ hours. Heat the oven to 450°F. I place a pizza stone in the oven on the rack I plan to use and an empty metal pan in the bottom of the oven. If using the pizza stone, allow time for the oven to be at 450°F for about an hour so that the stone is completely heated.

8. Score the boules with an oiled razor blade, spray lightly with water, sprinkle with the fleur de sel, and place the baking sheet on top of the pizza stone. The pizza stone will help keep the baking sheet at a constant temperature while the bread bakes. Just before closing the oven door, throw a bunch of ice cubes or pour some cold water into the hot metal pan at the bottom of the oven to create a little steam.

9. Bake the bread for 25 to 30 minutes. During the first 10 minutes of baking, open the oven door just long enough to squirt some water on the sides of the oven with a squirt bottle. If you don't have one, just get your hands wet and fling the water at the sides of the oven to create steam. Do this 3 times, but not after the first 10 minutes of baking. When you think the bread has about 5 minutes left to bake, open the oven door a bit. A crisper crust is encouraged by shots of steam in the beginning of baking, and by a dry oven at the end.

10. The bread is ready when its internal temperature reaches 200°F. To check, I pull the boule from the oven and stick a probe into the bottom. Because this is a wet bread, especially compared to French bread, let it cool before serving. Bon appétit!

TIPS AND TECHNIQUES

We skipped the scale when separating the dough in half and eyeballed it (your choice). Also, our bread took only 25 minutes to bake, so check it well before the 30-minute mark.

ChezSuzanne: "While I love the meditative activity of kneading dough by hand, this is a fairly wet dough and is best kneaded with the dough hook attachment on a standing mixer. To enhance the bread flavor, I made a pre-ferment (sometime referred to as "poolish") the day before I planned to bake the bread, which was then added to the other bread ingredients on baking day. Poolish also helps make a crusty bread with irregular crumb (bigger holes), which I was looking for in creating this recipe, and provides greater dough strength, better aroma, and increased shelf life. Important note: I use instant yeast when baking bread, making it much easier to work with. If you are working with active dry yeast, multiply the instant yeast amount in the recipe by 1½ to get the right amount of active dry yeast. Any kind of beer works, by the way, but the paler the beer, the less beer flavor you will have. You have to at least have a hearty amber to even taste the beer in the bread."

ABOUT THE COOK

For information on ChezSuzanne, and to see her recipe for Roasted Cauliflower Soup with Chimichurri and Poblano Crème Fraîche, turn to page 212.

WHAT THE COMMUNITY SAID

aussiefoodie: "Wow—this was wonderful bread! I couldn't find malt syrup, so I used golden syrup instead. I think it probably didn't have as strong a flavor as the malt syrup would add, but it still tasted delicious. The stout gives a lovely brown color, and the texture was very nice—small bubbles and enough denseness and airiness to give a lovely, chewy loaf. I forgot to fold the dough over on itself during the first rising, but this didn't seem to cause any problems; the bread turned out great. Would love to try this again, with some different beers and maybe even different herb flavors."

Risotto Rosso

BY ABRA BENNETT | SERVES 4

A&M: Earthy and tannic from the red wine, Abra Bennett's risotto is a carefully conceived juxtaposition of flavors and textures. It's also a study in umami: you start with a base of cubed pancetta and mushrooms, add shallots, and Carnaroli rice—which you then render creamy with red wine and beef broth—and finish the risotto with a shower of Parmesan and some butter. It's rich without being heavy, and we love how the Carnaroli rice holds its structure.

2 tablespoons olive oil

3 tablespoons unsalted butter

2 ounces diced pancetta

4 ounces diced mushroom caps (shiitake or cremini)

2 cups beef broth

3 cups chicken broth

¼ cup finely chopped shallot

1 cup Carnaroli rice (or use Vialone Nano or Arborio)

½ cup fruity red wine

½ cup plus 2 tablespoons finely grated Parmesan

2 tablespoons chopped flat-leaf parsley

Salt and freshly ground black pepper

1. Heat 1 tablespoon of the olive oil and 1 tablespoon of the butter in a heavy skillet with high sides over medium heat. Sauté the pancetta until the fat begins to render. Add the mushrooms and sauté over medium-high heat until the pancetta and mushrooms are golden and slightly crisp, about 5 minutes. Remove the pancetta and mushrooms from the pan with a slotted spoon and set aside.

2. Combine the beef and chicken broths in a large measuring cup or a saucepan. Heat the broth in the microwave or on the stovetop until simmering, and maintain it at a bare simmer. Add the remaining 1 tablespoon olive oil to the fat in the pan and briefly

sauté the shallot over medium heat until softened but not brown. Add the rice and sauté, stirring frequently, until the rice is completely opaque but not golden. Add the wine and stir until the rice is pink and the wine has evaporated. Reduce the heat to medium-low.

3. Begin adding the simmering broth, ½ cup at a time, stirring constantly. As soon as each addition of the broth is absorbed into the rice, add another ½ cup. When you have only 1 cup of broth left, return the pancetta and mushroom mixture to the pan to let the flavors blend into the rice. When all of the broth has been absorbed, the rice should be creamy, but not mushy. You may need a little more or less broth, depending on your rice.

4. Add the remaining 2 tablespoons butter and stir until melted. Add the Parmesan and stir to incorporate, then add the parsley and stir briefly. Season to taste with salt and pepper and serve immediately.

TIPS AND TECHNIQUES

Abra Bennett says: "I often create dishes to accompany specific wines, and I made this risotto in honor of Yellow Hawk's Mescolanza di Rosso, a delicious wine they're no longer making. You can make the risotto with any fruity red wine and still soar like a hawk when you serve it."

We like making risotto in a wide shallow pan so more of the rice is exposed to the heat and you have more control over it.

ABOUT THE COOK

To learn about Abra Bennett, and to check out her recipe for Autumn Olive Medley (Braised Lamb Shanks with Fennel, Celery Root, and Olives), turn to page 255.

WHAT THE COMMUNITY SAID

jas53: "This was *really* delicious. So flavorful that my husband, who usually throws salt and pepper on everything, commented that it didn't need any additional seasoning whatsoever. This is a keeper. Thanks for sharing!"

DeArmasA: "I have now made this recipe three times and the last time I made it I was informed by the family that it is henceforth the *only* risotto recipe I'm allowed to serve. Simply delicious, worth every minute it takes to make (37 for me). Thanks for posting; I don't know what I'd do without Food52 and all you generous chefs!"

Seared Scallops with Spring Onion and Tarragon Cream

BY LASTNIGHTSDINNER | SERVES 4 AS A MAIN COURSE, MORE AS A STARTER

A&M: Lastnightsdinner introduced her scallop recipe like this: "About a year ago I had a wonderful dish of halibut cheeks served with grilled baby leeks and asparagus and a spring onion soubise at one of our favorite Providence restaurants, La Laiterie. That soubise has haunted me, and I've been waiting for just the right opportunity to try my hand at making a similar sauce at home." How could we resist such inspiration? With just a few ingredients (spring onions—not the same as scallions or green onions—tarragon, butter, flour, and milk), lastnightsdinner has concocted a zippy, creamy sauce that's the perfect wading pool for the sweet scallops.

1 pound wild sea scallops, patted dry with paper towels

1 bunch spring onions, about ½ pound

4 tablespoons unsalted butter

Kosher or sea salt

1 tablespoon unbleached all-purpose flour

1 cup whole milk

2 tablespoons fresh tarragon leaves

Grapeseed or other neutral oil

2 tablespoons crème fraîche

Chopped fresh chives, for garnish

1. Place the scallops on a plate or platter and refrigerate, uncovered, for 30 minutes.

2. Trim the spring onions, separating the green tops from the small bulbs. Dice the bulbs and roughly chop the greens.

3. Melt the butter in a saucepan over medium heat. Add the chopped spring onion bulbs and a pinch of salt, reduce the heat to low, and cook 20 to 25 minutes until very soft. Add the green tops, toss through, and

cook an additional 5 to 10 minutes until soft but still bright green. Sprinkle the flour over, stir, and cook for a minute or two, just until the raw flour smell is gone. Stir in the milk, raising the heat to medium, and cook briefly until thickened. Add the tarragon leaves and stir them through, then turn off the heat and pour the mixture into a blender. Puree until very smooth, then return to the pan over low heat, cooking for several minutes until the mixture is thick enough to coat the back of a spoon.

4. Pour a thin film of grapeseed oil in the bottom of a sauté pan and warm over medium-high heat until shimmering. Carefully add the scallops, a few at a time, being careful not to crowd the pan. Sear them just a couple of minutes per side until they are nicely browned and caramelized. They should release from the pan easily once they're ready, and they should still be a little jiggly in the middle—they will continue to cook off the heat. Set aside and keep warm.

5. Taste the sauce and adjust the salt if necessary. Off the heat, whisk in the crème fraîche until the mixture is smooth. Then spoon a little of the sauce into the bottom of shallow, warmed bowls, place the scallops on top, and garnish with the fresh chives.

TIPS AND TECHNIQUES

Lastnightsdinner's technique of drying the scallops in the refrigerator before searing them makes for an impeccably caramelized crust.

ABOUT THE COOK

To learn more about lastnightsdinner, and to read her recipe for Smoky Pork Burgers with Fennel and Red Cabbage Slaw, turn to page 66. You can also find her recipes for Beef Chopped Salad on page 94 and Mussels for One (or Two) on page 234.

WHAT THE COMMUNITY SAID

mariaraynal: "Tarragon is one of those underused, underappreciated herbs. You've elevated it to something truly special in this dish. Congrats!"

Pasta with Prosciutto, Snap Peas, Mint, and Cream

BY LECHEF | SERVES 4

A&M: Although it may sound excessively rich, there are several details that keep this pasta sprightly and fresh. First, lechef is not shy with big flavors: 4 cloves of garlic, 4 shallots, and a heap of diced prosciutto make the cream sauce sing, and the pop of crisp sugar snaps punctuates every bite. A fistful of Parmesan gives the sauce body as well as a nutty tang. We folded in the mint rather than sprinkling it on top, so it infused the cream with its fragrance.

3 tablespoons olive oil

4 garlic cloves, minced

¼ pound prosciutto, finely diced

4 small shallots, minced

Salt and freshly ground black pepper

¾ pound pasta (farfalle or orrechiette)

½ pound fresh whole snap peas, roughly chopped

2 cups heavy cream

½ cup freshly grated Parmesan, plus more for serving

½ cup chopped fresh mint

1. In a heavy saucepan, heat the olive oil over medium heat and cook the garlic for 2 to 3 minutes until just beginning to color.

2. Add the prosciutto and cook for an additional 3 minutes.

3. Add the shallots and cook for 3 to 4 minutes to soften. Season with a pinch or two of salt and a turn or two of freshly ground black pepper.

4. Meanwhile, bring a large pot of water to a boil, salt it, and add the pasta. You want to time the pasta to be finished just as the sauce is finishing so that the cream doesn't sit long.

5. With about 3 minutes left for the pasta, add the snap peas to the prosciutto-shallot mixture and cook for 2 minutes. You want them to retain their crunch. With 1 minute remaining, add the cream and quickly bring to a boil, stirring constantly. Add the cheese, stir, and reduce the heat to low.

6. Drain the pasta and toss with the sauce to coat. Sprinkle liberally with fresh mint and serve with black pepper and extra Parmesan. Enjoy!

TIPS AND TECHNIQUES

Make sure not to cook the peas for too long—the key here is retaining just the right amount of crunch to offset the cream and starch.

Lechef: "I use whole prosciutto shanks because my butcher has them, but you can also ask for a ¼-inch-thick slice of prosciutto and chop that up instead. I think this works much better in pasta than thin slices."

ABOUT THE COOK

For more information about lechef, and for his winning recipe for Zesty Herbed Chicken Broth, turn to page 293.

WHAT THE COMMUNITY SAID

AmyNitrate: "I made this for dinner tonight, and even my kids cleaned their plates. Perfect spring recipe!"

Maple Yogurt Pound Cake

BY RIVKA | MAKES 1 CAKE

A&M: This pound cake drops the pounds of butter and sugar in favor of oil and maple syrup, creating a springy texture and glistening, shellacked exterior. The oil folded into the batter at the end was a new technique to us; we hold it responsible for the cake's sweet, crackly crust. Rivka's choice of Grade B maple syrup means that the maple aroma and flavor are pervasive without being cloying. The end result is moist and flavorful enough on its own, but fresh whipped cream and strawberries never hurt.

½ cup Grade B maple syrup

¾ cup yogurt, preferably not nonfat

3 large eggs

¼ cup sugar

1 teaspoon vanilla extract

½ teaspoon lemon zest

1½ cups all-purpose flour

2 teaspoons baking powder

¼ teaspoon salt

½ cup vegetable oil

1. Position a rack in the center of the oven and heat to 350°F. Generously butter a 9×5×3-inch metal loaf pan.

2. In a large mixing bowl, whisk together the maple syrup, yogurt, eggs, sugar, vanilla, and lemon zest. In a separate bowl, combine the flour, baking powder, and salt. Add to the wet ingredients and stir just to incorporate. Add the oil and fold gently until the oil is absorbed into the batter. Make sure not to overmix the batter.

3. Pour the batter into the prepared loaf pan. Place the pan on a baking sheet in the oven and bake until a tester inserted into the center comes out clean, about 50 minutes. Cool the cake in the pan on a rack for 5 minutes. Cut around the sides of the pan to loosen the cake. Turn the cake out onto the rack, then turn it upright on the rack and cool completely.

TIPS AND TECHNIQUES

Rivka: "The cake is extremely moist; unless eating it just out of the oven, toast your slice to get some contrast between the crust and innards. Really make sure to pull the cake out of the oven right when it's done. If it stays in longer, it'll dry out a bit."

ABOUT THE COOK

Rivka Friedman is a healthcare consultant and food blogger in Washington, D.C. You can find her recipe for Rhubarb Curd Shortbread on page 367.

Her favorite recipe from a cookbook: "Olive Oil and Sherry Pound Cake from Alice Medrich's *Pure Dessert*."

Her top cooking tip: "Freeze coffee into ice cubes so that iced coffee doesn't get diluted as the ice melts."

Her top entertaining tip: "Homemade pickles—I like a mix of green tomatoes, green beans, and maybe even sour cherries—makes an easy, elegant summer appetizer."

Here's her blog: Not Derby Pie (www.notderbypie.com).

WHAT THE COMMUNITY SAID

Bevi: "I have made this a number of times and always get the same response: delicious! Over Xmas I made the cake for my mom—a dyed-in-the-wool Vermonter. She was so happy."

vvvanessa: "I have this cooling on the windowsill and even though it just came out of the oven six minutes ago, I couldn't wait to taste it. It's great! I love that it isn't too sweet, and the texture is amazing—so moist and tender! Congrats and thanks for a great recipe!"

Faulknerian Family Spice Cake with Caramel Icing

BY ENUNN | SERVES 10 TO 12

A&M: ENunn introduced this showstopping cake with this charming declaration: "Being from the South, I come from a rather, ah . . . kooky family in which relationships are tangled but the food is straightforward and good." And in the true Southern tradition, this is a cake that makes a statement. The spices are pervasive, the icing concentrated and sweet, the height of the cake breathtaking. You expect a cake like this to be heavy, but ENunn's mother's recipe produces a cake that's finely textured and featherweight. ENunn rightly said, "Just like the South, you'll keep going back to it even past the point when it seems to be verging on an unhealthy addiction. It's that good."

CAKE
½ pound (2 sticks) unsalted butter, softened
½ cup shortening (yes, shortening)
3 cups sugar
5 large eggs
3 cups all-purpose flour
2 teaspoons ground cinnamon
½ teaspoon ground mace (don't leave this out)
½ teaspoon ground allspice
¼ teaspoon ground nutmeg
½ teaspoon ground cloves

½ teaspoon salt
½ teaspoon baking powder
1 cup plus 2 tablespoons whole milk
1 teaspoon vanilla extract

CARAMEL ICING
½ cup (1 stick) unsalted butter
1 cup packed light brown sugar
⅓ cup heavy cream
2 cups confectioners' sugar
1 teaspoon vanilla extract

---

1. To make the cake, heat the oven to 325°F. Grease and flour a tube pan and set aside. Using an electric mixer, cream together the butter, shortening, and sugar until light and fluffy. Add the eggs one at a time, mixing until smooth.

2. Sift together the dry ingredients, twice. Add the dry mixture to the creamed mixture, alternating with the milk. Add the vanilla. Pour the batter into the prepared pan and bake for 1 hour and 15 minutes, or

until a cake tester inserted into the center of the cake comes out clean. Cool in the pan on a wire rack for about 10 minutes, turn out of the pan, and allow to cool completely on the rack.

3. For the caramel icing: In a medium saucepan, melt the butter over medium heat and stir in the brown sugar and cream. Remove from the heat and stir until smooth. Return to the heat and bring to a boil for 1 minute. Let the mixture cool, then beat in the confectioners' sugar and vanilla. Ice the cooled cake.

TIPS AND TECHNIQUES

We used organic shortening made with nonhydrogenated fat.

To ice the cake, invert it onto a platter and spread the icing on the top and sides. We tried drizzling it, and you shouldn't.

ABOUT THE COOK

Read more about ENunn, and get her recipe for Lemony Cream Cheese Pancakes with Blueberries, on page 171.

WHAT THE COMMUNITY SAID

Daphne: "This is the cake of my dreams, literally! I made it yesterday morning and all who have tasted it since have agreed it's the best cake ever! Today, late morning after a long walk with the dogs, it's raining here in the SF Bay Area. I'm inside with a slice of your cake and a cafe au lait, sheer heaven! Thank you for the recipe!"

halfasiangirl: "Made this last night and it is totally, seriously, completely delicious. I had a little problem with the icing (it was too thick for spreading) so I added it to the bowl of a stand mixer, whipped it like mad, and dribbled in a little cream. Perfect! With other cakes, I often end up pushing the frosting to the side—but a thin layer really does add something. Thanks for the lovely recipe."

Mint Limeade

BY VVVANESSA | MAKES ABOUT 2 QUARTS

A&M: Tart and refreshing, this limeade is a perfect drink for getting into the spirit of spring. Vvvanessa said, "I love minty drinks when the weather starts to warm up. Add in some zippy citrus and bubbles, and I couldn't be more refreshed." The mint syrup is intensely flavored, so you don't need much, and vvvanessa applies a particularly light touch with this one sweet element—which we also found made for an invigorating drink. If you've got a sweet tooth, just add a little more of the mint syrup.

1 cup sugar

1 cup lightly packed fresh mint leaves, washed

1 cup freshly squeezed lime juice

1 to 2 liters club soda

Mint leaves or lime wedges, for garnish

1. Make the mint simple syrup by combining the sugar, mint leaves, and 1 cup water in a saucepan and bringing it to a boil over high heat, then reducing the heat and allowing it to simmer for 2 minutes. Remove from the heat and cool completely. Strain and discard the mint leaves.

2. To assemble the limeade: Pour about 1 ounce (⅛ cup) each of the simple syrup and lime juice into a tall glass filled with ice. Top with about 6 ounces (¾ cup) of club soda. Stir. Garnish with fresh mint or a lime wedge.

TIPS AND TECHNIQUES

Simple and lovely in its pure form, this recipe would make a great jumping-off point for all sorts of riffs. If you're so inclined, try adding a splash of vodka or light rum.

BigBear: "This is so good. We make up the syrup and freeze it in ice cube trays. It's perfect—so refreshing and instantly available when using the syrup cubes."

ABOUT THE COOK

Vanessa Vichit-Vadakan is a bartender based in Brooklyn, New York.

Her favorite recipe from a cookbook: "Fudgy Brownies from *The King Arthur Flour Cookie Companion.*"

Her favorite cooking tip: "Measuring spoons and measuring cups are much easier to use if they're taken off that little ring that holds them together. There's a lot less fumbling, and you only have to wash the one spoon or cup you used without dragging all the others along for the ride."

Here's her blog: The Beet Goes On (www.thebeetgoeson.blogspot.com).

WHAT THE COMMUNITY SAID

marzipanmarcia: "This is definitely going to become my summer standby beverage . . . but vodka might find its way in, too!"

Wild Ramp Pesto

BY SAENYC | SERVES 4 TO 6

A&M: Saenyc said, "Okay, this is basically just ramp pesto, but I think adding the 'wild' makes it sound a little more exciting." Fiery and bright, saenyc's pesto surprised us in a couple of ways: it's creamier than we expected it to be, despite a relatively small amount of olive oil and Parmesan, and it has a lovely mild sweetness from the combination of tender ramp bulbs and walnuts. We added a fair amount of salt to balance and heighten the other flavors, and the juice of half a lemon.

1 medium bunch ramps

½ cup toasted walnuts

½ cup freshly grated Parmesan

Sea salt and freshly ground black pepper

⅓ to ½ cup olive oil (you kind of have to eyeball it)

A squirt of lemon

1. Wash the ramps, trim the ends, and cut the leaves off.

2. Optional step: Blanch the ramp leaves for 30 seconds in boiling water. Some say this makes the pesto more bright and vibrant. I think it's plenty beautiful either way.

3. Chop the ramp bulbs and leaves and walnuts just a bit and put them in the food processor.

4. Add most of the Parmesan (save a sprinkle for serving) and a good dash of salt and pepper.

5. Pouring the olive oil in slowly, process the contents until they combine and look, well . . . pesto-y.

6. Taste for seasoning and add a good squirt of lemon.

7. Use to top your favorite pasta or grilled bread . . . and enjoy.

TIPS AND TECHNIQUES

Amanda folded the pesto into some spaghetti with bacon and peas for dinner, with very happy results.

Saenyc wrote: "You can add a number of other greens to this recipe . . . I've tried basil (which didn't really work, for me), parsley (which made it a little milder), and arugula (which had a real snappy, spicy flavor). My friend Lola threw in a little spinach, but she's always trying to one-up me. Also, use whatever nut you prefer. Some people love pine nuts, I tend to favor walnuts. Isn't this a great country?"

ABOUT THE COOK

Steve Elliott is a writer living in New York City.

His favorite recipe from a cookbook: "Shrimp Tamales with Roasted Garlic Sauce from Bobby Flay's *Bold American Food*–not because it's delicious, which it is, or easy, which it's not, but because I spent about five hours working on this dish with a woman I was dating and fifteen years–and three girls– later, we're still cooking."

His favorite cooking tip: "Season boldly and turn up the music, preferably Professor Longhair's *Tipitina*."

WHAT THE COMMUNITY SAID

littleclove: "I made this tonight and it's really really *yummy*! I altered two things: I used Pecorino Romano cheese instead of Parm because that is my fave and it's all I had, and I used pine nuts instead of walnuts (all I had). I added it to some homemade pasta and it was amazing. I had just gotten some ramps in my organic produce delivery box and had no idea (1) what they were and (2) what to do with them. This turned out to be a *very* tasty dinner thanks to you and my ramps. *Thanks!*"

ekpaster: "I doubled this recipe and made it Sunday night. I loved it! It made quite a bit of pesto. The taste was so fresh and zingy yet subtle. I gave some to my neighbor who had never heard of ramps and she loved it as well."

Rhubarb Curd Shortbread

BY RIVKA | MAKES 16 BARS

A&M: Rivka introduced her recipe thus: "When I saw this rhubarb curd on a couple blogs, I was instantly smitten and had to try it for myself. It's got the zing and intrigue of passionfruit curd, but it's . . . pink! I'm in love." On top is a silky and tangy blanket of the rhubarb curd (made just like lemon curd) and beneath is a pad of thick and crumbly spiced shortbread, adapted from a recipe by Karen DeMasco. Genius! We made the shortbread in the food processor and suggest that you do, too, if you have one handy. The curd takes some elbow grease, it must be said. Think of it as your workout for the day. Once you have the two basic elements, all you do is fuse them with an icing spreader and finish with a few minutes in the oven.

SHORTBREAD

12 tablespoons (1½ sticks) unsalted butter, cut into chunks

¼ cup confectioners' sugar, plus more for dusting

½ teaspoon salt

1½ cups all-purpose flour

¼ teaspoon powdered galangal or ginger

¼ teaspoon ground cinnamon

Pinch of ground cloves

CURD

¾ pound rhubarb (about 6 stalks), cut into 1-inch chunks

¼ cup plus ⅓ cup plus ⅛ cup sugar

4 egg yolks

3 tablespoons unsalted butter, cut into chunks

1 teaspoon lemon zest

2 teaspoons lemon juice

1. To make the shortbread: Heat the oven to 350°F. In a stand mixer or food processor, blend all the ingredients until combined. Wrap the dough in plastic wrap and refrigerate for about an hour. Then dump the dough into an 8×8-inch baking pan and use your fingertips to press it evenly into the pan. Bake for about 30 minutes until golden. Let the shortbread cool in the pan on a rack or on the counter, and leave the oven on.

2. To make the curd: Wash the rhubarb and trim as little off the ends as possible. In a small saucepan, heat the rhubarb, ¼ cup sugar, and 4 tablespoons water over medium heat. Cook until the rhubarb falls apart, adding water by the tablespoon if the rhubarb sticks to the bottom of the pan. At this point, either use an immersion blender to puree the mixture, or (if you're like me and your blender is otherwise occupied) push the mixture through a strainer—the first method is definitely easier.

3. Put a couple inches of water into the pot of a double boiler and set it over medium heat. Put the egg yolks, the remaining ⅓ cup plus ⅛ cup sugar, the butter, lemon zest, and lemon juice in the bowl of the double boiler and whisk to combine. When the sugar has dissolved completely, mix in the warm rhubarb puree by the spoonful, to temper the eggs. When all the rhubarb has been mixed in, set the bowl over the pot; the water should be simmering. Stir for about 5 minutes, until warm and slightly thickened. Remove from the heat. Press through a fine-mesh strainer—this will give your curd that smooth, puddinglike texture.

4. Use an offset spatula to spread the curd evenly over the shortbread. If you haven't eaten half the bowl right then and there, you should have enough curd to make a layer about the same thickness as the shortbread; I didn't. Bake another 10 minutes, then cool on a rack. Refrigerate about 20 minutes and you'll find that it has firmed up enough to slice cleanly. Cut into 16 equal bars. Dust with confectioners' sugar before serving—and do your best not to polish them all off in one sitting.

TIPS AND TECHNIQUES

Rivka: "If the curd doesn't firm up after a night in the fridge, try baking for ten more minutes or so—that should do it."

ABOUT THE COOK

To learn more about Rivka, and to see her recipe for Maple Yogurt Pound Cake, turn to page 355.

WHAT THE COMMUNITY SAID

donnaweaves: "Love these! The shortbread stays nice and soft. I would make them in a slightly larger pan next time—perhaps a 7 × 10" in order to make each bar a bit smaller and make the entire recipe go a bit further. I must admit I ate most of the pan myself!"

Broccoli Rabe, Potato, and Rosemary Pizza

BY TASTEFOOD | MAKES TWO 10-INCH PIZZAS OR 4 MINI-PIZZAS

A&M: This is simply one of the best white pizzas we've ever tasted. The crust, inspired by an Alice Waters recipe, is crisp and rich with olive oil, and gently perfumed throughout with garlic. The mozzarella creates an ultracreamy base in lieu of sauce. Applying attention to detail throughout, TasteFood blanches the broccoli rabe before sautéing it to get rid of excess bitterness; the crushed red pepper and garlic strike just the right balance of heat and pungency. Cooking the potato slices beforehand allows them to almost melt into the rest of the pizza, and a shower of rosemary, pecorino, and finally black pepper round out the wild symphony of flavors.

PIZZA DOUGH
2 teaspoons active dry yeast
3½ cups all-purpose flour
¼ cup semolina flour
1 teaspoon salt
¼ cup olive oil, plus more for rising

PIZZA
1 large Yukon gold potato, scrubbed and very thinly sliced
Extra virgin olive oil
Salt

½ pound broccoli rabe, washed, ends trimmed
1 large garlic clove, minced, plus 2 garlic cloves, lightly smashed but still intact
¼ teaspoon crushed red pepper flakes
2 uncooked pizza crusts (see recipe on this page)
8 ounces fresh mozzarella, thinly sliced
2 tablespoons fresh rosemary leaves, plus more for garnish
½ cup finely grated Pecorino Romano
Freshly ground black pepper

---

1. Make the pizza dough: Stir the yeast and ½ cup lukewarm water together in a bowl. Add ¼ cup of the all-purpose flour and all the semolina flour. Mix well. Let sit until bubbly, about 30 minutes.

2. Combine the remaining flour with the salt in another bowl. Add to the yeast along with ¾ cup cold water and the olive oil. Mix well to form a dough.

3. Turn the dough out onto a lightly floured board and knead with your hands until the dough is smooth and elastic, about 10 minutes. Or use a mixer with a dough hook and mix on medium speed for about 5 minutes.

4. Place the dough in a lightly oiled bowl and turn to coat all sides of the dough with oil. Cover the bowl loosely with plastic wrap. Let the dough rise in a warm place until it has doubled in size, 1 to 2 hours. Punch the dough down and let it rise for another 45 minutes.

5. Divide the dough into 2 equal disks (or 4 if you would like small pizzas). Cover with plastic and let it rest for 30 minutes before shaping.

6. Heat the oven to 375°F.

7. Toss the potato slices with 1 tablespoon olive oil and 1 teaspoon salt in a large bowl. Arrange the potatoes in one layer on a baking sheet. Bake until the edges begin to turn golden brown, 15 to 20 minutes. Remove from the oven and let cool. Increase the oven temperature to 475°F. If you have a pizza stone, put it in the oven on the lowest rack.

8. Bring a large pot of salted water to a boil. Add the broccoli rabe and blanch for 30 seconds; drain. Plunge the broccoli rabe into a bowl of ice water. Cool and drain again. Arrange in one layer on a kitchen towel to dry thoroughly. Cut into 2-inch pieces.

9. Heat 1 tablespoon olive oil in a large skillet over medium heat. Add the minced garlic and the red pepper flakes. Sauté briefly, about 30 seconds. Add the broccoli rabe and ½ teaspoon salt. Sauté for 1 minute, then remove from the heat. Taste and add more salt if necessary.

10. To assemble the pizzas: Lightly flour a work surface and, using your fingers or the heels of your hands, stretch one disk of dough into a 10-inch round and transfer to a pizza peel or baking sheet. Lightly brush the crust with olive oil and rub all over with a smashed garlic clove.

11. Arrange a layer of mozzarella over the crust. Top with a layer of potatoes and broccoli rabe. Sprinkle with 1 tablespoon rosemary leaves and top with half the pecorino.

12. Bake on the pizza stone or baking sheet until the crust is golden brown and the cheese is bubbly, about 15 minutes. Repeat with the second crust, making sure to serve each pizza while it's still hot.

13. Before serving, sprinkle with freshly ground black pepper, garnish with fresh rosemary leaves, and drizzle with extra virgin olive oil.

ABOUT THE COOK

To learn more about TasteFood, and to read her recipe for Southwestern Spiced Sweet Potato Fries with Chili-Cilantro Sour Cream, turn to page 159. You can also find her recipes for Smoked Ham with Pomegranate Molasses, Black Pepper, and Mustard Glaze on page 201 and Whole Baked Fish in Sea Salt with Parsley Gremolata on page 224.

WHAT THE COMMUNITY SAID

jelyapt: "I haven't been a fan of broccoli rabe, but I decided to try this recipe after reading A&M's comments. This was by far the best pizza I've ever eaten, and well worth the effort. Bravo to TasteFood! Thanks for sharing this wonderful creation."

STEsker: "My first successful attempt at pizza! No doubt due to your precise instructions. The only change I made was adding some pancetta. I browned it, removed it from the pan and used some of the rendered fat to soften the garlic for the rabe. I sprinkled the pancetta on top of the pizza before the Parm Reggiano. While my husband asked for more meat the next time around, I thought it was spectacular. Thank you!"

Heart of Gold

BY DYMNYNO | SERVES 2

A&M: This is a simple recipe that really showcases the best part of the artichoke: the heart. Dymnyno said: "Once, I spent a couple of hours watching Marcella Hazan fix an artichoke dish. An entire room full of students hypnotically watched her peel the leaves off an artichoke one by one until she had a pile next to her. Finally, someone asked, 'What are you going to do with those?' She looked puzzled for a few seconds and then announced that she was going to throw them away. 'What would I do with them?' Now I understand that the artichoke heart was all she needed. If you have a fresh, just picked artichoke, the heart is pure gold!" She's right: you get rid of all of the leaves (don't despair, it's worth it!), gently steam the artichoke hearts until just tender, and then coat them in egg and bread crumbs before crisping them in a shallow pool of olive oil. The richness of the crust and the slight bitterness of the artichoke are offset by the bright, aromatic lime and cumin dipping sauce.

CREAMY CUMIN-LIME DIPPING SAUCE
½ cup crème fraîche

1 teaspoon cumin seeds, toasted and ground

Finely grated zest and juice of 1 lime

Salt

ARTICHOKE HEARTS
2 globe artichokes, preferable with some stalk

½ lemon

1 large egg, beaten

1 cup dried bread crumbs (panko works well)

2 tablespoons olive oil

---

1. Make the sauce: Mix all the ingredients except the salt. Add salt to taste. Chill until ready to serve.

2. Prepare the artichokes: Peel all the leaves off each choke. Peel each stalk and with a paring knife neatly trim the bottom where you removed the leaves.

3. Cut the trimmed artichokes in half vertically and with a spoon remove the hairy choke. Be careful when cutting in half to cut the stem evenly, too.

4. Rub immediately with the cut side of the lemon so the artichoke doesn't get brown (which happens very quickly). Steam the hearts until tender. The time will vary depending on the size of the hearts, but it should take about 15 minutes.

5. Dip each artichoke half into the egg and then into the bread crumbs.

6. Heat the olive oil in a medium skillet over medium heat and fry the artichokes until golden, turning them so they brown evenly, about 5 minutes.

7. Set the artichokes on paper towels to absorb the oil.

8. Serve the golden hearts warm with the creamy dipping sauce.

TIPS AND TECHNIQUES

As dymnyno noted, the fresher the artichoke the better. Make sure to serve these warm, while they're still nice and crisp.

ABOUT THE COOK

To learn more about dymnyno, and to read her recipe for Lazy Mary's Lemon Tart, turn to page 180.

WHAT THE COMMUNITY SAID

Culinista Annouchka: "Great combination: this looks delectable, can't wait to try it!"

Salmon in Sorrel Sauce

BY MRSWHEELBARROW | SERVES 4

A&M: MrsWheelbarrow's salmon with sorrel has all the markings of a dish dreamed up by a professional cook; the unexpected beauty of this dish is that it can be executed from start to finish in under 30 minutes by even a relatively new cook. Once the herbs are chopped and the salmon sliced into two-bite slivers, all that's required is a quick broil (it barely took us 30 seconds to cook our salmon through) and an almost equally brief spell in a hot pan for the sauce. The result is an elegant, balanced dish that we'd pull out for a dinner party, or just a weeknight dinner we were looking to make a little special.

---

1 pound beautiful, wild, center-cut salmon
(Alaskan King is my preference here, but any
wild-caught salmon will do)

Vegetable oil

Salt and freshly ground black pepper

3 tablespoons unsalted butter

2 cups fresh sorrel leaves, roughly chopped

¼ cup chervil

½ cup chives, with flowers if possible, chopped

½ cup heavy cream

---

1. Slice the salmon into thin medallions. A flexible salmon slicing knife is my choice, but any long, thin knife will work well. It must be very sharp. Slice on a slight angle, cutting away the skin as you go. Aim for 16 pieces.

2. Place the salmon on a sheet pan lined with parchment paper and very lightly oiled. Brush the tops of the salmon very lightly with oil. Sprinkle salt and pepper over the fish.

3. Adjust an oven rack to be at the very top of the oven. Heat the broiler. Warm the plates (very important) in a sink of warm water, your extra oven (ha), or remove them from the just-run dishwasher.

4. Prepare all the ingredients and stage. This dish comes together quickly and you don't want to be scrambling. Reserve the chive flowers, if you have them.

5. When the broiler is ready, start the sauce. In a large, wide skillet, melt the butter until it starts to toast. It should be golden brown.

6. Add the sorrel, chervil, and chives to the butter and coat quickly. Allow them to wilt a little and then pour in the cream. Bring to a boil and reduce just until the sauce coats the back of a spoon. Taste and adjust for salt and pepper, keeping in mind that you have seasoned the fish.

7. Put the salmon under the broiler and cook until just opaque. Watch it carefully the entire time it's in the oven—it could take you as little as 30 seconds, depending on your oven.

8. Dry the warm plates. Place 4 medallions of salmon per person on each plate and decorate with the sauce, being very generous. Sprinkle with chive-flower petals and serve with crusty bread.

TIPS AND TECHNIQUES

If you can't find sorrel, you can substitute baby spinach.

MrsWheelbarrow added this note: "In a former life, I owned a fish market. In addition to selling fresh fish, we offered prepared foods to take home—a radical concept at the time—and this dish was prepackaged with instructions. I like to put the salmon skin under the broiler, too. Salt well. It's a delicious cook's snack."

ABOUT THE COOK

Learn more about MrsWheelbarrow, and find her recipe for Creamy Mushroom Soup, on page 119.

WHAT THE COMMUNITY SAID

Pierino: "Salmon with sorrel is sweet indeed. You might want to try this in *cartouche*, wrapped in parchment. When growing sorrel I try to keep it corralled in clay containers."

Goat Cheese Caesar Salad with Roasted Tomatoes and Parmesan Crisp

BY BROOKE'S KITCHEN | SERVES 4

A&M: This is a dish that has the veneer of a restaurant recipe, but the soul of a home cook's. Brooke's kitchen was inspired by a dish she had at Michel Richard's Central restaurant in D.C. "When I saw Caesar salad *and* goat cheese on the menu, I knew it was something I had to try. This is my 'home' version." Her salad has complexity—a bed of seasoned goat cheese beneath the Romaine, a sprinkling of blistered cherry tomatoes, and a cap made of a baked Parmesan crisp—but each part is easy and can be made ahead of time. So don't sweat it. Put this on the menu for your next dinner party.

CAESAR DRESSING
⅓ cup buttermilk

2 tablespoons good-quality mayonnaise

1 garlic clove, grated

1½ tablespoons lemon juice

½ teaspoon anchovy paste

2 teaspoons Dijon mustard

Salt and freshly ground black pepper

SALAD
4 ounces good, soft goat cheese

1 garlic clove, grated

1 teaspoon dried oregano

1 tablespoon heavy cream

16 cherry tomatoes

½ tablespoon olive oil

1 teaspoon balsamic vinegar

Salt and freshly ground black pepper

¾ cup freshly grated Parmesan

1 head romaine lettuce

---

1. For the dressing: Whisk all the ingredients together, adding salt and pepper to taste. Refrigerate until ready to use.

2. For the salad: Take the goat cheese out of the refrigerator to soften a little. Mix the grated garlic with the oregano and cream. Mix the softened goat cheese with this herb-cream mixture and set aside.

3. Heat the oven to 375°F. Toss the cherry tomatoes with the olive oil, balsamic vinegar, salt, and pepper. Roast on a rimmed baking sheet for about 20 minutes until the tomatoes burst and brown in a few spots. Take out of the oven and set aside.

4. Raise the oven temperature to 400°F.

5. Using ½ cup of the Parmesan, pour a heaping tablespoon of cheese on a silicone or parchment-lined baking sheet. Repeat, spacing the heaps of cheese at least ½ inch apart. (Reserve the remaining ¼ cup cheese for serving.) Bake until crisp and golden brown, about 5 minutes. Cool.

6. Clean the lettuce and trim. Place the leaves between damp paper towels and store in the refrigerator until ready to use.

7. Pipe a portion of the goat cheese mixture on the bottom of one salad plate (depending on how much goat cheese you like). I use a plastic storage bag with the corner cut off to make a pretty design, or you can always spoon it onto the plate. Repeat with 3 more salad plates.

8. Toss the lettuce very lightly with some of the dressing (be very sparing—I always put a little dressing on top of the finished salad). Divide the lettuce among the salad plates.

9. Divide the roasted tomatoes and arrange them on top of the salad. Drizzle a little more dressing over the lettuce and sprinkle with the reserved Parmesan. Add a cheese crisp to each plate and serve.

TIPS AND TECHNIQUES

We didn't break up the romaine leaves—instead, we used just the tender inner leaves and dressed them whole so we could stack them up, Suzanne Goin style.

ABOUT THE COOK

Brooke Moskovitz Dowdy works in marketing in Washington, D.C.

Her favorite recipe from a cookbook: "Wild Mushroom Risotto with Duck Confit from *Artisanal Cooking* by Terrance Brennan."

Her top entertaining tip: "Instead of making an appetizer, an entrée, and a dessert, buy one item that is prepared. You can pick up beautiful cheeses to make a lovely appetizer or a dessert from your local bakery. This leaves more time to mingle with your guests, plus you'll be relaxed and can focus on the preparation of your other dishes."

Here's her blog: Plum Pie (www.plumpiecooks.com).

WHAT THE COMMUNITY SAID

Jennifer Ann: "So delicious! We loved the fresh taste of the dressing, and will use the grated garlic trick again. The warm roasted tomatoes are a really nice touch."

Bell-less, Whistle-less, Damn Good French Toast

BY KAYB | SERVES 4

A&M: There's nothing to making this French toast. But there is one thing that makes it exceptional: cream. KayB cuts to the chase, forgoing spices and extracts, and focusing instead on eggs, cream, and challah. She said: "There are things in life that just ought to be simple, and to my taste buds, French toast is one of them." You whip together the eggs and cream, which form a custardy mixture, then dip the eggy bread slices into this custard and fry them in butter. Outside is a crisp crepelike shell. Inside, pudding. What are you waiting for?

1 small challah loaf

3 large eggs

½ cup heavy cream

Butter, for grilling and serving (unsalted or salted—it's up to you)

Good maple syrup, for serving

1. Cut the challah into ¾-to 1-inch-thick slices.

2. Whisk together the eggs and cream in a large bowl.

3. Heat a griddle or flat grill pan over medium-high heat, and add 1 tablespoon butter for every 2 pieces of French toast the pan will accommodate; swirl the butter around to cover the surface of the pan.

4. Dip a slice of bread in the egg and cream; flip and submerge again. Add to the pan and cook until golden on one side (approximately 90 seconds); flip and cook the other side. Repeat with the rest of the bread, cooking the French toast in batches. Keep the cooked slices warm in a 200°F oven.

5. Serve with additional butter, if desired, and good-quality maple syrup. The experience is enhanced by the addition of smoked bacon.

When dipping the bread into the custard, make sure to gently squeeze the bread with your fingertips to draw the eggs and cream to the center.

Kayb added: "It is critically important to use good challah for French toast. Fresh fruit is an acceptable add-on, but preserve me from cinnamon, confectioners' sugar, and the like."

ABOUT THE COOK

Kayb works in business development in Hot Springs, Arkansas.

Her favorite recipe from a cookbook: "Mark Bittman's fried rice recipe in *How to Cook Everything*. I'd never been successful at fried rice until I tried this recipe, and now I adhere slavishly to the basic ingredients and the technique, varying only in the 'extras' I add. On the sweet side are the Peabody Vanilla Muffins from Christine Arpe Gang's *Memphis Cuisine*, since they form the base for almost every breakfast muffin I've ever made."

Here's her blog: Kay at the Keyboard (www.kayatthekeyboard.wordpress.com).

WHAT THE COMMUNITY SAID

RaquelG: "This is exactly the same as my grandmother's recipe, except she would sprinkle with sugar after dipping in the egg/cream for a little brûlée action. Heaven!"

cookbookchick: "I made this today for Sunday breakfast served with a choice of fresh (real) maple syrup or a strawberry-blackberry-rhubarb compote. Rave reviews from my family, who called it the best French toast ever!"

gabrielaskitchen: "This is exactly how I make my French toast! I used to put a little cinnamon in the batter until I started cooking for my beau, who likes his French toast savory, served with eggs, bacon, and hot sauce . . . I still eat mine with powdered sugar and cinnamon, yum."

Smoky Minestrone with Tortellini and Parsley or Basil Pesto

BY WINNIEAB | SERVES 6 TO 8

A&M: We admire WinnieAb's talent for combining delicious, nutritious ingredients (like the many vegetables in this soup) with a dash of indulgence (bacon, cheese, tortellini). The smokiness of the bacon permeates the minestrone, imbuing the tomatoey broth with a depth it wouldn't have otherwise. The bright, rustic pesto (we used parsley, but basil would be great, too) is a superb final addition, with its garlicky, herbal kick.

3 tablespoons olive oil

2 slices preservative-free, all-natural bacon, chopped into small pieces

1 large onion, peeled and chopped

2 large garlic cloves, minced

1 leek, cleaned, trimmed, and sliced thinly

3 carrots, peeled and chopped into ½-inch dice

2 celery ribs, chopped into ½-inch dice

1 zucchini, chopped into ½-inch dice

1 potato, peeled and chopped into ½-inch dice

4 cups vegetable or chicken stock, preferably homemade

One 15-ounce can cooked chickpeas, preferably organic

One 28-ounce can peeled San Marzano tomatoes with juice

Salt

1 cup finely chopped kale

One 9-ounce package high-quality, all-natural cheese tortellini

Aged balsamic vinegar, for drizzling (optional)

Freshly grated Parmesan, for garnish (optional)

PARSLEY OR BASIL PESTO

1 cup loosely packed basil or parsley leaves

2 tablespoons pine nuts, toasted

2 garlic cloves, peeled

2 tablespoons grated Parmesan

1 tablespoon olive oil

1. Heat 1 tablespoon of the olive oil in a large pot over medium heat. Add the bacon and cook for a couple of minutes until it starts to brown.

2. Add the rest of the oil and the onion, garlic, and leek. Continue to cook over medium heat, stirring occasionally, until softened, about 5 minutes.

3. Add the carrots, celery, zucchini, and potato and stir for a minute or two.

4. Add the stock, chickpeas, and tomatoes, crushing the tomatoes with your hands as you go. Add a few generous pinches of salt (be judicious if your stock is salted already). Bring the soup to a boil, then reduce the heat to a simmer and cook for 20 to 30 minutes until the potatoes are just tender.

5. Meanwhile, make the pesto. Chop, chop, and chop the basil or parsley some more by hand until it's very fine. When you do this, you'll reduce it down to about ¼ cup.

6. As you chop the basil, start to incorporate the pine nuts, garlic, and Parmesan and chop them fine, too, until you have a lovely, finely chopped pesto.

7. Transfer to a small bowl and stir in the olive oil.

8. Add the kale and the tortellini to the soup and simmer until both are tender and cooked through, 5 to 7 minutes. Taste and add more salt if necessary. Serve garnished with a spoonful of the pesto, a few drops of aged balsamic, and a generous sprinkling of Parmesan, if desired.

TIPS AND TECHNIQUES

WinnieAb: "This recipe starts with just a little bit of all-natural bacon, but if you'd rather leave it out, go ahead and proceed with the rest of the recipe. You won't get the smoky flavor, but you'll still get a great soup. (You could also substitute pancetta for the bacon, but obviously you won't do that if you are a vegetarian!) As for the pesto, I went the hand-chopped route here. Because it's a small batch, I didn't want to drag out the food processor, and I wanted to use a minimal amount of olive oil. You can also use your own favorite homemade or store-bought pesto instead of this one, if you prefer."

Abra Bennett said: "For anyone who wants to omit the bacon, a spoonful of pimentón (Spanish smoked paprika) is a great way to get some smoky flavor in there."

ABOUT THE COOK

To learn more about WinnieAb, and to read her recipe for Turkey Pho, turn to page 174.

WHAT THE COMMUNITY SAID

Mookie: "This is a great recipe! We don't eat meat, so I skipped the bacon and used some alderwood smoked salt to substitute for the smoky bacon flavor. It worked out well! Thanks!"

Carrollmontreal: "*Pesto perfecto*! I made your pesto with parsley and planned to serve it with grilled salmon tonight. But it is so fresh and delicious, we were eating it by the spoonful long before dinner was ready. There are thousands of recipes for pesto, with so many different balances of the ingredients, but your ingredients and proportions are the best! I can't thank you enough. (And I can't wait to make the minestrone.)"

Lemony Green Bean Salad with Feta, Red Onion, and Marjoram

BY MIDGE | SERVES 4

A&M: In her introduction to this recipe, Midge explained: "During the Maryland summer when it was too hot to turn on the oven, our friend John would grill a couple of steaks or whole fish to perfection and toss together a simple Greek salad of ripe tomatoes, red onion, feta, and marjoram. I use lemon juice here instead of red wine vinegar and green beans when tomatoes aren't in season, and when they are, both are terrific." On the surface, this salad seems like one you see at every barbecue—except that it's more lemony, only gently oniony, fragrant with marjoram, and entirely balanced. The secret? A dash of agave nectar in the dressing, which sweetens and smooths the lemon and feta.

---

1 pound green beans, tops removed

1 lemon, juiced and zested

¼ cup best-quality olive oil

Dash agave nectar (or sugar to taste)

¼ red onion, super-thinly sliced

4 ounces feta, crumbled

3 to 4 fresh marjoram sprigs, leaves stripped and roughly chopped (oregano is great, too)

---

1. Bring a pot of salted water to boil. Throw in the green beans and cook for about 4 minutes, or until al dente. Drain and rinse in cold water.

2. In a small bowl, whisk together the lemon juice, zest, olive oil, and agave nectar.

3. Combine the beans, red onion, feta, and marjoram in a large bowl. Toss with the dressing. Chill until those steaks come off the grill.

TIPS AND TECHNIQUES

Make sure you don't overcook the green beans—you want them to snap under your teeth.

Midge said: "Regarding raw onion, I was just paging through one of my Nigella Lawson cookbooks and she suggests letting sliced onion steep in the oil and vinegar (in this case, lemon juice) for 2 hours to take the edge off."

ABOUT THE COOK

Margaret Loftus is a writer and editor living in Boston, Massachusetts.

Her favorite entertaining tip: "Was it Julia Child who said never call your guests' attention to the fact that you've botched a dish?"

Her top cooking tip: "Always finish your chopping before you start drinking wine."

WHAT THE COMMUNITY SAID

Elise: "I've made this several times for having people over, and it's always a hit with dinner guests—not to mention that I love it (I'd eat it every day if I could). I've used shallot instead of red onion, and that works well, too."

Spanish Roasted Potato Salad

BY MYSOCIALCHEF | SERVES 3 TO 4

A&M: "A few years ago my sister and her husband invited me to a Spanish restaurant in New Jersey for dinner," wrote MySocialChef, "I really don't like leaving the city, but they promised me it was well worth it. I got my visa, filled the car with gas, and punched the address into Paula, my GPS navigation device. All the food seemed pretty typical, but I had these amazing roasted potatoes that I couldn't get enough of. I asked the waiter what was in them, and the only thing he would tell me was garlic. I asked another waiter, and he said mayonnaise." Attempting to re-create his discovery, MySocialChef came up with this smart play on Spanish *patatas bravas*. Instead of frying the potatoes, he has you roast them, and rather than making your own homemade mayonnaise, you sharpen store-bought mayonnaise with lemon juice, Dijon mustard, and a whole lot of garlic. You'll breathe fire for days, but the suffering you inflict on others is worth it!

---

1 pound small potatoes (white or red), scrubbed

3 tablespoons olive oil

1¼ teaspoons salt

½ teaspoon freshly ground black pepper

4 garlic cloves, finely chopped

¼ cup mayonnaise

1 tablespoon lemon juice

1 teaspoon Dijon mustard

---

1. Heat the oven to 400°F. Cut the potatoes in half or quarters and put them in a bowl. Add 2 tablespoons of the olive oil, ¾ teaspoon of the salt, and the pepper and mix to coat. Spread the potatoes on a baking sheet in a single layer. Bake the potatoes for 40 minutes, flipping twice during baking. Make sure they turn a nice golden brown. Take them out of the oven and allow to cool.

2. In a medium bowl, combine the remaining ½ teaspoon salt, 1 tablespoon olive oil, the garlic, mayonnaise, lemon juice, and mustard. Mix and pour over the cooled potatoes. Toss to coat. Serve warm or at room temperature.

TIPS AND TECHNIQUES

OldGrayMare: "Suggest you add a tad bit of paprika (smoked or plain) to the seasonings before roasting . . . this just deepens the flavor."

Seshirkey: "My only adjustment was to use 1½ pounds of potatoes, and I still didn't need to use all of the sauce. It's got a lot of kick, and I think too much mayo overwhelms it. Also, my boss mentioned that she substituted Greek yogurt in place of the mayo and she loved it."

ABOUT THE COOK

Petrit Husenaj is a caterer and event planner in New York City. You can read more about his culinary adventures on his blog, MySocialKitchen.com.

His favorite recipe from a cookbook: "Paul's Zucchini Fritters from *I Like You: Hospitality Under the Influence* by Amy Sedaris."

His top entertaining tip: "Always buy bread and fish the day of your party."

WHAT THE COMMUNITY SAID

Seshirkey: "This really is the best potato salad I have ever had. I took it to work (where we tend to share recipes *a lot*) and everyone who tried it had to know where the recipe came from. Thanks for a recipe that I will use over and over!"

Lori: "I made these for a party and they were a huge hit! I have a little of the aioli left and am considering using it to marinate chicken. Can only imagine how tasty that combo will be."

Caramelized Pork Bánh Mì

BY MONKEYMOM | SERVES 4 TO 6

A&M: The caramelized pork could be a recipe all its own, but we sure do like it in this sandwich as well. Most bánh mì are made with a rich and fatty ground pork; this seasoned pork tenderloin gives the sandwich character. Make sure you use a light, airy roll with a crisp crust—bánh mì is all about the interior. About the addictive pickled veggies, Monkeymom said, "This is a good starting point for pickling, but feel free to adjust the vinegar and sugar levels to your taste. I tend to pickle these guys for only a short time, and they can be ready to eat in less than an hour!"

PICKLED CARROTS AND RADISHES
¼ pound baby carrots, peeled

1 bunch red radishes, preferably breakfast radishes (daikon are more traditional; I just think red radishes are beautiful)

1 cup apple cider vinegar

1 tablespoon salt

2 tablespoons sugar

BÁNH MÌ
1 to 1½ pounds pork tenderloin

3 tablespoons fish sauce

2 tablespoons maple syrup

1 tablespoon light or dark brown sugar

2 tablespoons soy sauce

½ teaspoon sesame oil

2 garlic cloves, minced

One ½-inch piece of ginger, peeled and minced

1 scallion, sliced thinly

½ teaspoon freshly ground black pepper

2 tablespoons vegetable oil

1 loaf sweet French baguette (thin) or French bread sandwich rolls (try to get the kind of French bread with a crisp crust and tender light center)

Mayonnaise

Pâté (optional, but recommended)

Red leaf lettuce

Several cilantro sprigs

Sliced jalapeño peppers

1. Make the pickled carrots and radishes. Slice the carrots and radishes into quarters (or sixths for thicker guys) lengthwise. In a large bowl, mix all the ingredients together with ½ cup water. Taste for seasoning.

Let stand at room temperature for as little as 1 hour or as long as overnight. They keep for several days in the refrigerator.

2. Cut the tenderloin across the grain into ½-inch pieces. Flatten each piece to an even ¼ inch between 2 pieces of plastic wrap using a meat pounder, rolling pin, or glass bottle.

3. In a large bowl, combine the ingredients from the fish sauce to the black pepper. Taste and adjust the seasoning—it should be sweet and savory, so add more soy sauce, salt, or sesame oil as you like. Add the pork and use your hands or a large spoon to make sure all the pieces of meat are coated in the marinade. Marinate for 10 to 30 minutes.

4. You can cook the pork on the grill outdoors (best), or indoors using a grill pan or cast-iron skillet (something that you can get very hot). Heat the grill or grill pan to high, and turn on that vent fan! Add the vegetable oil to the meat and marinade and stir to coat. Sear the first side of the meat until very dark brown, then flip and sear on the other side. The meat is thin so it cooks quickly, 1 to 2 minutes on each side. Be careful not to overcook it.

5. To assemble the sandwiches, slice the baguette and spread the mayonnaise on one side, pâté on the other, if using. Add lettuce, pork, pickled vegetables, cilantro, and peppers. Dig in!

TIPS AND TECHNIQUES

Monkeymom: "Pâté is typically found in bánh mì, and though I list it as optional, doesn't French bread just taste great with pâté?"

ABOUT THE COOK

To learn more about Monkeymom, and to read her recipe for Wishbone Roast Chicken with Herb Butter, turn to page 283.

sdr1959: "That sandwich looks delicious, but I am over the moon about the radish-carrot salad recipe. That little, simple salad is one of my family's favorite things about Vietnamese cooking, and I have never been able to properly replicate it at home. This recipe is slammin', and I have a big bowl of it in the fridge, waiting to be devoured on any sandwich they can think of. Yum and thanks!"

RaquelG: "Congrats Monkeymom! Made the pork tenderloin last night and it is *fab*! A big hit with my protein-loving husband and extra for sammies for me. A wonderful foray into Vietnamese food."

Pistachio Meringue Stack with Rose Cream and Strawberries

BY HEENA | SERVES 8

A&M: As Stephanie, Food52's head recipe tester, said, "It's like pavlova revved up." The pistachio-laden meringue disks are both chewy and crisp, and the combination of whipped cream and mascarpone lightly scented with rose water and a dash of balsamic vinegar makes for a brilliant and delicious "glue" to hold the layers of this stack together. Mounds of fresh strawberries, macerated with sugar and a bit more rose water (enough to evoke a summer garden without making them taste soapy), cut through the sweetness of the meringue and the mellowness of the cream. Heena said, "This recipe was originally inspired by Nigella Lawson's Gooey Chocolate Stack. Summer, and leftover ingredients from a recent tryst with kheer (Indian rice pudding), inspired this version."

MERINGUE

6 large egg whites (at room temperature; make sure there is no trace of egg yolk)

Pinch of salt

½ cup light brown sugar (not packed; pulsed in a food processor if crystals are large)

1 cup superfine sugar

1 teaspoon balsamic vinegar

1 cup pistachios, finely chopped

BERRIES

2 pounds strawberries

2 tablespoons sugar

1 tablespoon rose water

CREAM

1 cup chilled heavy cream

1 cup mascarpone

1 tablespoon rose water

1 tablespoon pistachios, chopped or slivered, for garnish (optional)

1. Heat the oven to 250°F.

2. Lightly grease three 8-inch round cake pans and line with parchment paper. Alternatively, line 3 baking sheets with parchment paper and draw an 8-inch circle on each one (you can use a cake pan as a guide to draw the circles).

3. In a clean metal or glass bowl, whisk the egg whites with the salt till they hold soft peaks. (You can also do this in a mixer, which will make your life a little easier.) Whisk in the sugars, 1 tablespoon at a time, beating well after each addition. Add the vinegar and whisk until the mixture looks glossy and holds stiff peaks. Fold in the chopped nuts, gently but thoroughly.

4. Divide the meringue mixture equally among the 3 cake pans or the 3 circles drawn on the baking sheets. Smooth the tops with the back of a round spoon. Bake until the tops are crisp and dry, 1 hour to 1 hour and 15 minutes. Switch off the oven and leave the pans to cool in the oven for 1 hour with the door slightly ajar.

5. For the berries: While the meringues cool, hull and then halve or quarter the strawberries, depending on their size. Place in a large bowl, sprinkle the sugar and rose water over the berries, toss gently, and let stand for 30 minutes.

6. For the cream: Beat the cream and mascarpone with the rose water in a bowl until the mixture just holds stiff peaks.

7. To assemble: Invert the cooled meringue disks onto a plate and gently peel off the parchment paper. Invert onto another plate so they are right side up.

8. Spread a third of the cream over one meringue disk, followed by a third of the strawberries. Repeat with the remaining meringue layers, cream, and strawberries. Garnish with the slivered pistachios, if you desire. To serve, cut this delicate cake with a long, sharp serrated knife.

TIPS AND TECHNIQUES

Although the dessert must be assembled just before serving, the meringue layers can be made ahead of time; they will keep well wrapped in parchment paper in an airtight container for up to a week.

Heena: "You can locate pistachios and rose water at any Indian or Middle Eastern store; if not, I'm sure the combination of almonds and pure vanilla would be equally delightful. This delicious dessert also happens to be gluten-free."

She added, "You can also make this as individual meringues or one large meringue like a traditional pavlova." We actually like that you start out with this beautiful, regal dessert and that it crumbles as you cut into it—the destruction is part of the pleasure.

ABOUT THE COOK

Heena Punwani is an analyst in Waterloo, Canada.

Her favorite recipe from a cookbook: "It has to be the Espresso-Chocolate Shortbread Cookies from Dorie Greenspan's *Baking: From My Home to Yours*. It is one of the few recipes I've never felt a need to tinker with. It produces a delectable and addictive cookie, and Dorie's trick to freeze and roll cookie dough in a zipper-lock bag is genius."

Her top entertaining tip: "When entertaining, don't sweat the small stuff. Your friends don't notice the small imperfections, and even if they do, the real friends don't care."

Here's her blog: Tiffin Tales (www.tiffintales.com).

WHAT THE COMMUNITY SAID

ChezSuzanne: "This is gorgeous! I love the combo of the rose water and balsamic vinegar with the strawberries."

Creamy Cucumber "Side"

BY LIZTHECHEF | SERVES 4

A&M: The success of this recipe lies in the details: salting the cucumber and onion slices to keep them from getting soggy; augmenting the sweet tang of the yogurt with a dash of vinegar and a bit of sugar; and adding Meyer lemon zest and fresh dill to achieve subtle layers of perfume. The resulting dish, as Lizthechef said, "gives a cool note to summer suppers and works well with salmon or lamb." We think it would be excellent picnic fare.

1 organic English cucumber (about 1 pound)

½ Vidalia onion, peeled

1 teaspoon kosher salt

1 teaspoon organic cane sugar

1 tablespoon rice vinegar

½ cup best-quality whole-milk Greek yogurt

2 tablespoons chopped fresh dill

Zest of 1 Meyer lemon

1. Slice the cucumber and onion as thinly as possible. Put the slices in a colander, sprinkle with the salt, stir, and sit the colander over a bowl to catch the released liquid. Refrigerate for 1 hour.

2. Discard the extra liquid and rinse the salt from the cucumber and onion. Drain well and pat the slices dry using kitchen towels.

3. Turn the cucumber and onion into a medium bowl and add the sugar and vinegar, stirring to dissolve the sugar. Fold in the yogurt, dill, and lemon zest. Chill for 1 hour, stir again (the juices will have settled), and serve.

TIPS AND TECHNIQUES

Lizthechef: "I prefer the crisp crunch of an English cucumber to the waxy ones that require peeling. You may substitute sour cream for the yogurt. I've discovered that draining the yogurt releases even more liquid. Put your yogurt in a small, fine-holed sieve and place the sieve over a small bowl. Place in the fridge while you drain the cukes and onions."

mdm said: "I *love* this, and have been adding radishes as well. Then yesterday I added blanched green beans, too—yum!"

Elizabeth Schmitt is a retired clinical social worker living in San Diego, California. Her favorite recipe from a cookbook: "Chicken Roasted with Sour Cream, Lemon Juice, and Mango Chutney from *Cooking for Mr. Latte*. I use my Meyer lemons and homemade mango chutney from my pantry. I serve this over and over at home, just for the two of us or for simple dinner parties."

Here's her blog: Liz the Chef (www.lizthechefblog.com).

WHAT THE COMMUNITY SAID

dymnyno: "I made this Friday night to 'side' with BBQ lamb loins, and it was wonderful! Finished the rest for lunch on Saturday."

TasteFood: "I am a huge fan of tzatziki and this recipe is a dream, since it gives me an excuse to gobble it up as a side dish instead of a condiment."

Veal Chops Lombatina with Roasted Garlic

BY THIRSCHFELD | SERVES 4

A&M: This recipe treats veal chops with the respect they deserve, highlighting rather than overpowering the tender meat. Thirschfeld employs a nifty technique of stacking the chops to flavor them with layers of lemon zest, garlic, and whole thyme sprigs sandwiched between; while the chops absorb all these great flavors, you roast whole heads of garlic and whip up a simple vinaigrette. Then it's just a few short minutes on a hot grill (we recommend you stop at medium-rare), and dinner is served. Thirschfeld's sage advice? "Maybe the hardest part about this is waiting for the grill to heat, but I have never found that to be too trying as long as a nice chilled bottle of rosé from Provence is on hand."

---

1 bunch fresh thyme

4 to 6 garlic cloves, minced

Zest of 2 lemons

4 veal chops, about 1½ inches thick

Kosher salt

4 garlic heads

2 tablespoons unsalted butter, softened

Freshly ground white pepper

4 tablespoons extra virgin olive oil

1 tablespoon lemon juice

1 teaspoon Banyuls vinegar or good balsamic vinegar

2 teaspoons minced thyme

---

1. Place a large piece of plastic wrap on a flat surface. Spread out 4 to 5 sprigs of thyme on the plastic wrap to match the size of one of the veal chops. Sprinkle on some minced garlic and lemon zest.

2. Season each side of the 4 chops evenly with kosher salt. Place one chop on top of the herb mixture and top it with more thyme, garlic, and lemon zest. Place another chop on top and also top it with

thyme, garlic, and lemon zest. Repeat until the chops are all stacked and topped. You want all sides covered.

3. Pull the plastic wrap up and over and wrap the chops tightly. Place them on a tray to catch any possible drips and put them in the fridge for no less than 6 hours and no longer than 12 hours.

4. Heat the oven to 325°F. Slice the top third off each head of garlic and smear them with the butter; season with salt and pepper. Place the heads in a small casserole dish and cover with aluminum foil. Bake for 1¾ hours for an 8-clove head, maybe less for smaller heads. Remove from the oven and let them sit.

5. In a small bowl, whisk together the olive oil, lemon juice, vinegar, and minced thyme. Season with salt and pepper and set the dressing aside.

6. When you are ready, heat your grill to the highest temperature you can. While it is heating, remove the chops from the fridge, unwrap them, and scrape off all the thyme, garlic, and lemon zest. Season the chops with pepper and leave them out to warm while the grill is heating.

7. When the grill is hot, cook the chops until medium-rare or medium, 5 to 6 minutes per side. Near the end of the grilling time, put the garlic on a tray and place it on the edge of the grill to warm it up. Transfer the cooked chops to a platter or plates, top them with the dressing, and garnish with thyme. Place a head of roasted garlic next to each chop and serve.

TIPS AND TECHNIQUES

Thirschfeld said: "I like to use the stack and wrap method, as I call it, just to give the veal a little more time to absorb the flavors I want to pair with it. I really like to serve this dish with a whole head of roasted garlic for each diner so they can smear it onto the chop if desired."

Tom Hirschfeld is a former culinary arts instructor who now runs a family farm in Indiana.

His favorite recipe from a cookbook: "Without question there is one recipe I have never altered and don't want to: Thomas Keller's Moules au Safran et à la Moutarde, or Mussels with Saffron and Mustard, in the *Bouchon* cookbook. Just a side note: it is a crime not to serve this without one or two loaves of crusty French bread."

His top cooking tip: "Get the best knife you can afford and learn how to use it, because it will make food prep enjoyable, or at the very least tolerable."

Here's his blog: Bona Fide Farm Food (www.bonafidefarmfood.com).

WHAT THE COMMUNITY SAID

Aliwaks: "I love the stacking technique . . . Will have to try with my next meat dish."

Monkeymom: "I can confirm that this is wonderful with pork chops as well. Subbed some sage for a couple of chops and that was very tasty, too. Well done, thirschfeld, and congrats on another stunner!"

Grilled Bread with Thyme Pesto and Preserved Lemon Cream

BY FIVEANDSPICE | MAKES 6 SLICES

A&M: Fiveandspice described the first time she made this dish: "I found myself staring down at my bread and saying, 'Where have you been all my life?'" We felt the same. We love it's rusticity and its ability to inspire endless adaptations: you can use a different herb for the pesto, dab with ricotta instead of lemon cream, or, as fiveandspice suggested, top with a fried egg. Grilled bread is so much better than toasted, and the heady perfume of the thyme pesto seduces you before you can even get the toast to your mouth. The preserved lemon cream acts as the calm yet bewitching sidekick.

2 cups baby spinach, cleaned and torn into small pieces

½ cup fresh thyme leaves (stems removed)

½ cup toasted pine nuts

3 garlic cloves, peeled and smashed

½ cup freshly grated Parmesan

½ teaspoon salt

½ cup olive oil, plus more for brushing

½ cup crème fraîche

2 teaspoons minced preserved lemon (page 313)

6 thick slices good Italian country bread

1. In a food processor, combine the spinach, thyme, pine nuts, garlic, Parmesan, and salt. Process until the ingredients are roughly chopped. With the processor running, gradually drizzle in the olive oil until you have a chunky pesto. Set aside. (This will make more pesto than needed; the rest can be kept refrigerated for about a week and used to accompany other dishes, such as pasta, chicken, and fish.)

2. In a small bowl, combine the crème fraîche and preserved lemon. Allow to stand in the refrigerator for about ½ hour for the flavors to combine.

3. Heat a grill or grill pan to medium-high. Lightly brush each slice of bread with olive oil on both sides. Grill the slices for a minute or two per side, until they are crusty and have charred grill marks but are still soft in the middle.

4. Spread each slice of bread with a layer of pesto and top with a generous smear of the preserved lemon cream. Enjoy!

TIPS AND TECHNIQUES

Fiveandspice: "You can top the bread and spreads off with slices of grilled chicken or a runny fried egg and grilled asparagus, and your life will never be the same."

Unless you have many people to feed—and to help you strip the thyme leaves from their stems—we recommend halving the pesto recipe.

ABOUT THE COOK

Emily Kuross Vikre is a graduate student in Boston, Massachusetts.

Her favorite recipe from a cookbook: "I'm fairly obsessed with the recipe for Herb Jam from Paula Wolfert's *Slow Mediterranean Kitchen*."

Her top cooking/entertaining tip: "Set the table before guests arrive, and you'll look like you've got it together, no matter when the food actually winds up being ready. And there's almost no cooking disaster so bad that it can't be fixed by throwing it away and serving eggs and toast instead."

WHAT THE COMMUNITY SAID

cheese1227: "This is lovely! It's in my saved recipe files, and I'll have it on the menu all summer long!"

{Contributors}

Abbie Argersinger–
aargersi

Abbie Burke–
Abs

Abra Bennett–
Abra Bennett

Adriene Goldstein–
ADRIENE

Aleatha Parker-Wood
–kamileon

Ali Waks–
Aliwaks

Allison M. Veinote–
DolcettoConfections

Allison Parker–Feeding the
Saints (A.C. Parker)

Amreen Karmali–amreen

Amy Nichols-Belo–
Amy_N-B

Arielle Arizpe–
arielleclementine

Ashley Hooker Jons–
wanderash

Berna Bader–
Berna

Brenna Alexandra White–
Brenna

Brigid Callinan–brigidc

Brooke Herman–
notlazy.rustic

Brooke Moskovitz Dowdy–
brooke's kitchen

Caitlin Wheeler–Savour

Camille Béland-Goyette –
camille

Cara Eisenpress–
SmallKitchCara

Cathy Barrow–
MrsWheelbarrow

Casey Benedict-Pendergast
–kitchenwitchcookie

Diana Chu–monkeymom

Colombe Jacobsen–
colombedujour

Dagny Prieto–
dagny

Dax Phillips

Deena Prichep–
deensiebat

Drew Lambert–lechef

Elizabeth Schmitt–
Lizthechef

Emily C. Swantner–
epicureanodyssey

Emily Kuross Vikre–
fiveandspice

Emily Nunn–ENunn

Eric Liftin

Erin Culbreth–
Hotplate Gourmet

Erin Hanusa–ErinH

Erin McDowell–
apartment cooker

Gabrielle Marie Lopez–
gabrielaskitchen

Giulia Melucci

Gwen Ashley Walters–
Chef Gwen

Heather Schroder–
sweet enough

Heena Punwani—Heena

Helen Allen—
Helenthenanny

Helen Leah Conroy—
AntoniaJames

Helen Johnston—
Helen

Ian FIsher—
fisheri

Jaclyn Kolber—JackieK

James Briscione—
Chef James

Jane Lopes—janeymax

Jennifer Hess—
lastnightsdinner

Jennifer Perillo

Jennifer Vandenplas—
Jennifer Ann

June Jacobs, CCO—
ChefJune

Karen Kwan—kaykay

Kelsey Banfield—
KelseyTheNaptimeChef

Lauren Shockey—
lauren

Laura Chávez Silverman –
gluttonforlife

Lauren Sozmen—loli

Leitha Matz—MissGinsu

Leslie Shatz—Leslie

Lindsay Meisel—linzarella

Liz Larkin—mrslarkin

Lynda Balslev—TasteFood

Margaret Loftus—Midge

Maria Raynal—
mariaraynal

Maria Teresa Jorge

Marissa Grace Desmond &
Ian Kaminski-Coughlin–
Marissa Grace

Mary Fairbanks
Constant–dymnyno

Mary Murphy–machef

Melissa Villaveces–
melissav

Meredith Shafer–
The Internet Cooking
Princess

Meredith Shanley

Michelle McKenzie
Waltman–porktopurslane

Nancy Jo Iacoi–Nancy Jo

Nicole Lang–NicoleCLang

Peter Steinberg

Petrit Husenaj–
MySocialChef

Phoebe Lapine–
BigGirlPhoeb2

Rebecca Lando–
wcfoodies

Rhonda Hesser Thomson–
Rhonda35

Rivka Friedman–Rivka

Rebecca Palacovics–
RebeccaP

Robert Lee and David
Rollins–The Dog's Breakfast

Robyn Michelle-Lee
Thompson–robynmichellelee

Sandy Smith

Sara Robillard–Sara

Sasa Stucin + Jan Vranje

Shayma Owaise Saadat–
shayma

Sonali Ruder–Sonali

Stacie Bills–One Hungry
Mama

Stefano P. Coppola–
Stefano Coppola

Steven Dunn–Oui, Chef

Susan MacDougall–Susan

Susan Pridmore–ChezSuzanne

Tammy Hepps–Tammy

Teresa Parker

Tom Hirschfeld–thirschfeld

Veronica Stubbs–Veronica

Winnie Abramson–WinnieAb

Ying Lee–ying

NOT PICTURED:
Collin Seals–Collin
Hila Grinsberger–Cordelia
Naomi Rosen–Naomi

{Menus}

SUMMER

Summer Breakfast Dishes

Mom's Blueberry-Coconut Muffins, 32

Strawberries with Lavender Biscuits, 22

Blueberry Almond Breakfast Polenta, 140

Lemony Cream Cheese Pancakes with Blueberries, 171

Sweet and Savory Tomato Jam on Toast, 80

Magical Coffee (aka Cafe Davio), 207

Summer Picnic Dishes

Blackberry Caipirinha, 82

Ginger Sangria, 34

Mint Limeade, 362

Amagansett Corn Salad, 48

Spanish Roasted Potato Salad, 395

Lemony Green Bean Salad with Feta, Red Onion, and Marjoram, 391

Moroccan Carrot Salad with Harissa, 147

One-Pot Kale and Quinoa Pilaf, 219

BLT Panzanella, 74

Salad Dressing, for a green salad or sliced tomatoes, 39

Classic Southern Buttermilk-Bathed Fried Chicken, 86

Caramelized Pork Bánh Mì, 397

Seriously Delicious Ribs, 84

Luciana's Porchetta, 329

Strawberries with Lavender Biscuits, 22

Simple Summer Peach Cake, 58

Zucchini-Lemon Cookies, 52

By the Sea

Mediterranean Octopus Salad, 100

Spicy Shrimp, 45

Grilled (or Broiled) Oysters with a Sriracha Lime Butter, 252

Whole Baked Fish in Sea Salt with Parsley Gremolata, 224

The (Not Barefoot) Contessa's Fish Pasta, 61

Fourth of July

Mint Limeade, 362

El Chupacabra, 43

Amagansett Corn Salad, 48

Spanish Roasted Potato Salad, 395

Lemony Green Bean Salad with Feta, Red Onion, and Marjoram, 391

Creamy Cucumber "Side," 404

Steak for a Brooklyn Backyard Barbecue, 65

Smoky Pork Burgers with Fennel and Red Cabbage Slaw, 66

Lemon Basil Sherbet, 72

Moroccan Merguez Ragout with Poached Eggs, 231

Christmas Dinner

Norma's Eggnog, 199

Hot Spiced Drunken Apple Cider, 194

Autumn Olive Medley (Braised Lamb Shanks with Fennel, Celery Root, and Olives), 255

Ciabatta Stuffing with Chorizo, Sweet Potato, and Mushrooms, 150

Mashed Potatoes with Caramelized Onions and Goat Cheese, 261

Sweet Potatoes Anna with Prunes, 188

Grilled Brussels Sprouts, 144

Smoked Ham with Pomegranate Molasses, Black Pepper, and Mustard Glaze, 201

Leg of Lamb with Garlic Sauce, 321

Wishbone Roast Chicken with Herb Butter, 283

Airy Rosemary Citrus Pignole Bread Pudding, 275

Figgy Pudding Butter Cookies, 205

Secret Cookies, 8

New Year's Eve

Bubbly Manhattan, 142

Hot Spiced Drunken Apple Cider, 194

Norma's Eggnog, 199

Salted Almonds, 30

Smoky Fried Chickpeas, 123

Spicy Shrimp, 45

Olive all'Ascolana, 268

Creamy Sausage Stuffed Mushrooms, 280

Grilled (or Broiled) Oysters with a Sriracha Lime Butter, 252

Rosemary Thyme Pita Chips, 50

Yogurt and Spinach Dip, "Borani Esfanaaj," in the Persian Manner, 304

Tuscan Chicken Liver Pâté, 335

Ancho Chile–Cinnamon Chocolate Bark, 196

Super Bowl

Smoky Fried Chickpeas, 123

Yogurt and Spinach Dip, "Borani Esfanaaj," in the Persian Manner, 304

Creamy Sausage Stuffed Mushrooms, 280

Lentil and Sausage Soup for a Cold Winter's Night, 215

Classic Southern Buttermilk-Bathed Fried Chicken, 86

Seriously Delicious Ribs, 84

Smoky Pork Burgers with Fennel and Red Cabbage Slaw, 66

Meat Loaf with Blackberry Barbecue Sauce, 301

Barbacoa Beef Cheek Tacos, 241

Southwestern Spiced Sweet Potato Fries with Chili-Cilantro Sour Cream, 159

Eggplant Parmesan, 89

Spanish Roasted Potato Salad, 395

Valentine's Day Menu

Tuscan Chicken Liver Pâté, 335

Mussels for One (or Two), 234

Arugula, Pear, and Goat Cheese Salad with Pomegranate Vinaigrette, 161

Not Red Velvet Cake with Fudge Glaze, 16

Grilled (or Broiled) Oysters with a Sriracha Lime Butter, 252

Cowboy Rubbed Rib-eye with Chocolate Stout Pan Sauce, 182

Mashed Potatoes with Caramelized Onions and Goat Cheese, 261

Lazy Mary's Lemon Tart, 180

Salad with Sweet and Spicy Horseradish Dressing, 298

Risotto Rosso, 347

Feta Frozen Yogurt with Blood Orange and Mint Granita, 295

Weeknight Suppers

Daddy's Carbonara, 36

Roasted Bagna Cauda Broccoli, 237

Lemon Posset, 271

Wishbone Roast Chicken with Herb Butter, 283

Grilled Brussels Sprouts, 144

Double Chocolate Espresso Cookies, 138

Shrimp Biryani (Indian Shrimp and Rice), 177
Lemon Basil Sherbet, 72

Broccoli Rabe, Potato, and Rosemary Pizza, 371
Toasted Coconut Gelato, 128

Dinner Party Menus
Roasted Cauliflower Soup with Chimichurri and Poblano Crème Fraîche, 212
Secret Ingredient Beef Stew, 257
Mashed Potatoes with Caramelized Onions and Goat Cheese, 261
Lemon Posset, 271

Creamy Mushroom Soup, 119
Leg of Lamb with Garlic Sauce, 321
Autumn Celeriac (Celery Root) Puree, 133
Rum Apple Cake, 111

Red Leaf Salad with Roasted Beets, Oranges, and Walnuts, 4
Luciana's Porchetta, 329
Pink Greens, 156
Saffron Semifreddo with Cherry-Cardamom Syrup and Salted Honey Hazelnuts, 317

SPRING

A Garden Party
Herb and White Wine Granita, 164

Ginger Sangria, 34
Prosciutto and Fontina Panini with Arugula Pesto, 135
Absurdly Addictive Asparagus, 338
Wild Ramp Pesto (on Crostini), 364
Mediterranean Octopus Salad, 100
Leek, Lemon, and Feta Quiche, 246
Griddled Polenta Cakes with Caramelized Onions, Goat Cheese, and Honey, 289
Rhubarb Curd Shortbread, 367
Lazy Mary's Lemon Tart, 180

Easter Dinner
Leg of Lamb with Garlic Sauce, 321
Mashed Potatoes with Caramelized Onions and Goat Cheese, 261
Absurdly Addictive Asparagus, 338
Lemon Posset, 271

Spring Lunches
Creamy Mushroom Soup, 119
Grilled Bread with Thyme Pesto and Preserved Lemon Cream, 411

Prosciutto and Fontina Panini with Arugula Pesto, 135
Chewy Sugar Cookies #2, 333

Lamb Burgers with Cilantro Yogurt, 19

Creamy Cucumber "Side," 404
Rhubarb Curd Shortbread, 367

Weeknight Suppers
Wishbone Roast Chicken with Herb Butter, 283
French "Peasant" Beets, 286

Pasta with Prosciutto, Snap Peas, Mint, and Cream, 352
Herb and White Wine Granita, 164

Steak for a Brooklyn Backyard Barbecue, 65
Absurdly Addictive Asparagus, 338
Foolproof Ice Cream, 56

Dinner Party Menus
Heart of Gold, 374
Seared Scallops with Spring Onion and Tarragon Cream, 349
Rhubarb Curd Shortbread, 367

Preserved Lemon and Vegetable Risotto with Grilled Pernod Shrimp, 313
Leg of Lamb with Garlic Sauce, 321
Lazy Mary's Lemon Tart, 180

Wild Ramp Pesto (on Crostini), 364
Salmon in Sorrel Sauce, 377
Herb and White Wine Granita, 164

{ Acknowledgments }

This book began in an unconventional fashion. Rather than researching and cooking and cooking some more, and then writing recipes as you would for a regular cookbook, we instead built Food52.com, a site that would crowd source recipes by hosting weekly recipe contests. Once this virtual test kitchen was built and 52 weeks of contests were completed, all the winning recipes would go straight into this cookbook.

All we needed were the talented and passionate home cooks who would provide the actual recipes. We knew there were thousands of them out there, and we could only hope they'd find us. Thankfully, they did. They came from Hawaii and Denmark, Indiana and Portland. They were lawyers by day and obsessed cooks by night. They were gardeners who made charcuterie and farmers who took beautiful photos. And they have made this cookbook what it is, a true celebration of cooking at home.

We have come to know a great many of our community members on the site and in person—we've met Food52ers all over the country and have been lucky enough to attend a couple of the Food52 potlucks in San Francisco, New York City, Washington, and Austin.

We're so grateful to them not only for creating extraordinary recipes week after week, and for voting on the best, but for nurturing a meaningful community, an online social hub for food that is now visited by hundreds of thousands of people every month. We built a wonky site that was a kind of bare pantry, and our users filled its shelves with beautiful food. We're sending a special thank you to some of our earliest members, who did so much to set the tone and spread the word: Lynda Balslev, Kelsey Banfield, Cathy Barrow, Helen Conroy, Steve Dunn, Jennifer Hess, Liz Larkin, Jennifer Perillo, Maria Raynal, and Meredith Shanley.

Our site and this book would not be what it is without the deft eye and creative vision of our photographer, Sarah Shatz. Sarah was a portrait photographer who had never shot food. Every Tuesday for these 52 weeks, we spent a full day with Sarah in Amanda's kitchen and photo studio (aka her bedroom), cooking and shooting finalist recipes, and creating the visual sensibility of Food52 that can also be found throughout this book. She photographs food as if it's a person, always in search of its expression. She sees melancholy in a pear when most of us just see a tasty fruit (yes, we tease her relentlessly for this). And when Sarah was away, her friend—and now ours, too—Melanie Einzig would fill in (see pages 57 and 59 for examples of her fine work).

A ton of recipe reading and testing, editing, writing, tweeting—and eating!—goes on behind the scenes, and we have worked with an amazing group of editors and writers, including Helen Johnston, Jennifer Steinhauer, Allie Chaden, Francesca Gilberti, Kristy Mucci, Emily McKenna, Rebecca Palkovics, Martine Trelaun, Anabelle McLean, Lily Taylor, Lauren Shockey, Helen Hollyman, Alaina Sullivan, Will Levitt, Brette Warshaw, Lily Taylor, Rachel Berkman, Katie Essenfeld, and Rona Moser. We could not have produced this book without the serene and talented Kristen Miglore, who joined us halfway through the first year as our first senior editor, expertly tackling everything from blog posts to community management to recipe testing. Every week, an army of us read through and tested recipes. At the helm of this team is Stephanie Bourgeois. She plans the testing, tames the large and unwieldy testing spreadsheet we keep, and makes sure on chocolate weeks to call dibs on most of the recipes!

Thanks to the community and to an excellent group of advisors and investors, including Jason Rapp, Kenneth Lerer, Joanne Wilson, Rob Stavis, Eric Arnold, Scott Puritz, and Jordan Cooper, among others, our company has grown, and we have an office team we love: Alexandra Lutz, Kristen Miglore, Francesca Gilberti, Jonathan Stavis, Kfir Shay, and Peter Steinberg.

Along the way we've had the opportunity to work with some fantastic developers and designers, like Alain Benzaken, Ben Lim, Peter Kamali, Eric Liftin, Pat Stern, Becky Carpenter, and Christine Yom.

Over a lunch at Aquavit in the fall of 2009, Bob Miller asked us about our vision for Food52, and after three sentences, signed us up for the first two Food52 cookbooks. We are grateful not only for his faith but for his prescient wisdom in not making us write a proposal.

We've had a ball working with Cassie Jones, who has patiently dealt with our the-dog-ate-our-homework approach to deadlines, and who's a truly collaborative and thoughtful editor. Also at William Morrow, we're grateful to Jessica Deputato, Leah Carlson-Stanisic, Karen Lumley, Joyce Wong, Ann Cahn, Sonia Greenbaum, Shelby Meizlik, Liate Stehlik, Lynn Grady, Tavia Kowalchuk, and Shawn Nichols.

Thanks, as always, to Heather Schroder, Nicole Tourtelot, and Tabitha Schick at ICM; to Debbie Stier, the social media master who helped us set out on the right path; and to our friends Gretchen Holt and Bena Shah at OXO, who have sponsored our contests from day one.

When we launched Food52, we were blessed with enthusiastic reviews from people like Erick Schoenfeld at Techcrunch, Gwyneth Paltrow at GOOP, and the fab editors at Daily Candy. They shooed us out of the nest lovingly, and we're grateful for it.

Getting this book and site in motion required enormous support from our friends and families. We'd especially like to thank Jennifer Steinhauer, Eliza and Mike Anderson, Veronica Stubbs, Rhonda Thomson, Walker and Addie (Amanda's kids, who happily embraced a succession of themed meals from "broccoli rabe week" to "lamb week"), and, particularly, our lovely and sweet husbands, Jonathan Dorman and Tad Friend.

{ Index }